Coming to terms with

Coming to terms with mental handicap

Ann Worthington M.B.E.

Foreword by
Brian Rix C.B.E., M.A.,
(Secretary General of MENCAP)

HELENA PRESS
1982

First published 1982
Reprinted 1983 and 1985

Edited by Barbara and Peter Saunders
©Copyright Ann Worthington
ISBN 0 9507930 0 0

All rights reserved. No part of this publication may be reproduced, stored in a retrieval system, or transmitted in any form or by any means, electronic, mechanical, photocopying, recording or otherwise, without the prior permission of the copyright owner.

British Library Cataloguing in Publication Data
WORTHINGTON, Ann
Coming to terms with mental handicap.
1. Mentally handicapped children – Care and treatment
I. Title
362.3'088054   HV891

Set in 10 pt Times series by
Bury Phototypesetting Limited, Peel Mills, Bury, Lancashire
and printed in Great Britain by
Ashworths Print Services, Peel Mills, Bury, Lancashire

Published by Helena Press, Orchard Lane, Goathland, Whitby, YO22 5JT

FOREWORD BY BRIAN RIX, CBE, MA
Secretary General, Royal Society for Mentally Handicapped Children and Adults

It gives me great pleasure to comment on this most useful book by Ann Worthington. She has been associated with mentally handicapped children and their families for very many years and for fourteen years she has published a Newsletter putting parents in touch with each other. Many parents of children with rare forms of mental handicap have been grateful to her for being able to receive advice and help from the parents of similar children.

The book covers very many areas of great concern to parents, including the adjustments which become necessary within the family when a child is born with a severe handicap and the part which parents can play in cooperation with teachers to help the child to develop his abilities to the maximum. There is a very full list of organizations concerned with disability in general and mental handicap in particular and an excellent bibliography.

I am sure that her long experience and real concern for families faced with the situation of coming to terms with the life-long care of mentally handicapped children will find much to help and guide them in the pages of this excellent book.

Editor's notes:

1. *Illustrations*

   (a) The cover photograph is of Nicholas Anthony, a Downs syndrome boy aged 10 years.
   (b) Page 86: Helen (aged 11) with Mister James.
   (c) Page 91: Colin (aged 3½) finishing his meal.
   (d) Page 103: Helen (aged 14) and Jackie (aged 13) working with their Headteacher, Miss Marilyn C. Simpson, at the Turnshaws School, Kirkburton, Huddersfield.
   (e) Page 112: Andrew (aged 13) at a Riding for the Disabled Gymkhana.
   (f) Page 132: Andrea and Peter (students at Huddersfield Social Education Centre) with Mr. Bryan Nichols, Head of the Centre.

2. *Letters written to IN TOUCH by relatives*

These have not been edited; however, names and initials have been changed in order to preserve confidentiality.

CONTENTS

Page

FOREWORD

CHAPTER ONE 1
BREAKING THE NEWS
Disclosure of the diagnosis; approach of medical staffs;
parents' reactions.

CHAPTER TWO 7
CONSIDERING PARENTS' NEEDS
Privacy; the need for further discussion; parents' experiences

CHAPTER THREE 16
FINDING OUT GRADUALLY
Problems of development; the strain of uncertainty;
parents' experiences

CHAPTER FOUR 23
THE FAMILY: PARENTS
The mothers; the fathers; first reactions

CHAPTER FIVE 30
THE FAMILY: BROTHERS AND SISTERS
Effect upon other children; the handicapped child as a firstborn;
having another child; parents' accounts

CHAPTER SIX 39
THE FAMILY: GRANDPARENTS
Accepting the diagnosis; letters from grandparents and parents

CHAPTER SEVEN 43
STRESS IN THE FAMILY
Hyperactivity; physical handicaps; parents looking back

CHAPTER EIGHT 52
COMING TO TERMS
Emotional adjustments, parents' expectations; problems of
acceptance; financial circumstances; religion; parents' suggestions

CHAPTER NINE 61
ONE DAY AT A TIME
Finding the best approach; accepting help; telling other people;
parents' suggestions

CHAPTER TEN 74
HELPING DEVELOPMENT
Parents as teachers; Teaching at home; training for parents; parents' suggestions

CHAPTER ELEVEN 81
BEHAVIOUR
The undemanding child; behaviour problems; pets; parents' suggestions

CHAPTER TWELVE 88
TEACHING THE BASIC SKILLS
Play; feeding; speech; mobility; parents' ideas

CHAPTER THIRTEEN 101
EDUCATION (SCHOOL, CENTRE AND COLLEGE)
Pre-school education, special schools; further education

CHAPTER FOURTEEN 106
FINDING OUT MORE
Forward planning; organisations; local sources; leisure; residential care; finance

CHAPTER FIFTEEN 118
SHALL WE LET GO?
Deciding on residential care; independence; short and long term care; parents' experiences

CHAPTER SIXTEEN 128
ADOLESCENCE AND ADULTHOOD
The adult at home; continuing education; work; social and sexual problems; parents' accounts

CHAPTER SEVENTEEN 142
REWARDS
Achievements and abilities; parents' accounts

APPENDIX ONE 145
THE IN TOUCH SCHEME

APPENDIX TWO 149
INFORMATION SECTION

APPENDIX THREE 181
PUBLICATIONS AND BIBLIOGRAPHY

INDEX 192

ACKNOWLEDGEMENTS

Acknowledgement is gratefully made to the following organisations:

Huddersfield Community Health Council
(for permission to quote from their Survey on Community Support Services for the Mentally Handicapped (1979))
(page 14)

Souvenir Press Ltd., 43 Great Russell Street, London, WC1B 3PA
(for permission to quote an extract from the book "LEARNING TO COPE" by E. Whelan & B. Speake (1979))
(page 140)

B.B.C. Publications, 35 Marylebone High Street, London, W1M 4AA
(for permission to quote an extract "from ACCIDENT OF BIRTH by Fred Heddell published by BBC Publications 1980".)
(page 78)

DEDICATION

To John, Sarah, Richard and Kate

ABOUT THIS BOOK

The In Touch scheme began fourteen years ago, with a simple purpose; the linking up of parents of children with similar disabilities so that they could exchange ideas and encouragement. (A more detailed account of the In Touch scheme is given on page 145).
 This book has grown out of the In Touch scheme and has similar aims. It brings together the experiences of members in order to pass them on to anyone, parent or professional, concerned with the day to day care of mentally handicapped people. In addition, it provides basic information on services for the mentally handicapped and sources of further advice.
 Parents of mentally handicapped children and adults, when asked to contribute their views to a book of this kind, needed no persuasion. Given the opportunity to pass on their knowledge (as well as their mistakes) their response was immediate and enthusiastic. Second only to their concern for their own child was the wish to ease some of the problems facing others for the first time. Many felt that it was equally important to convey to professionals some of the less obvious needs of parents; they were sure that their early contact with medical and paramedical staffs had some bearing upon their subsequent adjustment, or even upon their handling of the child.
 Those who contributed to the book did so to reassure 'new' parents that they too can come through. It would be wrong to imply that it is roses all the way, but it would also be wrong to present a picture of unremitting gloom. In the letters of hundreds of parents over fourteen years, determination gradually takes the place of the intense despair felt at the beginning. Those who join In Touch in search of help and information soon begin to offer themselves as supporters of others. When their child's handicap is discovered, parents are enveloped by anxiety and dominated by thoughts of all the problems to come. But, according to one In Touch member,
 "I was so worried about how I would cope as she grew older. But there was something I didn't account for then – that after I had looked after her for a few months, nursed her and got to know her personality, I would also *love* her. It became impossible *not* to care about her happiness and welfare or to fight for the best for her. That's what made all the difference, and that's what made it possible to cope".
Another mother, with a 22 year old son, wrote,
 "A. continues to grow and develop – a joy and a pleasure to everyone he comes in contact with. He's so helpful in the house, and to his 87 year old grandmother he is such a lifeline, doing all her heavy jobs such as digging or lawnmowing. We hear so much about the quality of life these days. This severely handicapped boy enriches all our lives with his sweetness and love."

A cynical view might be that parents have no choice but to recover, or that they are deluding themselves rather than face the reality of the situation. But, they are not a band of martyrs, smilingly taking it all on the chin; there is much more to it than that.

Whatever it is that turns the unacceptable into something which can be adjusted to, or at best can become a source of real pride and pleasure, it seems to happen in many families. New parents may find some comfort in the fact that it is likely to happen to them too.

* * *

I should like to express my thanks to Brian Rix, C.B.E., M.A., Secretary-General of MENCAP for reading my manuscript and for the kind remarks which he has written in the Foreword.

Finally I wish to record my appreciation of the advice and encouragement which I have received from my Publishers.

Ann Worthington

Chapter One

Breaking the news

On two occasions, in 1971 and again in 1977, mothers of mentally handicapped children and adults were asked a series of questions about their child's early years. In 1971, 153 mothers gave their answers and 183 replied in 1977. This was not a scientific survey but it gave a general picture of the situation and it was interesting to see how remarkably similar in proportion were the answers.

Who gave you the diagnosis?

	1971	1977
Specialist/Paediatrician	74	104
Hospital doctor	36	33
General Practitioner	23	33
Psychologist	4	0
School Medical Officer	8	3
Never told officially	8	10

The specialist or paediatrician is now most likely to take the responsibility for passing on the diagnosis, though sometimes the job is delegated to one of his or her assistants (who may have had little dealings with the child's case.)

If the baby has gone home before the results of tests are known or if testing was done as an out-patient, the hospital may send details to the family doctor and he informs the parents. If the handicap was not apparent at birth, but has become evident because of behaviour or development problems, the mental retardation is sometimes diagnosed by a psychologist or school medical officer. In a few cases there was never any official confirmation, just a growing knowledge by parents that their child was retarded and an assumption by education and medical consultants that they had been fully informed.

Were you satisfied with the way you were told?

	1971	1977
Yes	80	91
No	73	92

There can be no 'pleasant' way of giving such news, and no easy way of receiving it. The position of the person responsible for telling parents is an unenviable one. It is extremely difficult for a doctor to decide how and when to tell them; whether to be frank and to the point (which may be interpreted as callousness or abruptness), or whether to break it gently, a little at a time (which may be taken as skirting the issue, or perhaps *a refusal* to be frank).

But, even taking into account the difficulty of the task and the possibility that the parents' emotional state might colour their impression, there were still too many complaints to be explained away as misunderstandings. For parents, the moment of discovery is so loaded with emotion that it is remembered in vivid detail ever after. Those who felt that they had been dealt with honestly and sympathetically remained very grateful to the doctor for his respect for them. They left the interview feeling that they were all 'on the same side', and so did not feel brushed off or resentful towards him.

Many parents, however, felt exactly the opposite. In addition to their confusion about the child's handicap they came away with an additional burden of anger, embarrassment and a sense of hopelessness.

They described the doctor's attitude as off hand, abrupt, callous. What may have been his attempt to be straightforward had come across as a lack of concern.

They felt intimidated and unable to ask the questions that ran around their minds by the dozen. Or, they left with a list of all the very worst things that could happen, including all the things their child would *never* do.

This pessimistic approach was presumably designed to prevent the raising of false hopes – yet many parents seeing how much their child achieved in later years were not so much grateful that it turned out better than predicted, but resentful of the unecessary distress caused by the picture of a gloomy future.

It was very clear in the accounts given by dissatisfied parents that they felt very strongly about these aspects of the early relationship with doctors and nursing staff. It was also very clear in the accounts of those who felt that they had been fairly dealt with that it was the *presence* of those very same points which sustained them through a very difficult time.

Mrs. G. . . . .
> "I would not have taken so much of what doctors said as gospel. If they were rude, unfeeling or discourteous I'd tell them so now. Also, if you are told a child will never walk, make house adjustments and improvements there and then. Don't delay extensions etc. If the child walks, great! If not and you are still in a cramped house with bedrooms and bathrooms upstairs, you may find things getting on top of you – literally!"

Daughter, tuberous sclerosis.

Mrs. G. . . . .
"I would have asked more questions at the first doctor's appointment. Apparently, as I have found out now, they had a pretty good idea of what was wrong with S then. I would have paid more attention to maintaining high standards of behaviour — perhaps this could be put better if I said that I should have treated him more like a normal child. Most important, I would have made my husband come to doctors' appointments, or if he couldn't, I would have explained the situation more fully to him".
Son, hypochondroplasia.

Had you suspected something was wrong before you were told?

	1971	1977
Yes	119	115
No	34	68

Both in the first days after birth and in the first year of their child's life, some mothers were remarkably (sometimes uncannily) sensitive to there being something 'different' about their child, even if there were no obvious signs. Often they described this feeling as haunting them from the beginning of pregnancy or from the moment of birth, despite their own attempts to rationalise it and the reassurance of others.

How often this 'hunch' was unfounded cannot be proved, but in some cases the vague suspicions did turn out to be justified. Mothers noticed the forced cheerfulness or briskness of the nurses who came to take the baby for yet another test (usually described as routine, but as one mother remarked — 'it did not seem as routine for the other babies in the ward')

They picked up odd phrases of conversation or looks between nurses, and attempts to find out what was happening, (or even the direct question 'Is something wrong?') were not always satisfied. Obviously, when conclusive diagnosis had not been made it was impossible to give full details. But, many mothers felt that it would have been kinder to tell them of the concern for the baby and the information gained so far, than to reply with an emphatic denial.

A similar situation can arise with the gradual realisation of mental handicap, in a child of a year or two old. Here, too, there were occasions when parents found themselves trying to convince doctors that there was a problem, but being given vague reassurances (perhaps because the doctors themselves were not sure) that their fears were groundless. When they finally reached someone who said the words 'mentally handicapped' it was almost a relief because someone else had acknowledged it. At least the suspicions had been given an explanation and the uncertainty was over.

If parents are sufficiently uneasy about their child's development to approach the specialists, that is the time for honest discussion of the facts. Uncertainty can be the hardest thing of all.

Mrs. A. . . . . .
"I had a normal birth with L. She weighed over 10 lbs. Though she was a pretty baby, I knew there was something wrong. I had to press for an E.E.G. at nine months. Then, a young student doctor told me in a corridor, as I was leaving, 'the test results are through. You were right, she is retarded — come back in six weeks'.
Daughter, unspecified retardation.

"We should have been told straight away"

Sometimes a diagnosis was held back (perhaps because the doctor felt that the parents should have time to get to know the baby and form a relationship, before being told). Occasionally, if further tests were necessary, the mother went home before her baby. Several mothers who left the hospital first had been told nothing about the handicap and later presumed it was to avoid the risk of their rejecting the child. However, other mothers who came home first, knowing about the handicap, expressed only readiness to have their baby home. Where there had been no thoughts of rejection in the hospital, none were created by the temporary separation in itself. All of these mothers spent as much time as they could with their babies while they were still in hospital.

Much more discontent was expressed by those who had been allowed to believe that all was well, only to discover that the diagnosis had been made weeks or months before and withheld from them. Instead of seeing it as something done in their interests, they felt it to be a deception and a pretence which underestimated them.

Almost without exception, parents wished to be told as soon as the handicap was suspected. They did not want to be 'protected' from the news and led to believe that all was well. Many mothers, already suspecting that something was wrong had expressed their fears, and even then had been told 'not to be silly'.

"We should have been told straight away" or "I wish we had been told earlier" were comments frequently expressed.

Finding out together

A number of parents complained bitterly that they had not been together when the diagnosis was given. Because the mother was in hospital or taking the child for examination she was often alone when told, then left to break the news to her husband. Occasionally, if the mother was still in hospital the father was drawn aside and told, "She might take it better from you" — a most unfair relegation of responsibility. In this situation the father has to absorb the shock and control his own feelings, and also has to find some way of putting it in a way that his wife will accept. He is in no position to explain the medical implications or to answer questions, yet is expected to relay what information he has to his unsuspecting wife.

If the mother has been told in the ward, her husband may arrive quite cheerfully at visiting time to find that his wife has been crying for hours, and somehow has to accept both her distress and the child's handicap in one blow. There can be few occasions when it is necessary to inform one parent on his or her own, or when it is impossible to arrange for quiet and private discussion with both parents.

Some couples have been acutely embarrassed by having the diagnosis given to them in a busy corridor or crowded waiting room. In this situation they find it impossible to express their immediate feelings or to ask questions. One or two mothers told how they heard in an even more clumsy way; hearing nurses discuss the child's handicap when they thought they were out of earshot, or in one case, seeing her baby's name on a list at a baby care talk as 'Baby W-Mongol'.

Mrs. H. . . . .
"When I was seven months pregnant with my third child, the paediatrician at the local hospital phoned me when I was alone and told me that some tests done on my 4 year old daughter had shown that she had a progressive disease and that the baby I was carrying would have to be tested as soon as it was born — the possibility was that it could have the same condition. Fifteen months earlier we had been told that our older daughter had quite a different condition, which was definitely not genetic. After advice from our G.P. the paediatrician and a gynaecologist we went in for another child, having been told that a second handicapped child was as likely as 'having lightening strike twice'. Our new baby did have the same condition — she should never have been born. Results of tests on my older daughter done more than a year before had only come to light. If our older girl had been diagnosed properly I could have had a test in my other pregnancy, which I am told is 100% accurate. The system has now been changed and I am assured that the same mistake with test results cannot be made for other parents. We were utterly disgusted with the way I was phoned at home, instead of being seen with my husband".
Two daughters, San Fillipo syndrome.

Mrs. B. . . . .
C's physical handicaps were obvious to a certain extent at birth but he was wrapped up and whipped away before I had time to notice. My husband wasn't with me or immediately available so it was a couple of hours before he could get in to be with me, to tell me (he knew, but as it was my first baby I hadn't realised that the baby would have been with me longer if he had been OK). Even then, my husband had to give his permission before I was allowed to hold my baby — even after 5 years this still rankles tremendously. I was just told in a bald fashion, with no idea of future prospects or guidance."
Son, Möbius syndrome.

Were you given information about relevant organisations etc?

	1971	1977
Yes	37	37
No	116	146

It is not the job of the consultant in charge of the child's case to hand out leaflets and give addresses, and parents would be unlikely to ask him or her about them. But every area has a local society for the mentally handicapped, and there are many organisations which cater for specific conditions such as Down's syndrome, autism, epilepsy, spasticity and so on. There is a vast amount of literature in the form of Government leaflets, directories of local facilities, practical handbooks etc. But the information is so scattered that parents would need to know a great deal before they could begin to find out anything.

They would need to know that their local reference library kept copies of local directories and lists of organisations, that their Social Services Department or Department of Health and Social Security would have leaflets about grants and allowances, that their local clinic might know of aids available – all this on top of trying to find out more about mental handicap in particular. Medical Social Workers and Health Visitors exist in all areas and are in an ideal position to pass on printed material to parents.

At the very least, some information about the local Society for the Mentally Handicapped might lead the parents to make enquiries. The Society will have done the searching on behalf of its members, and should be able to tell the new parents about all the facilities available in the area. (see Chapter 14).

Mrs. R. . . . .
"I am 24 my husband is 26 and we have a little mongol son of 4½ months old. Little or no help seems forthcoming – I was refused the address of the Society for Mentally Handicapped Children on the grounds that I would get emotionally involved, or some such pointless excuse. I have yet to understand why no-one, not even my own doctor wanted to give me information. I have been to see many people, but found I just had useless bits of information which common sense alone could provide. I am very lucky to have a family and group of friends who are wonderful, and they give me every help they can."
Son, Downs syndrome.

Chapter Two

CONSIDERING PARENTS' NEEDS

Privacy

Some mothers who learn of their child's handicap soon after birth find the ward a strain. They are surrounded by other mothers with new babies in an atmosphere of general happiness. Once their own happiness has been overshadowed, it becomes difficult for all concerned. Their distress is intensified by watching and listening to other mothers handling their babies and their only wish is to be allowed to go home.

Those who were unable to go home immediately felt that it would have been helpful to have some relaxation of visiting times so that they could have more time with their husbands and begin to come to a mutual understanding of the many things they had to talk about.

Mrs. B. . . . .
"When my son L was born, my other child was a girl, almost three years of age, so it seemed to me that I now had a perfect family. Less than twenty four hours later I discovered that my baby was a mongol. To my shame, I must admit that all my life I have been repelled by mental subnormality. If I saw a mentally handicapped child I would turn away and shudder. As I was 39 before I conceived my second child, I realised there was a risk of it being born a mongol, but of course, I thought, "This can't happen to me." When I realised it had happened it seemed as if I was in the middle of a nightmare. My immediate reaction was to plead to be allowed to leave hospital. I felt I could not face the pitying looks of the other mums, and above all, I wanted the comfort and support of my husband — to be with him all the time, not simply during visiting hours. The doctor said he could not allow the baby home so soon after the birth, he was a few weeks premature and besides being a mongol, he might have feeding difficulties — we would have to wait and see how he progressed. I could see he was very reluctant to let me go home without the baby, and although at this stage I had not heard about mothers rejecting subnormal children, I sensed that he was afraid that if we were separated so soon after birth I might go home, slip into my old routine, and not want him. However, I managed to convince him that this was not so. It seems strange that although I had this terrible revulsion for subnormality,

> I never doubted that I would love my little son and want to care for him, but I thought it would be a purely compassionate and one-sided love. I never dreamed that not only would he respond to, but return my love, or that he would grow into a mischevious, lovable little boy.

Son, Downs syndrome.

The need for hope

Most couples agree that they should be prepared for the possibility that their child *may* not walk, talk, or become toilet-trained. And certainly it would be wrong to allow them to believe that their child would one day become miraculously cured of all his disabilities.

Usually parents are realistic enough to accept that this will not happen. They ask only that they are not given the impression that anything they do for the child will be a waste of time. The difference between *'he will never be able to do anything, so expect nothing'* and *'he is severely handicapped and may not be able to walk and talk, but let's see what we can do to help him'* is similar in content but very different in implication.

No-one, however expert, can predict every detail of a child's life with total accuracy, and when sweeping generalisations are made in his first weeks it seems like closing the book after reading only the first word. Parents need some hope to spur them on and most will hope, regardless of what they are told. They want to be allowed room for hope in small and gradual improvements, so that they are worth working for. Where there are obvious and severe physical handicaps or deformities, the parents can see them and little extra emphasis is needed. If they must be 'told the worst', it should be followed by advice and support. If there is reassurance of readily available help they can meet each difficulty, if not with optimism, at least without despair.

It can be just as distressing, and very frustrating, to be told nothing at all. Sometimes the child is examined and tested in almost complete silence, notes written down and the parents given their next appointment. They come away knowing nothing and feeling as though the child and his problems have no connection with them at all.

Mrs. C. . . . .
> "We were lucky, L showed no sign of heart defect and apart from feeding very slowly had no difficulty in sucking or swallowing, so he was home with us in less than a week. The following day our G.P. brought a Paediatrician to the house. He examined L, said that there was no doubt that he was a mongol and told us that at some future date we might have to place him in a mental institution, possibly out of fairness to our other child. On the other hand, we might be able to cope with him most of the time, but send him to a residential home for two or three weeks each year, to allow the rest of us to 'escape' for a little while. Escape! That word hit me hard. What was life going to be like for us if we found it necessary

to escape? I'm sure he was a kind man, his manner was sympathetic, but how tactless! When he spoke to my husband and I, he must have realised that we both accepted the situation completely. Why did he think it necessary to paint such a grim picture of our future? As soon as he left the house I wept bitterly. Later, I stood looking down at L sleeping so peacefully and I felt angry. Why should this man spoil my pleasure in my baby? I would enjoy him like any other baby and meet problems when they arose."

Son, Downs syndrome.

Mrs. D. . . . .

"My own personal experience of having a mongol son was some 21 years ago. He was my third child. To suspect, to know there was 'something wrong' just moments after birth was shattering. The actual birth from start to finish lasted hardly two hours. It wasn't difficult, no instruments, just very straightforward. So why? Why me? What for? Why should I be a parent of such a baby? What had I done? Out of all the mothers who had given birth to a baby that day, why did this happen to me? (Strange to say, many years later I discovered that another mother not far away also gave birth to a mongol boy, and more than likely had the same thoughts as me.) No one, doctor, nurse or sister offered any explanation, and after a few days of worry and secret tears, I asked the night sister, "Why all the fuss and attention by the doctors − the little peeps behind the ward door by Matron when A and I were together − what is wrong with him?" Straight away the lady doctor arrived and for the next two hours she and I discussed this 'very special boy' who was going to need a great deal of caring, loving, and most important of all, understanding. To say that I had accepted my lot and had come to terms with this challenge, would be a lie. It was many weeks after, once I was home, I realised that A depended upon me so much, and also that not only he needed help, but so did I. Where to get it, who to ask, no one knew − and I felt, no one cared."

Son, Downs syndrome.

Mrs. C. . . . . .

"However kindly meant, no-one should withold this sort of thing from a normal parent any longer than absolutely vital, and no-one should tell parents about handicap without real *modern* knowledge of the fantastic help one gets with the child, and without being able to convey the hopeful, good side of any handicap. I don't mean fairy stories or miracle cures but experience of the extra gift of joy these children can give, and facts of the limited but positive achievements which are accomplished are a vital part of the bringing of bad news! There is no *ideal* way to tell parents this kind of news but I think the way we were told was unnecessarily ignorant and even dangerous."

Son, Downs syndrome.

Mrs. D. . . . .
"The doctor at the maternity hospital who told me that I had a mongol baby said, "These things happen, nothing can be done about it, so it is no use making a fuss or crying." He left me to break the news to my husband. The sister at the hospital when my husband asked if there were different degrees of mongolism, told him, "If you have a mongol baby, you have a mongol baby and that's all there is to it. The same sister, when I asked if I could go home earlier to my family than scheduled said. "What about the baby? We can't look after her for you." The Health Visitor has visited once and hasn't been since. She was too busy to get me the address of the Society for Mentally Handicapped Children. The Clinic doctor has shown a noticeable lack of interest in her. When I remarked conversationally that we were pleased with her progress, he said, "Don't get too excited it's unlikely that she will keep it up. Her backwardness will show up soon." Still, she is fifteen months now and we have managed to pick ourselves up each time we are slapped down so far!"
Daughter, Downs sydnrome.

Keeping it clinical
Another frequently expressed disatisfaction is that of apparent insensitivity on the part of medical staffs − (and according to many parents, the more senior the doctor, the more this seems to apply.) The impression of a doctor's handling of the situation tends to be subjective, and depends too much upon the personalities and sensitivities of those involved to be judged as right or wrong. No doctor would knowingly increase the distress of those in his care, so it can only be assumed that some are unaware of the importance of their attitude.

One rarely hears criticism of the way a doctor breaks the news of a serious illness or death of a patient to the relatives. It is usually done with sympathy and respect. Yet some parents describe the discovery of their child's handicap as similar in effect to the death of someone close.

For mothers, particularly, the child's birth is not the beginning of the relationship but a continuation of it. Throughout the whole pregnancy there is an awareness of the child and a feeling of closeness and affection for it which increases as it become more active. When the resulting child is damaged, there is a very real sense of having lost someone close: they have lost the child they expected and they mourn for him. One mother believed it was worse than experiencing a death,

"If someone close to me died I would know that however grief stricken and desolate I felt at first, the pain would ease with time. I wouldn't have to worry about their suffering any more, even though I would probably always miss them. But, for all I knew, the arrival of my severely handicapped baby was only the beginning of my grief − I couldn't see it being healed by time or my getting over it and living a normal life again. As it turned out, it wasn't as bad as that, but I had no way of knowing that then."

This may seem to be a over-emotional or dramatic reaction, but it is not an uncommon one. For most people it *is* an emotional experience, the distress is very real and is never forgotten.

There seems to be a policy among some specialists to avoid at all costs any sign of personal sympathy creeping in with the cold facts, so that the situation remains clinical and parents will not get too upset. Usually, this policy has the desired effect; the parents say thank you and leave, reserving their emotional reaction until they get outside the door. Some are acutely conscious of the fact that the doctor is a busy man and assuming that he can spare them only two minutes, don't feel they can waste his previous time by asking questions — which they feel may be silly ones anyway.

One mother remembered that not only was she worried about wasting the doctors time, but was also concerned about asking questions which might embarrass him. She didn't want to 'put him on the spot' by probing into the problem and forcing him into telling her unpleasant things —

> "I just acted as though it wasn't all that bad, and I just wanted to let him off the hook." Years later, after numerous visits to doctors she was hardly able to believe her own reaction in that first interview, having become as she described it 'much more thick skinned'.

With experience most people become more confident in their child. Looking back they blame themselves for their lack of knowledge because 'they were not pushing enough'.

But unlike medical staffs, most parents are unused to hospitals, sickness and disability. When they are summoned to an interview with a specialist who is going to tell them something vital to the future of their child, they are under considerable stress even before they go through the door. The training of doctors gives them the ability to end the discussion when they have finished, and it takes courage and presence of mind for shocked parents to refuse to be dismissed.

Mrs. M. . . . .
> "We were not satisfied with the way we were told. The Specialist was too abrupt and didn't appear to have any sympathy or give us enough understanding. Although we learned at 10 months that C was handicapped it was not until he was nearly 3 years old that Klinefelter's syndrome was diagnosed. During the first year we had very little help from anyone and went for a year without a Health Visitor calling. Now, we have a very good Health Visitor, who is helpful and understanding. A Social Worker calls too, about twice a year".

Son, Klinefelter's syndrome.

Mrs. E. . . . .
> "I don't think I shall ever forget the feeling of desolation when I first knew about T's handicap two years ago. All I wanted to do was to be able to talk to someone in the same position, to know and see someone who had come through and come to terms with it.

> Unfortunately we live in an area which seems to be shielded from this sort of handicap to a large extent and I only knew vaguely of one or two mongols. I even began, right inside myself, to hope that one of my many friends who were expecting babies would have a similar child, so I wouldn't be alone. This was awful, and none of them did, thank goodness."

Son, Downs syndrome.

The need for further discussion

Most couples felt very strongly that they would have been greatly helped by a follow up interview with their consultant. If they knew that they had a 'second chance', they would prefer the first discussion to be brief and simple, so that they would not have to absorb everything at once. Many say that after the words 'mentally handicapped' had been spoken they heard very little else anyway. They felt the need to have a few days to let the news sink in, to talk together and to gather together their confused feelings. They could then have gone to a second consultation with their most pressing questions prepared.

The parents who were given a second interview found it of immense value. They felt respected, supported and understood. Having the co-operation of a doctor or hospital Social Worker who spared time to listen to what they had to say increased their confidence and certainly helped them to adapt more quickly.

Mrs. T. . . . .

> "I have now got over the first shock. V is now nearly 8 months old and I feel life is back to normal again. When you are told your child is a mongol it is such a shock, and in my case it was some time before I found out much about the condition. If only the hospital had given me some idea it would have helped me. When I mentioned it to the doctor at 3 months that I had read in a book that a mongol was an 'idiot', he arranged for a little explanation of mongolism.
>
> If only this had been given in the hospital we would have still had the shock, but we would have had a better idea. I think the hospital people presume you know but when they don't say anything you imagine the worst and are so intent on keeping a stiff upper lip in front of the other mums, you daren't ask."

Son, Downs syndrome.

Mrs. S. . . . .

> "My husband was initially told by the specialist, but not in detail. I remember different nurses giving me vague answers about K's condition. I had not heard of microcephaly so naturally wanted to get some books or any information I could on the condition, but I was told "That would be a silly thing to do". I felt K was used as a guinea pig. I had no idea what problems we would have. If I had been given some information and guidance at the time, I'm sure things would have been a lot easier for me."

Son, microcephaly.

Mrs. H. . . . .
"A psychiatrist told me that F was severely retarded with autistic tendencies. Nobody ever told me definitely that he was autistic. Doctors, Specialists etc., seem reluctant to make that diagnosis on their own. Also, I didn't like being told that he would be better off in a home as he would never make any real progress. You can't say that of a normal looking 2½ year old child. Anyway it was untrue as it turned out — and this is where lack of specialised training shows."
Son, autism.

Mrs. F. . . . .
"A specialist came to see T in the nursing home and we were told that they had no idea if he would be able to walk or talk at that stage. He was seen again at 6 months and I was told they could do nothing for him, and that somebody would be in touch with us before he was 5 to assess if he would be able to have any education. We had no specialist attention in the first five years."
Son, Rubenstein-Taybi syndrome.

Mrs. H. . . . .
"I was satisfied with the way I was told, but not whole-heartedly. We were told that all the tests were normal except for the chromosome count, but the Specialist stressed that they had discovered this almost by accident as it wasn't one of the tests they considered particularly concerned with M's problem. He said it was a 'big medical name' (Luckily I remembered it and was able to do some research in the local library) he said it wouldn't be of particular concern to us until he was older — around puberty. However, our Health Visitor was able to arrange an interview with a lady who was doing research and who was able to give us some notes on the syndrome. These revealed that boys with this condition could be difficult to handle after a docile first few years of life. Though it made quite depressing reading (I had been warned that it would!) it did solve quite a few problems. Quite often I had been made to feel a complete failure because he was difficult to control. When you realise that anti social habits are not totally deliberate you see the problem from a different perspective, though of course you must still use discipline."
Son, Klinefelter's syndrome.

Mrs. T. . . . .
"F was our first child, born when we were both twenty. By the time she was eleven weeks old we were told she would be backward. It wasn't a shock. We had been expecting it. We were told she would do everything very slowly. I wasn't very upset because I didn't realise how bad she would be. It was a quick birth and the pain was very bad at the end. The sister insisted that I was not 'pushing' and told me she was going out of the room until I did. When she came

back she cut me and then decided to go for a doctor. A minute after the doctor came F was born. The morning after she was examined and said to be normal. After the first day she started having convulsions and because the nurses had not seen her having a convulsion it was three days before I could convince them that there was something wrong, and she was put in the intensive care unit. After a fortnight she was allowed home, still having convulsions, which the doctor said would disappear. Another fortnight later she was re-admitted and after extensive tests was found to have severe brain damage. We were told that we would have to go back to the hospital for check ups and if I had any problems I should raise them then, The Health Visitor came but she didn't know much about handicapped children and just came to see if she was physically well.

It was just like having a normal child at first although we had sleeping problems with her. I think if they had given me some idea how her brain damage was caused, even though it can't help now, I'd be more content.''

Daughter, brain damage.

A later survey

At the end of 1979, Huddersfield Community Health Council conducted a survey on community support services for the mentally handicapped. This contained similar questions to those put to the *In Touch* membership in 1977. One section of the survey related to the response of parents to the disclosure of their child's handicap, and included the following analysis. (95 families gave their answers.)

The Birth of the Child

The time when parents were told, or realised that something was wrong, varied between 3 weeks before the birth to 7 years after. In some cases, medical staffs had to be prompted by parents before a final diagnosis was made. 17 families were never really told. In 3 cases the children were not born handicapped.

The Setting for Disclosure

Most of the families were told about their child's handicap by a hospital doctor; other informants included a health visitor, school psychologist or hospital nurse. Approximately 42% said that they were not told in a sympathetic setting.

Immediate Action

Little was done to help parents during this period and before their children went to school. However, half of the families of children under 11 said that the hospital doctor took some sort of immediate action, e.g. making regular appointments, writing to the education authorities, arranging a blood test. 19 families said they had received help from the G.P. or health visitor. Most families had little if any contact with the Social Services.

51% were not satisfied with the help from the Health and Local Authority. The main failings complained of, and typical comments were . . .

a) Lack of information
"We should have been visited by the Social Worker to give us all the information with regard to local services."
"I recently applied for an Attendance Allowance which I only learned about this year. I was told I could have applied 8 years ago so I suggest families should be informed".

b) Lack of Care
"Until last year the health visitor did not know that 'A' existed (11 years old).
"We have noticed over the years that assistance is not readily forthcoming".

c) Lack of liaison
"A need for follow up visits from Health and Social Workers. We never had a visit from a Social Worker until our daughter was 10 years old."
"The hospital should have been in close contact and related to the Local Authority services. The Local Authority services should have visited and advised on how they could assist. None of this happened".

d) Lack of Facilities
"Need for more short stay places".
"More Social Services initiated offers of help on practical matters such as short stay or emergency accommodation and specialist equipment".

For most parents receiving the news is a short sharp introduction to the world of mental handicap, which they enter blindfolded and apparently alone. It is the beginning of a constant search for answers to a multitude of questions, and of continuous effort to provide a worthwhile life for their child.

Those who are lucky enough (if anyone can be described as lucky in those circumstances) to be given the basic tools of professional support and information from the beginning are spared the hopelessness of ignorance and are better equipped to build a solid future for their child.

Climbing a mountain without special preparation seems an impossible task. With the right equipment, it becomes a challenge which can be met.

Chapter Three

FINDING OUT GRADUALLY

Some parents leave the hospital with a perfect, beautiful baby, to the congratulation of everyone, then after a few months, may notice that he doesn't seem to be thriving, is having feeding difficulties or does not seem responsive to movement or sound. Or they may notice nothing at all until the baby makes no attempt to sit up or grasp objects. Some may be unaware of a problem until even later; the child may eat and sleep well, crawl and walk, but lack of speech may begin to worry them.

They may even regard themselves as having a perfectly normal child until the first developmental test is done and they are told that he is not progressing at the average level for his age. This is especially likely to happen with a first child when the mother has not had the experience of bringing up a non-handicapped child.

'Over anxious' parents

Parents will often consult a doctor about what they believe is a purely physical problem, wondering if he is seeing or hearing properly, whether his lack of speech needs attention or if they are imagining his clumsiness, odd movements or behaviour problems. If they are referred to a specialist and tests show that their child is mentally retarded it can be a severe shock. Some may have had secret fears about the child's progress when compared with that of other children they knew, but had dismissed them with the often-quoted phrase 'all children develop at their own rate'. Others may actually have voiced their worries to their doctor or clinic – and have been dismissed as 'over-anxious'. This phrase is frequently applied to parents and it could hardly be less constructive. No mother wants to admit that her child might be backward and will only mention it to a doctor if she has enough evidence and experience to make her pretty sure. By the time she has summoned up the courage to come and discuss her fears she probably *is* over-anxious – and understandably so. From the moment a child is born mothers are urged to be vigilant, to protect against overheating, to sterilize feeding utensils carefully, to see the necessary injections are done, and so on.

Sometimes, when they seek help about a medical problem they are asked, "Why didn't you come earlier?" Yet if they tentatively mention something which worries them they are often sent away feeling rather stupid.

Too often these 'over-anxious parents' are proved right in their fears: they knew something was wrong but found it impossible to get anyone to listen to them and take them seriously.

One mother began to be concerned about her son when he was about two years old.

It had been a difficult birth but nothing was said to indicate that any damage had been done. He was very sleepy for a few days, (unusually so) then fed ravenously and developed well. He crawled, walked and played at the right time and in a normal way. But when at two and a half he was talking very little, constantly dribbling and presenting behaviour problems his mother became worried. His unpredictable behaviour seemed to coincide with the arrival of his new baby brother, so she thought he was jealous and seeking attention. But he became so hard to handle that she got him into a Day Nursery, thinking that it might be good for him to be with other toddlers and more fully occupied. She became convinced that it was she that was at fault. She felt that she must have been doing everything wrong and was a bad mother.

She told her family doctor about his dribbling and was told it might be cured by the removal of his tonsils and adenoids – but it wasn't. Slowly she began to wonder if there was something really wrong.

She read as much about autism as she could, and thought he had some of the features, but this was ruled out.

She read that lead poisoning could cause brain damage, and as he had chewed everything (window sills, his cot, toy cars) she suggested this, though feeling rather hesitant about it. She was considered over-anxious – obviously one of those mothers who couldn't read anything without believing her child had got it – and still she was told he would come out of it. She asked for every test available but they were all negative. Yet she was still frantically trying to cope with his problems as well as with a younger child.

Almost a relief

Not until he was due to start school, at five years of age, did the School Medical Officer tell her that he was retarded. After believing herself to be going crazy for several years, it came almost as a relief to hear someone else acknowledge her beliefs. It hadn't been her ineptitude or lack of attention which caused it, as she had come to believe. Suddenly so many things had a reason: she knew why he became frustrated, why he was clumsy, why he seemed to need telling over and over again about the smallest thing.

Mixed with the relief, though, was some anger that she had spent years alternating between hope and despair, of wondering what on earth she was doing wrong. Most of all she felt that she would have understood him so much more and handled him differently had she known his difficult behaviour was not sheer disobedience.

She felt that five years had been wasted. Five years in which she could have geared her approach more precisely, found ways of helping him learn, asked for advice about education, and sought speech therapy. She thought of the time she had been completely exasperated with him, exhausted by endless broken nights and angry to the point of having to walk out of the room to avoid hitting him.

She had had to endure the looks and comments of people in shops and on buses when he had decided to be awkward. Being a tall and well-made boy, with an attractive face, it was acutely embarrassing to have him throw a tantrum, in the manner of a toddler, when he was four years old – and looked six. If she could have countered the disapproving looks with the reason – or at least had been able to explain it to herself – she would have been spared so many unpleasant experiences.

The strain of uncertainty

Parents whose children are diagnosed at birth suffer a sharp and sudden shock. But at least they know from the beginning what they are faced with and can begin to adjust to it and tackle it.

Those whose children bear no outward sign of any handicap, who may be physically sound and of beautiful appearance have, instead, a series of small shocks, piling one on top of another, over months or even years. The strain is considerable. They, and those round them, spend half their time thinking they are imagining things. They read all they can on child development, looking to prove or disprove their child's lack of progress. In many ways finding out gradually is much more traumatic than having the facts presented early and all at once. Uncertainty can be harder to cope with than a positive set of facts. Looking after a child one cannot understand and who is 'different' in achievement and behaviour is doubly hard if it cannot be balanced against the reason for that difference.

Families may disagree about the child's problem – mother is told she is worrying too much and father refuses to believe it because he hasn't spent as much time with the child or would rather only believe something he is told officially. Relatives may consider the child in need of a good smack, grandparents that he will grow out of it ('after all, our Jim didn't talk properly until he was three').

When at last there is some confirmation of a problem, it is still a shock and a great sorrow, but it can now be discussed as a mutual problem, not as a search for who to blame. Now at least, parents can concentrate their thoughts and energies on finding out what they can do instead of on finding out what is wrong. They can look ahead and plan, and work together to make up for so much wasted time. One advantage of this kind of discovery is that the child has had complete acceptance and love from birth; and however many problems he has presented he is firmly integrated into the family. He remains the same child after diagnosis as he was before – only his 'label' has changed. He does not suddenly become a problem because he is officially a mentally handicapped child. He has already been a source of worry to his parents and will not become more so because of the diagnosis.

In fact, the reverse may happen. The parents can look at him with a greater understanding now that so many of the earlier problems are explained. The release from the strain of years of ignorance enables them to be free to deal with him in a much more relaxed way. The problems are still there — but with some of the doubts removed they can be recognized and tackled.

Mrs. A. . . . . .
"We were never told officially that G was mentally handicapped. I just asked to see my G.P. when he was a year old as I realised he was behind in his development. We were referred to a specialist at the local hospital, where various tests were done over a period of time. No particular name was given for what was wrong with him. It took me another two years to accept that he is what is called mentally handicapped. It seemed to be assumed right from the start that I knew this. I should have liked to have been told as soon as it was apparent. I feel a lot of time has been wasted in which I could have been doing more to help him, if only I had had more understanding of his problems."
Son, retarded.

Mrs. F. . . . .
"At 2¾ years, my son M was diagnosed as having Rubenstein-Taybi syndrome. It wasn't a shock to me, in fact I was relieved, maybe that's the wrong word, but I knew for sure that my baby was not like other children. All his little physical abnormalities, and feeding problems etc. . . I felt sure all this stemmed from the one thing — I couldn't know what. I used to say to my husband, "Our M is a special little fellow with a condition our doctor has never even heard of." I said as much to my doctor, but both he and my husband said I was too anxious, and that he was just a little slow. So, when we were told finally what his condition was, I felt that I could help him more."
Son, Rubenstein-Taybi syndrome.

Mrs. P. . . . .
"I had attended the hospital with J (he had a 'clicking hip') for over a year, at 2 monthly intervals, when on one visit the orthopaedic consultant dictated to his secretary (he rarely spoke to parents) that J had spastic muscles in his leg. When I asked if J was a spastic he just said, "Yes", and moved onto the next child on the conveyor belt. It was then that I asked to see another specialist — and what a difference! We haven't looked back since."
Son, brain damage.

Mrs. G. . . . .
"S is 9 years old now, and totally deaf and severely mentally handicapped. Our main problem is her deafness, we had been telling doctors that we believed her to be deaf, and no one would listen. It was only 6 months ago that we were proved right — and then only by accident. Naturally, we are very angry that 8 years of her life have been wasted, the most important years too."
Daughter, brain damage.

Mrs. N. . . . .
"M went to an observation centre at 3 years old. My nerves were so bad and no-one wanted to listen, or even believed half of what we had to put up with, with him. I took an overdose, consequently M was taken in the next day, just for a break. They said for 2 weeks – it ended up as 6 months before they could do anything with him. One good thing came out of it – they told us he was an epileptic, and mentally half his age. They told us not to tell anyone. My husband and I couldn't understand this at all – just not talking about something doesn't make it go away. We have never been told anything directly, just in conversation, or if we asked about the brain damage. He was normal at birth, but after an operation at 4-months peritonitis set in, and his right side was affected. He was then having small fits, unknown to us. We asked the doctor about the fact that when he sat up, he fell to the right, but nothing was said. Having read books etc., we assumed that the peritonitis had poisoned the brain, thus causing the fits."
Son, brain damage.

Mrs. A. . . . .
"Our daughter developed like any other baby. My two other children had had german measles when I was pregnant and I had to have an injection of gamma globulin. When she was approaching 2 years old, doubts began to creep in – she seemed unaware of things, and wasn't trying to speak. I brought her to the attention of the Health Visitor and the doctor, and they suspected she was deaf, and was diagnosed as such. But, her peripatetic teacher of the deaf thought there might be more to it and advised us to press for further tests. She had these when she was 4 years old. After several tests, my husband was told to take E out, and I was told quite bluntly that there was no hope of her ever being normal, and to place her in a hospital school as soon as possible. Perhaps it seemed a little cruel to be told quite brutally, but having survived the experience I'm grateful. At least we knew where we stood. You can't get any lower than rock-bottom and can only climb upwards. I cried the hundred miles home, but managed to put on a brave face for my parents and other children the next day."
Daughter, brain damage.

Mrs. T. . . . .
"Looking back, F's retardation started right from the start though it didn't show itself until he was about 3. By then he was clearly behind, but we were told by a paediatrician there was nothing wrong – he was just very slow and there was no sign of him being a spastic – which was a relief. We were getting advice from family and friends – "don't worry, he'll catch up, so and so has a son or daughter and they caught up", etc., – this made us wonder all the more. It wasn't until he was 5 and allocated to a school for the

educationally subnormal that we really knew — he doesn't fit into any category so is difficult to assess. When talking to doctors I'm always on the defensive. Many times the doctors, psychologists, paediatricians etc., do not tell us in full detail what the tests are about, and don't use laymen's language. People should make sure parents understand, and not treat them as stupid. Doctors don't get co-operation from parents if they treat them like half-wits."
Son, retarded.

Mrs. T. . . . .
"J is not a typical child. He is brain damaged and autistic, and I have never met anyone with the same severe behaviour problems that we have encountered with him. Most children are easier to handle than he has been. However, from talking to other parents, some of the problems seem common to many families, at least to some extent. We had felt that J was not developing normally for about two years. It was not easy to pinpoint exactly what was wrong, and every time we went to see our doctor we were told we were worrying too much. When I took J to our doctor, complaining that his speech was not developing normally (he was nearly 4), he sat himself in the doctor's chair, picked up his pen, and said, "Now, how are you today, doctor?" Eventually, after tests, we were told that part of his brain was severely damaged, and he would have to spend the rest of his life in institutions. The most we could hope for was to have him home for another two years. In fact, he lived at home until he was 12. After the initial shock, it was a relief in many ways, knowing what was wrong. It had been like living on a tightrope, being pulled first one way and then another. We were trying to believe those who told us not to worry, that everything would be alright (I.Q. test at 3 years — 100. A bit slow on the uptake but got there in the end!) We could now, at least, get to grips with living with the problem."
Son, brain damage, autism.

Mrs. F. . . . .
"For 2½ years we had "he's slow but he'll catch up", and we feel it is very wrong to build up hopes, instead of laying it on the line at birth, when you can get the period of adjustment over earlier."
(This condition gives rise to certain physical differences, and specific recognisable features which could have been seen very early.)
Son, Rubenstein-Taybi syndrome.

Mrs. D. . . . .
"A. . .s retardation didn't show itself until he was about 3 (though looking back, it started right at the beginning.) He did sit up at nine months, and he wasn't able to walk until he was 2¼, though we had been assured there was nothing wrong. Up to the age of 5 everything was fairly normal as far as the family were concerned.

His toilet training was causing a bit of a problem, but we took it in our stride. This became more obvious when we had our second son, as he progressed normally. A's speech was very poor, just a few words. Fortunately, he attended a nursery school with me until our second son was born, mixing with normal children helped him a great deal — he was loved by all who came in contact with him. At 5 he was sent to a local ESN school, but as he was constantly wet and dirty the headmaster wouldn't tolerate him anymore. The head of the local state school had him straight back and they put up with him until we found another ESN school. It wasn't until about 2 years ago that we realised what extra attention A needed compared with that for a normal child of his age."

Son, mildly retarded.

Chapter Four

THE FAMILY: PARENTS

When they look back over the early years, parents can sometimes recognize factors in their personalities or their family situation which influenced their adjustment to the handicap.
  As one mother said,
   "I can now see that there were many things affecting me that I wasn't aware of. Viewing the situation at a distance I realise that my own feelings were affected by all kinds of emotional and practical pressures. They were not things which could have been easily changed, but I'm sure it would have helped if I had recognized some of the things which were clouding my judgement, and holding me back. Also it would have been useful if I had been able to appreciate fully, the many advantages I had compared with other people."
Son, unspecified retardation.

The mothers
Some mothers, on the discovery of their child's handicap, had a remarkably philosophical approach. They had a good cry, then told themselves, "Crying will get me nowhere and won't change things. It's our responsibility and up to us to make as good a job of it as we can."
  It didn't mean that from that moment on it all became easy, nor that there were no more periods of sadness. Nor did it mean that they were braver or more noble than anyone else. It was just that, on the whole, their determination overrode their despair. Usually they were the kind of people who approached most aspects of life in a practical and matter of fact way. Rather than torturing themselves with endless questions ("Why me? What will everybody think? Will I be able to cope?") they had the capacity to meet the problem head on and to deal with each situation as and when it occurred. The sadness they felt tended to be for the child himself rather than for themselves, and because of the child's special dependence on them rejection never entered their minds. From the beginning they were able to identify with the child and felt a fierce, protective love for him. One mother made up her mind very early:
   "I wasn't having people avoid asking questions about him or being embarrassed. I came right out with it so that they would see I wasn't ashamed of him."

There are others, though, who find it hard to be so fatalistic. For them, this is not only a child with special needs. He is a blow to their confidence and to their self-esteem. The whole thing seems a cruel trick of nature, impossible to understand or accept. The baby who had been anticipated with pleasure now appears to be a threat, the future fraught with disappointment and uncertainties. These mothers have described themselves as feeling completely helpless and were convinced that they would never be able to cope. They tended to isolate themselves, feeling that no one but the immediate family could understand why 'she can't pull herself together'. They were upset by seeing other mothers with normal babies. They exhausted themselves by wondering why it had happened to them; they suffered agonies remembering all they had seen and heard about mentally retarded adults shuffling around some outdated hospital.

This feeling can last for months but for the majority the initial shock eases as they recover from the birth. For a few however, it never disappears entirely. It isn't a constant thing, but a little of the bitterness remains. Often, these are mothers who have other problems: domestic or financial – or who have felt completely unsupported by health and social services staff.

A few could not accept the diagnosis at all. Even as the child grew older and his lack of development became more and more obvious they would not acknowledge it as a fact. They managed to find other explanations: he was 'lazy', 'delicate', 'jealous of his brother', but he'd grow out of it. Some must surely have known, deep down, that there was more to it.

But they simply could not say it out loud; so they pretended, to themselves and to others. These mothers probably suffered the greatest conflict of all; they deprived themselves of the understanding of others by being unable to share their own problems, and deprived themselves of peace of mind by clinging to the conviction that one morning the child would wake up completely cured. By excluding themselves from any involvement with other parents of handicapped children and from available sources of help they risked depriving their child of the early stimulation or specialized teaching he needed so much.

For mothers like these the approach of school age posed some anxiety. Sooner or later the need for special education had to be faced, and the situation had to be discussed with school and health authorities. Usually after the first difficult adjustment the mother actually felt relief that there were teachers and other mothers willing to suggest ways of helping her child. Years of denying the reality and of alternating between secret hope and secret despair were replaced by something much more positive.

> "It was funny," said one mother, "but I had always been able to explain away what the doctors and clinics said. I'd tell myself that he was only a baby, then that he was only a toddler and there was plenty of time for him to catch up. But when he got to school age I really knew that he couldn't compete with other five year olds. I felt almost glad – I could stop kidding myself. Knowing and admitting what I had to tackle was a great relief. Suddenly I found myself able to say, 'So what does it mean?' It means that he cannot

learn as quickly as others but he's happy and healthy and very loving. He's at a marvellous school where they do great things with the children.

All those years of tearing myself apart! I'd never have believed I'd accept it, but I think I do now."

These, perhaps, are extreme examples of the range of emotion. Most parents experienced a little of each – moments when they were full of fighting spirit, times of utter dejection when their efforts didn't seem worthwhile – and times when they wished that they could shut their eyes and the whole situation would disappear. The prospect of a completely changed life is too great a thing to be absorbed quickly and it takes time to filter out the important things and dismiss the unproductive ones.

Every parent is changed by having a mentally handicapped child.

The reserved ones amaze themselves with their insistence on what they think is right: challenging decisions, demanding information, refusing to be put off. Those who thought themselves helpless find that the reverse is true; they discover reserves of strength they didn't know they had. Those who said, "I'll never have the patience" have it in abundance.

Mrs. G. . . . .
"Before we had H I had a terrible abhorrence of mental subnormality. Some say mongols are lovely children. I used to try not to look at them. It never ceases to amaze me that feeling as I did, I found it comparatively easy to accept H. I knew he was a mongol less than twenty four hours after he was born. They did not intend telling me but I was suspicious right from the birth, so they had to tell me. I never felt like rejecting him – in fact it would not be an exaggeration to say that my maternal instincts started working overtime right from the start. Of course I have shed a few tears but any periods of depression I've had have been of very short duration and few and far between. Before H was born I wouldn't have set foot in a hospital for the mentally handicapped – the thought would have made me quite sick. Some people believe everything happens for a purpose. I don't know if this is right but if it is, then H must have been sent to cure me of this unnatural aversion. I think in my own mind, I must have equated subnormal with subhuman."
Son, Downs syndrome.

The fathers

The feelings of fathers tend to be given far less attention than those of the mother. Obviously this is because some of the worst strains are applicable to the mother. She has carried the baby, imagined how he or she will look, has given birth, and will be the person responsible for his day to day care in the early years. Her involvement with the baby before and after the birth is both physical and emotional, so she is particularly bereft when she is robbed of the expected sense of achievement and pleasure. The birth itself leaves her tired and sensitive so the implications of handicap are especially daunting. Her disappointment and her practical problems are more obvious than those of her husband and probably more openly expressed. On the whole, fathers are less willing to talk about their fears and find it harder to confide their sadness to others. Nor are they likely to express their feelings in tears. But it does not mean that they are less deeply affected.

Mr. S. . . . .

"Our daughter K was born two years ago, after we had been married for eleven years and had virtually given up hope of having a family. Strangely enough, my wife now tells me that she had a feeling all was not well when she was carrying her. It became obvious as she grew, that she was not progressing normally. After an examination she was found to have a slight hole in her heart. This of course was a shock but the hospital assured us that if the condition did not right itself they would be able to operate. We both felt, during the first few months, that she was not progressing as she should − her hands were clenched, and there were other signs. At nine months we took her for a routine hearing test. We were absolutely staggered when an elderly woman doctor said, almost without preamble, "She seems to be spastic in the hands." Spastic was a dreadful word to us. She was seen by a paediatrician who diagnosed cerebral palsy, but we are not sure of the degree. We still find it hard to accept, but I suppose we should reconcile ourselves to the idea. Fundamentally we are very much in the dark about it all. We have a sense of frustration, we don't know what we can expect from her or how best we can help her. She will never be without love, but can we fit her for a normal life?"

Daughter, cerebral palsy.

Another father who described his feelings perhaps summed up those of many others.

He felt that he had given the child to his wife and felt that he was therefore responsible for imposing so many problems on her. He was very conscious of having let her down. This was his first child and he admitted that his feeling of proving his manhood was undermined by the child's handicap. In the same way that his wife had to explain to neighbours, he felt self-conscious when he returned to work and told his colleagues. Before he could do so he was greeted by one friend who joked: "Now your problems are really beginning − no more nights out with the lads!" A harmless enough remark but full of new significance in the circumstances.

A father has to come to terms with his own sadness and try to find an extra reserve to support his wife in her more obvious distress. He may be called upon to play a more positive role in the care of his other children if one of them is going to need more attention than the mother alone can provide.

Many mothers also feel somewhat responsible for the feelings of the rest of the family. One talked of being torn apart by the knowledge that her husband had to go home and ring everyone for the second time, to amend the good news he had celebrated hours earlier.

One mother said,
> "Poor thing walked around the hospital for nearly two hours, unable to come in and see me, but dreading going home to tell my parents."

A mother might even wonder if her husband will blame her for the child's handicap or if he would begin to feel differently for her. Rational thought does not come easily with so much to absorb all at once. This fear is not usually borne out: husbands are generally said to have been 'marvellous about it'. No doubt many men feel that this is a time for them to provide extra strength, concentrating on assuring their wives that they will come through — saving their own grief for the times when they are on their own.

Occasionally a husband will refuse to believe the news and carry on as though it hadn't happened. Sometimes, part of this approach appears to be deliberate; an attempt to make it easier for his wife. But it is just as likely to be a way of escaping the pain of facing the facts and as several mothers have observed, "Fathers do seem more able to switch off as a method of defence." In fact this kind of reaction only serves to make a mother feel even more isolated and convinced that the father wants nothing to do with her or the child.

Mothers often regard talking to others as vital if they are to keep their problems in proportion. Fathers, just as often, want to talk about it as little as possible and certainly not to anyone outside the family circle.

Some close up altogether and won't even discuss it with their wives, believing, "You can't change the facts so why go on and on about it?" The wife may openly subscribe to his view and keep her fears to herself because "He has enough pressure at work all day and doesn't want to listen to me moaning the minute he gets home."

The increased understanding about mental handicap and the general trend towards parents working together with their children in equal partnership shows itself in the *"In Touch"* correspondence. Nowadays, fathers seem more inclined to seek out information and give as much practical support as they can.

Some go much further and discover in themselves talents for speaking, campaigning and organisation. They throw themselves into finding out every scrap of useful information, into work with local societies for the mentally handicapped, and attend parents' workshops or conferences. Their involvement widens, and becomes geared to improving facilities for mentally handicapped children in general.

Mr. S. . . . .
> "K is blooming! We really are very happy to have her share our lives and she has contributed more to us than I thought any child could. Happily she seems to be coming along well in her own time. We are so lucky — she has just started to walk, which is an enormous step forward (literally!).

She has a very real personality. Of course, she is no angel, nor would we have her so. She can be as 'ratty' as the next and in turn as sweet. She may present us with problems that others only have fleetingly, but the reward of seeing her accomplish each step is great indeed. My wife is marvellous with her and K is a very lucky girl to have chosen her. We counted ourselves very lucky before she was born but we are more complete now. I have been very bucked by the activities of our local society and I've recently helped to start a Gateway Club for older children. I enjoy it immensely and I really look forward to seeing them all each week. They get so much pleasure from the club and get on fabulously together. We have a pretty wide age range from twelve to mid thirties and a wide range of disabilities. It gives me heart to think that our K will aspire to a happy social life, probably without any of the tensions of the so called normal children. It is difficult to reconcile my old ideas of mentally handicapped children with these happy and often very cute children. The different levels of achievement even in one classification is staggeringly wide.

Before our K was born, we thought a spastic was a spastic and that's where it ended. I don't mean that I was unconcerned but that they all seemed objects of pity – how can one be so wrong! I know that there are many extremely difficult cases, but much can be done for them now."

Daughter, cerebral palsy.

There are some families in which the mother elects to take most of the responsibility for the child upon herself. It is she who contacts people who may help, looks into the educational alternatives, takes the child for assessments, devises ways of improving his behaviour or development at home.

This does not means the role was forced upon her by her husband's indifference – but that she sees herself as in the best position to take it. If her husband is behind her, giving support and encouragement, it is no less a partnership.

Because they go out to work, fathers do get more breathing space and to some extent they are able to distance themselves from the day to day stresses. This can enable them, if they are sensitive and willing enough, to provide balance and perspective when problems do occur.

The arrival of a handicapped child does not automatically draw a couple together. There are occasions when this is the 'last straw' and the marriage breaks up.

On the other hand couples can become closer in the face of a mutual problem. The special dependence of their child upon both his parents promotes a desire to put less important difficulties on one side, and rearrange their priorities.

Mrs. F. . . . .
"Living with a handicapped child is bound to cause stress to some extent. There is the physical strain of actually caring for the child continuously. J slept about five hours a night when he was six to eight years old. Looking back, I wonder how we did it, but somehow you are given the strength to cope with what has to be done. He also had to be watched very closely throughout the day, because of his aggressive and destructive behaviour. It can cause mental and emotional stress and in some cases, can result in marrage difficulties too. Somehow you tend to blame each other for everything that goes wrong. It is as if you have to let off steam, and the marriage partner is usually in the line of fire!"
Son, brain damage, autism.

Chapter Five

THE FAMILY: BROTHERS AND SISTERS

If there are already other children in the family, their presence does emphasize the need to 'pick oneself up'. They have needs to be met and want their share of time and affection. Having them to consider provides a continuity and a comfort. Knowing something about everyday handling of children, potty training, suitable foods and toys and so on, removes some of the practical worries. Of course, the mother has some other worries – how will she explain the handicap to them? Will the new baby restrict their lives? Will they understand the extra care he needs or resent it? The relevance of these questions depends upon the ages of the other children. If they are also very young immediate explanation will be unnecessary and can be given step by step as they grow.

Older children will probably glean that all is not well, though how quickly will depend upon the slowness of the baby's development, whether there are any physical disabilities, and how much information they pick up from the rest of the family.

Most people find that they can best explain it by saying something like "sometimes people have something wrong with their eyes or their legs. Our baby has something wrong which means that he can't learn as quickly as other children. So, we must help him as much as we can by playing with him and showing him what to do." One mother told her son, "Our brains are like boxes in which we keep all the things we learn. Your brother's box is a bit small so it takes longer to fit everything in, and to find things when he needs to remember something."

Some older children worry about having friends home, or wonder how to explain their handicapped baby to their friends. Mothers who dealt with this by giving their children a simple explanation to use, and who took the trouble to invite other children in from the beginning found most children soon accepted the handicap without question. Young friends are more likely to tease or stare if the situation is one they don't understand. If a parent or teacher provides an explanation and suggests ways in which they can help, most children will respond. They like to feel responsible. The willingness of children to help those less able than themselves is demonstrated by their involvement in television appeals in programmes like Magpie and Blue Peter.

As the handicapped child grows bigger there are moments when it can be hard for brothers or sisters to make allowances for behaviour for which they would be punished. They may, for instance, wonder why they must feed themselves, or use a knife and fork when their brother, despite being older and bigger, is still spoon fed. But, on the whole changes are gradual and they grow up with an awareness that the handicapped child has to have special attention.

Mrs. E. . . . .
> "C's mental development is improving so well. She has been made head girl at her school (a feather in her cap). She is a very independent child and doesn't fret at all when away from us. We have always treated her like a normal child as far as we have been able and I think this has helped her to be more self sufficient. Being reared with other children in the family she has had to take the rough with the smooth and has had to learn to stand up for herself. We have never insisted that the other children 'give way' to her, and she likes nothing better than to be out of doors playing with other children."

Daughter, Downs syndrome.

Mrs. B. . . . .
> "I adore my little 'A stream' daughters but was not very good with them until they reached talking age, then they fascinated me. Luckily, they both love A dearly and don't mind at all that he is 'backward' baby. I have explained to them as fully as I can (they are only 4 and 6) and I have even used the word 'mongol' — it has no unhappy associations for them and they are bound to hear it sometime. I hope that their devotion and unconscious stimulation will make up for my shortcomings. A is nearly two and won't even hold his spoon — just throws it around the room! I don't go much on his chances of holding a knife and fork at 2½. However, we are having great potting success — two dry nappies today and no dirty ones for over three weeks!
> We have been having a hilarious evening with him dressing up in his sister's panties on his head and her tights round his neck — as you can imagine he's quite lively!"

Son, Downs syndrome.

From 1977 Questionnaire:
Would you say that the presence of a handicapped child in the family has been a disadvantage to the other children, or have there been any advantages in terms of character building etc?
> "A disadvantage, yes, but not a serious one. Yes, it does build character, though I think this depends greatly on the age difference and also possibly whether the children are of the same sex, or the alternative sex. What has surprised me is the attitude of M's (brother) friends. None of them has ever been unkind to R, nor teased M about having a handicapped brother — though others at school have taunted him from time to time. This has not bothered him greatly, and as he grew older he pitied them for their lack of understanding (which has made us very proud of him) but, then again he has taken his cue from our attitude."

Son, Downs syndrome.

Mrs. T. . . . .
"It can be both. At one stage when J was at his worst he was aggressive towards A, and his behaviour made it impossible for her friends to come. We lived behind locked doors, but now we are over that stage (hopefully) and it has been a great character builder. A says it has made her more understanding and tolerant ultimately, and this also applies to neighbours, friends and relatives."
Son, autism.

Mrs. G. . . . .
"No, having a handicapped sister has not been a serious disadvantage to my son. He is very loving towards her, and has made his own life and friends. He also realises that health and the ability to walk, talk etc., are not the automatic God-given right of everybody, and is more tolerant of those who have problems."
Daughter, tuberous sclerosis.

Mrs. K. . . . .
"Very hard to say. H (sister) is already a more considerate and gentle child towards other children, very tolerant and understanding of A — and so far, A hasn't cramped her style — e.g. Brownies, swimming regularly with her father and so on. I think it would have been better if we had had another child soon after A — but that didn't happen — because in some ways A is like an only child, especially as she is the elder, and 'pioneer' as the mental age gap widens. I do sometimes feel that we have only one child to be launched out into the world — one hopes happy and successfully."
Daughter, Downs syndrome.

Mrs. J. . . . .
"In some ways, disaster I would say. Basically now the others are 22, 19, and 16 years they seem to be starved of love. The eldest (a boy) asked me the other day, why I loved the handicapped one more! that hurt deeply but I answered that I spent more time with her, so that they could get on with their 'doings' without her spoiling it. I notice they are 'jealous' of me — also that all of them are extra selfish. They have too many scars!"
Daughter, vaccine damage.

Mrs. R. . . . .
"I think the disadvantage of having G in our family has been that over the years, when the three girls were younger we could never enjoy ourselves together — i.e. go on walks. He would create, so someone always had to come and look after him. His tantrums have upset the whole family — particularly his father. There were occasions when we would have a miserable weekend because G had upset Daddy. In some ways I think it has helped the girls though.

They are very aware of the sick and handicapped, and can cope with other children. My two eldest girls are doing medical jobs — physiotherapy and nursing. I do feel now that we are getting older (in our 50's) we should be enjoying a little freedom. We always have to think of what to do with G if we want to visit relatives — all in Ireland. I feel, myself, that one loses what little freedom one has. When one has a handicapped child, even though we all love G very much, he has caused a lot of frustration and sadness. These children need time and money — most people don't have this. Parents must have a lot of support."

Son, Downs syndrome.

Mrs. S. . . . .
"So long as the family's life does not revolve around the handicapped one all the time, and they each get their fair share of attention — yes possibly, they do develop into 'better' adults. There have been times when my hyperactive mongol child could easily have dominated us as a family, but fortunately, help was available."

Daughter, Downs syndrome.

Mrs. P. . . . .
"In general, having a handicapped brother has not made a great deal of difference to my daughter. I think it has made her and relatives more aware of any disability — mental or physical. Allowances have had to be made, but the only thing my daughter felt was that there was more emphasis on doing well at school, to 'make up for' her brother."

Son, brain damage.

Mrs. L. . . . .
"It has been a wonderful experience seeing their help and love for their little brother as well as that of their friends. Both my daughters are older than B — one 3 years and the other 5 years, and are devoted to him. They do a lot of work with mentally handicapped children — my eldest daughter chose to do a degree in developmental psychology at the age of 17, and is now working in a home for handicapped children as a house parent."

Son, Downs syndrome.

Mr. S. . . . .
"R is the youngest of four. The eldest got an Open Scholarship to Oxford and the middle two girls became very successful teachers — no sign here of any disadvantage in having a handicapped brother. Our older daughter may in fact have benefitted in her career from her experience with, and looking after R."

Son, unspecified retardation.

Mrs. G. . . . .
"I didn't think that having a handicapped child was a serious disadvantage to his brother until recently, when I found we weren't leading a normal social life, and E (brother) had to fend for himself a lot. However, S is now in a hostel so that solved that. I do feel E has more understanding of people and children, and in some ways is mature for his age. It is hard to be sure, but what he has gained on the roundabouts he lost on the swings (or the other way round!) − it probably balanced itself out."
Son, hypochondroplasia.

Mrs. E. . . . .
"Having a handicapped brother has not been a serious disadvantage to my children. They accept him as he is, their own friends have always been told exactly what is wrong, they are encouraged to come to our home and get to know S. Having said this, I must say that the family is not as 'free' to do things as a group, as other families are, and so they miss out on some things."
Son, brain damage.

Mrs. R. . . . .
"I have only one other child, aged 7. I think in some ways having N for his brother has its advantages, and disadvantages. J (brother) does miss not being able to play games with N. Often he pretends N is playing at being a cowboy − in fact N is just sitting oblivious of the game in progress. One game I saw on another occasion was J (after a circus trip) training lions. N was just sitting on the floor while J leapt about − how much better if both were playing those games! But, an advantage − J loves going to the toy library with his handicapped brother, and gets toys out I couldn't afford to buy. He's also been on Toy Library outings. I often wish I had another child so J would know what it was like to have others in the family."
Son, unspecified retardation.

Mrs. M. . . . .
"Problems can arise with other children, who can feel neglected (and indeed, may be) or perhaps jealous of a child who commands so much attention. Their lives may be restricted or perhaps they may have to accept too much responsibility at too young an age. We had to keep all our doors locked for years because of J's aggressive behaviour. At one stage his sister showed emotional reactions whenever he came home from the hospital, yet she cried when it was time for him to go back!

"Actually, now my daughter is grown up she is able to look back and say that in many ways, she thinks it was good for her in terms of understanding and learning to be unselfish and tolerant."
Son, brain damage, autism.

Mrs. A. . . . .
"I grew up with a physically handicapped sister myself, and I feel it was a slight disadvantage emotionally. I'm sure it did little for my character. In the light of this I do worry about my other two children, and it was mainly for their sakes that A started as a weekly boarder when he was seven. Now, we seen him every four weeks or so and they look forward to seeing him and don't mind giving in a little when he's home. They are lovely with him but they must be able to lead their own lives as other children do. They must not always have their horizons limited because 'A can't do it".
Son, Downs syndrome.

Mrs. M. . . . .
"I think that C's trouble is that he was an adored only child, and although he looked forward to having a brother, he didn't realise how much of a back seat he would have to take. He is four years older than R. and very sensible for his age. He said a pretty wonderful thing the other day, I thought. My husband and I were talking about using our bikes for excursions etc., C said, "When I get big enough, I'll be able to take R out on the tandem won't I Dad?". My husband said, that was a good idea and a kind thought. C said, "I shan't relish it Dad, but after all he is my brother, and can't help being like he is, can he? And, if anyone laughs at him, I'll bash them on the nose!" This is the sort of thing that brings a great lump to my throat, and makes me feel sorry for the brothers and sisters of the handicapped ones, though no doubt it makes better people of them. But, it's hard, isn't it, for a little lad of 7½ to have to think like this, and shoulder his responsibilities so to speak. Another time, we were talking to each other about what would happen should R outlive us. We didn't know C was listening, or even within ear-shot, when he suddenly entered the room and said, "You're not putting him in a home when you are dead, I shall look after him." So, we explained that he might be married by then and his wife wouldn't want R as well to live with them. So, he said he wouldn't marry anyone unless they would have R as well, and ended by saying that he hated girls anyway, and wasn't going to get married. So we asked where he was going to live – he said he was going to buy a big house with lots of bedrooms and four bathrooms and he and R would live there. We asked where he was going to get the money for his big house. He gave us both a withering look and said, "From the money you leave me in your Will, of course." We hooted with laughter, particularly as we have just been in the red at the bank. But, it just shows what goes through their minds, and since then we've taken care he doesn't hear any of our comments on R's future."
Son, Downs syndrome.

Mrs. T. . . . .
"A (sister) says she now feels that J is sometimes left out of things because of his handicap, but admits to having felt left out many times herself (and justifiably so.)"
Son, brain damage, autism.

Mrs. C. . . . .
"As P is an only child this doesn't apply to me. But, having seen parents with a handicapped child as well as others, it does seem to awaken a sense of compassion in the other children. I had my young niece to live with me for six months when she was 12 years old, and P. was then 18 – she was marvellous with him. He would often do things for her that he wouldn't do for me. She even cleared up his sick and made his wet bed!"
Son, brain damage.

Thoughts from a brother and sister

From Timothy, aged 8 –
"When Abi was born, I thought what a lovely girl she was. The first thing I did when I saw her was give her a kiss. I did not learn that she was handicapped until a few years after she was born. I thought it was nice to have someone to play with. Now she is five I am happy that she can come to school with me. Abi is a person in our family whom we all love a lot. I like looking after her. She is improving her speech tremendously. We are all very glad that she is managing to read and is now on Ladybird 4A reading book. She is enjoying reading but she is sometimes a bit shy when she reads to other people. She likes school and every day she tells us what she has done. She looks nice in pretty dresses. She also likes Sunday school and likes joining in the hymns. She likes listening to records and music. She also likes people reading books to her."
Sister, Downs syndrome.

From Helen, aged 9 –
"I love my sister very much. I am glad she is not normal because she might not be nice, she might spoil a game. I wish she would not grind her teeth, she gets me annoyed. I am sad that she might not live as long as we do, and I do not want her to go into a home. But people make me upset when they say nasty things about her. No one ever plays with her but me. I wish she could talk like us but she does not. I am afraid she might get hurt because she might run into the road and get knocked over or touch the iron, fiddle with a plug, or something like that."
Sister, Downs syndrome.

Another child

A mother whose first child is handicapped feels cheated of something which others seem to acquire so easily – the pleasure of her first baby. She wonders if subsequent children will also be affected and she doubts if she would be able to face another long pregnancy which might end in the same way. Even if she could be assured of an unaffected second child, could she cope with another child now that the present one is going to bring problems?

The first baby is something very special. It is felt to be a presentation to the husband and is perhaps a first grandchild for the grandparents. The sense of loss, therefore, is so much greater and there is a feeling of letting them down. On the practical side, the mother has no experience of looking after a baby; in fact she may feel nervous about the thought of handling any baby at all. Now, not only is she expected to learn the new skills of being a mother but she is expected to specialize in something she knows even less about.

There seems to be a tendency for parents with a handicapped child to wait longer than usual before having a second child. When the firstborn takes longer to achieve the basic skills mothers often want to concentrate on helping him, before bringing another child into the family. Sometimes it is not until the handicapped child is three or four years old that parents feel sure enough that they can cope with a larger family. Or it can simply take that long to find the courage to make the decision.

Most mothers say, once they find they are coping, that they have a very strong need to have another child, for their own sakes and that of the handicapped child. They want him to have brothers and sisters to grow up with, often speaking of it being unnatural for him to grow up in a family of adults.

And, of course, the parents themselves are anxious to have the experience of bringing up a child without special needs. The arrival of a healthy normal baby after an anxious nine months is all the more joyful because of the contrast with the previous birth. Watching the baby go from stage to stage as a completely natural process gives continuous pleasure. Mothers feel that they are a complete family at last and look forward to observing a relatively problem free childhood. The new baby's presence often enhances the love for the handicapped child rather than detracts from it. Parents talk about feeling happier, and more relaxed. Instead of their everyday life being dominated by handicap the 'problem' becomes part of a wider range of experiences and interests. Some of the intensity goes out of their life, and they feel themselves more 'normal'. All of them find it hard work physically but almost always are convinced that it is worth it.

Sometimes a second child arrives before the parents have discovered that their first child is handicapped, so the decision is already made. Most are very glad that they were unaware of the first child's problems when they enlarged their family – they wonder if they would have gone ahead if they had known. They might have deprived themselves of their other children, or at least might not have had them until much later. They breathed a sigh of relief when they remembered how they had gone into a second pregnancy without knowing about the handicap and whether it could recur. In some cases, fortunately rare, mothers had given birth to a second handicapped child – a cruel blow indeed.

There are some types of mental handicap which can occur in subsequent children so it does seem advisable for couples to seek genetic advice through their doctor. Recent advances have made it possible to identity some parents who are at risk and to detect certain abnormalities in an unborn child. For parents who are found to be at risk there are special decisions to make. They might decide to take the risk and hope that they will be 'lucky' — but few feel prepared to do that. Some decide to try again and have prenatal tests to detect any abnormalities. Of course this can force another difficult decision if the foetus is shown to be affected. Should there be a termination, and if so what effect will the termination itself have upon the mother?

Adoption

The alternative of adoption is not usually a very productive one, because the presence of a handicapped child in the family is often seen as a disadvantage and adoption societies are reluctant to place their children there. From the parents' view point this seems most unfair — they argue that they are sure that they could offer a secure and happy life to a child. They point out that most families with a handicapped child have other children of their own and seem to bring them up successfully. Ironically, there have been cases where families who have a handicapped child of their own have been allowed to adopt a second handicapped child. The reason is of course that there are many handicapped children available for adoption and few families who feel able to take them. But there are not enough non-handicapped babies to meet the waiting lists of parents wanting to adopt them.

One couple who were advised not to have any more children of their own were unable to arrange for an early adoption. They were put on the waiting list but were warned that they might not be considered for at least two years. Finally, this couple opted for A.I.D. (artificial insemination by donor) which was effective in six months and gave them the second child they wanted.

These decisions are deeply personal and need a great deal of thought by both parents. All they can do is seek advice from medical experts, then take time to decide whether or not to extend their family. Fortunately in the majority of cases, the handicap has arisen from an isolated accident, before, during or after birth and is unlikely to happen again.

Brothers and Sisters
Useful books

Sibs — quarterly magazine

Me Too, V. & B. Cleaver (Collins, 1975)

Don't Forget Tom, H. Larsen (Black, 1974)

My Brother Steven Is Retarded, Harriet L. Sobol (Gollanz, 1978)

About Peter (R.S.M.H.C. books)

(further details in Publications Section)

Chapter Six
THE FAMILY: GRANDPARENTS

There is often a worry about the reaction of grandparents to the arrival of a handicapped child, particularly if this is the first grandchild. The mother feels that it will hit them particularly hard; her own parents will be heartbroken for her; her husband's parents may think it is her fault. For grandparents, who have brought up their own children happily and successfully, it is deeply distressing to have a tragedy in the family just when they thought the worst of their worries were over. Now, instead of being able to relax into the usual role of grandparents, enjoying the child without having total responsibility for him, they are beset by worries all over again.

Like the parents themselves they have to make swift adjustments and learn to become experts in a new field. They must try to offer comfort and support as well as try to set aside any long-held prejudices about mental disability.

It is hardly surprising that some grandparents find acceptance hard at first — and show it. They are in a difficult position. They want to advise and help but they don't want to interfere. They must be careful not to spoil the handicapped child at the expense of other grandchildren nor to appear to favour the other children at the handicapped child's expense. They wonder if they will be able to find the courage to look after the child in order to give the parents a break, or to support the parents' handling of the child regardless of their own instincts.

Their deep emotional bond with the parents can be both an advantage and a disadvantage. Being so close to the emotional issues can sometimes get in the way of constructive and practical discussion.

So mothers can find that their parents' reactions add one further worry to the already considerable list. Perhaps because they are older grandparents may be influenced by old superstitions and misinformed ideas. One mother heard her husband's mother remark, on receiving the news of the handicap,

> "I just don't understand it. There's never been anything like that in our family."

Sometimes grandparents simply will not accept the diagnosis, especially if there is no outward sign of handicap. They insist that parents have heard wrongly or have misunderstood. Some change the subject as soon as it is brought up; others suggest it might be better for everyone to put the child into care. Many are convinced that the other children in the family will be damaged in some way.

These reactions are caused by their great distress, which makes them deny the situation or seek a way of making the problem disappear as quickly as possible. Their distress is not entirely selfish. For them it is a double tragedy: seeing their son or daughter suffer and their life changed is coupled with sadness for their new grandchild. Often this is only an early panic reaction; gradually most come to realise that they are needed in a very special way.

A few persist in the belief that the child will catch up; only slowly do they accept the handicap as a fact. The more normal the child looks, the more difficult it is for them to accept that he has any handicap at all.

Mrs. H. . . . .
"I feel I must write to you as a very upset grandma. My daughter and her husband have two lovely children and in October they had a baby daughter. She is a mongol. You can imagine how shocked and upset we were, and so desperately sorry for my daughter and her little family. They say A is a 'regular' mongol, with a heart murmur, but they don't know how serious that is yet. My daughter has been marvellous, but the strain is telling. A is very sweet, and as a tiny baby doesn't seem different to a normal one. I see them often and help as much as possible not letting anyone see how frightened I am of the future. I can only hope and pray that they may not have her long – that may be wrong of course, but as I see it, time can only make things more and more difficult. All the love and care lavished on the baby are to no purpose. For years I have done voluntary work at a spastic centre, but I just can't adjust when it comes so close."
Granddaughter, Downs syndrome.

Mrs. L. . . . .
"My daughter has a little boy – he is now two, and a few months ago, a doctor told her he was a mongol. His eyes are crossed, but we expect to have them seen to next year. He hasn't the strong look of a mongol – do you think after his eyes are corrected, he will lose the little look he has sometimes? He is so natural usually, then other times he has that look again. Are there any books so I can study them to help him? If I can get the right books on the subject maybe he would learn more than we are teaching him just now."
Grandson, Downs syndrome.

MRS. S. . . . .
"When we first sent out birth announcements we had hardly any acknowledgements, then as friends recovered from the shock, we had a slowly accumulating pile of cards, letters, flowers and presents. It was amazing how sympathetic people were.

Just about everything that arrived made me cry, although about a week after she was born I had a 'dry' period when I felt hard and cold as if I'd never cry again.

"The attitude of our parents was difficult. I felt terribly guilty talking to my father because he wanted to stop all the discussion and just accept her as our daughter, it was the first time I just could not agree with him on such a major point. My mother was very upset and disappointed and often repeated "Oh I didn't want anything like this to happen to you two". When D came home she petted and nursed her, but still, like me, had frequent times of remembering and saying "Oh, isn't it a shame." My husband's parents and sister were upset and shocked. His father was most indignant that it should have happened like this, and probably wished there was someone one could complain to about such events. Then they got around to accepting the idea and welcomed her as a granddaughter, and seemed to be coping with the situation by ignoring it, and taking her at face value as a little baby girl. They also commented on how good she was – hardly ever crying, and sleeping well at nights. We took this to be a clear indication of mental deficiency – she never cried for her bottle like a normal baby."
Daughter, Downs syndrome.

All grandparents enjoy spoiling their grandchildren. But parents sometimes feel irritated when their handicapped child is regarded as a 'poor little thing' who must be indulged in everything. Grandparents may be upset when the child is reprimanded and this can lead to conflict of opinion. One mother felt very guilty that she was sometimes angry with her own mother.

"She really has helped me in so many ways and I don't know what I'd have done without her. Right from the start she has taken the child out so that I could shop or have my hair done. But he's no longer a baby and he has to be taught that he can't do just what he wants. She always says, "He doesn't understand" and lets him do anything when he's with her. How can I make her see that he never will understand unless we are firm when he's young and that such behaviour won't be acceptable when he's older? I've tried to explain but she just says she feels sorry for him and can't bear to see me get cross with him. She also seems to want to feed him all the time as though she is desperate to see him show pleasure. I know she loves him and does it out of kindness and I am very grateful to her. But I don't think she'll see what I'm getting at unless I put my foot down – which is impossible without hurting her feelings."

Of course, mothers who live away from their parents, or whose own mothers are dead, would consider such irritations small and unimportant ones, which they would willingly endure to have the practical help that went with them. And on the whole those who do have occasional differences with **grandparents appreciate how fortunate they are to have them around at all.**

One unfortunate couple were virtually cut off by both sets of grandparents — an exceptional situation. Looking back over the years since her daughter was born the mother said she was no longer hurt by this situation. Instead she felt that it was the grandparents who had lost out, missing, as they had, all the struggles and achievements. The parents had produced a pleasant and capable teenager and wished only that their pride in her could have been shared with their parents.

Many mothers feel guilty about what others might see as 'complaining'; but they are usually coping with several relationships at once; with husband, handicapped child, and their other children. It can be hard work handling grandma and granddad as well. Yet most of the time gratitude is uppermost; when irritations do occur it is very therapeutic if these can be expressed to other mothers. Then, the occasional 'little moan' is all that is necessary for the situation to be seen once again in perspective.

Chapter Seven

STRESS IN THE FAMILY

In the questionnaire (referred to in Chapter one) parents were asked: —
Question
"Do you feel that the presence of your handicapped child in the family presents —
a) no more stress than a non-handicapped child
b) some extra stress at times
c) great stress most of the time

Answers	Number of parents
a) no more stress than a non-handicapped child	31
b) some extra stress at times	91
c) great stress most of the time	31

It was noticeable that all those whose response was category a had children with Downs Syndrome.

The amount of stress imposed on the family by their handicapped child seems to depend, not upon how backward he is intellectually, but upon the presence of physical or emotional difficulties which interfere with normal family life.

A child who is of pleasant temperament, co-operative behaviour and is socially acceptable is usually described as 'no trouble at all' or 'a real blessing', even though he may be severely retarded in the intellectual sense. On the other hand, those whose children are given to bizarre or wild behaviour, who have aggressive or hyperactive outbursts, who seem totally unresponsive to the requests of others or prohibit outings, feel that their lives are dominated by the stress.

In most cases, however, the child's handicap is something parents are aware of and make allowances for, but it does not overwhelm their whole existence.

Hyperactivity
It is not lack of intellectual ability in itself which causes the stress. Almost always, those who find the going hard are those whose child presents problems of behaviour which require constant vigilance, the ability to shut out persistent noise, or which deprive the family of the right amount of sleep.

Hyperactivity and diet

During the last few years, it has become evident that hyperactivity can be reduced or even eliminated by the detection and treatment of food allergies. The Hyperactive Childrens Support Group (see Information Section) has been treating children with great success for a number of years. Most of their work has been done with children who are not mentally or physically handicapped, but increasingly they are advising parents of mentally handicapped hyperactive children and adults. It has been found that other conditions such as epilepsy, eczema and migraine respond to adjustment to diet. Speech, hearing and bed wetting have often improved once the hyperactivity has been reduced.

The diet consists of eliminating harmful chemicals found in processed food, and does not involve the taking of drugs or medicines.

Epilepsy

Epilepsy can occur in many forms — the fits may be mild or severe, frequent or infrequent. Because it demands constant vigilance on the part of parents, it can be a considerable strain. Families may restrict their social life, outings or holidays. Usually a drug or a combination of drugs can be prescribed which effectively controls the fits, but it can sometimes take time to find a treatment which does so without side effects. Work is now being done on the treatment of epilepsy by dietary means and there have been cases in which the fits have been considerably reduced in number and severity. (see Information Section.)

Physical handicaps

Lifting, bathing, dressing and feeding a child with a severe physical handicap is very hard work. Inevitably such a child, unable to co-operate, makes great demands on the parents.

Yet very often, parents of children who are quite helpless in the physical sense, speak of them only with the greatest affection. They talk warmly of the child's happy, contented and undemanding nature.

In accounts of their experiences mothers seem able to accept such helplessness in their child. What grinds them down much more is helplessness in themselves.

A mother who has to see to all her child's physical needs does know what is demanded of her, and can see some result from what she does. On the other hand, the mother whose child taps obsessively on walls, throws screaming tantrums, races off at full speed unless his hand is held, or refuses to be touched or handled, simply does not know what she should do. She feels helpless and alienated from her child instead of drawn to him. The physical effort of lifting a disabled child seems less likely to cause stress than continual emotional battering and jangled nerves.

Parents looking back

Unlike parents of non-handicapped children who view their child's future with optimism, parents of a handicapped baby regard the future with understandable pessimism. They see themselves as having an immediate problem, and nothing but problems to come. Within a space of a few hours, days, or weeks, they anticipate a lifetime of difficulties, preparing themselves for the very worst.

To try to find out how much of this early pessimism turned out to be justified, a group of parents were asked: –

Question
"Remembering your feelings at the beginning, would you say that life with your handicapped child has turned out to be: –

a) better than you expected?
b) about as you thought it would be?
c) worse than expected?"

Their replies: –
Mrs. F. . . . .
"As I had worked with handicapped children, the various stages of R's development (sitting, walking, feeding etc.) occurred much as I expected. But, I was unprepared for the sheer physical hard work that looking after a healthy active mentally handicapped child can entail. I had had no previous experience with very young Downs syndrome children, and I was given the impression at the Maternity Hospital that these babies are lethargic, incurious and very little trouble.

On the contrary, I found R full of energy, and interested in all that went on about her. In fact she was far more fascinating than I had ever imagined, and at the same time, a great deal more trouble."
Daughter, Downs syndrome.

Mrs. H. . . . .
"I had no idea at all what it would involve and therefore, had no idea what to expect. I do find, however, that the older I get, the harder it gets (all my other four children are grown up) so I live from day to day, not thinking of five years hence."
Son, unspecified retardation.

Mrs. C. . . . .
"On the whole I would say it was better than expected. A, now seven, fits in fairly well with all family activities. She is a lot prettier and has more character than we expected. The hardest part after the diagnosis was the first two years – coming to terms with the fact that she was so slow (slower than expected) – with the physical milestones, like sitting, standing etc. The mental ones weren't so apparent until later."
Daughter, Downs syndrome.

Mrs. G. . . . .
"On the whole, things are better. The terrible hurt, despair and fear diminish, and the feeling 'life must go on' takes over. Every so often, the wounds re-open, and the tears and rage come, but the 'here and now' takes up most time and thought. It is a revelation how ones character and tolerance develops — not at once, but gradually. You realise what is really important, and find kinship and support amongst those who have suffered like yourselves."
Daughter, tuberous sclerosis.

Mrs. D. . . . .
"On the whole, it has been better than we thought it would be. She may be handicapped, but she is still our child, and we love her for what she is."
Daughter, Downs syndrome.

Mrs. N. . . . .
"I don't know how I expected my child to progress as his cause of handicap is not known. In some ways I am glad to say he is better than I expected because, for example, he will definitely walk. He now crawls up the steps, and comes down again. On the other hand, I had hoped his speech might have developed by now, so I'm resigning myself to the fact he may never speak."
Son, unspecified retardation.

Mrs. G. . . . .
"S is 2½ now and we have overcome many obstacles. He has spent much of his time in hospital. He has just had his valve refitted and we were in hospital for 4 weeks, then another 5 having antibiotics injected into the pumping chamber of his valve. Our life has been very limited as he has no resistance to infection and we are virtually housebound in the winter. But, we consider ourselves extremely lucky to still have him, and although we never know what each morning will bring we are grateful for each day. He is a lovely natured little boy, very happy, who demands nothing but our love. He never cries, which I know sounds wonderful but it has its disadvantages — it means I can't leave him out of my sight at all. I have stayed with him all the time in hospital because, although it's an upheaval I feel that even though he's backward mentally and physically the constant contact has been very important to both of us. I think that's why we've got so far, I had to fight for things to keep him alive at times, but I find I've always had somebody who mattered behind me. My Health Visitor has been like a mother to me. Each time I've been in hospital I've met somebody worse off than me so I've always made them a coffee, invited them to my room and just let them talk and talk. S's progress is as follows, (despite even the paediatricians saying he wouldn't) . . . He can at last support his head, roll over to get to places on the floor, almost

sits, talks in a babble, picks sweets off a tray, says 'daddy' and 'es' for yes, hold his left arm out be be picked up (the other is spastic) has started to eat mince and bread without the crusts (another big step). He can mimic people, wave 'bye bye', and at long last has started pushing with his legs − so there is reason to believe he will eventually walk. I would be happy to help or support any other mother with a baby with such a severe form of meningitis plus hydrocephalus, in any way I can. I could tell her that if you fight on, you get the strength from somewhere. Providing the child is wanted by his parents no one has the right to decide against you and withdraw treatment. I think I could take on the Houses of Parliament now if I had to!"
Son, meningitis plus hydrocephalus.

Mrs. H. . . . .
"Our great sorrow is not that B is a mongol − this aspect of her life has brought us as much joy as sorrow, as she is high grade and attractive to look at. She is happy and loving. The terrible thing is that she has leukaemia and the doctors only give her about two years to live. Five months of that have gone already. I have made many interesting friends through her. I have one great friend who has a mongol girl of 13. The welfare worker asked her to visit me when B was diagnosed. Seeing her daughter so sensible and happy, enjoying the lovely new Training Centre, it made it seem not such a tragedy after all that B was a mongol. My biggest problem has been the sheer weight of a large toddler with the mind of a baby, and my kind husband decided to manage with his old car for some years longer and bought me an old mini. It has made so much difference to my life. I would never have had the courage to learn to drive if it hadn't been for other friends with backward children, who urged me on. Now I can help those less well off with transport etc. I just don't know how we will cope with losing B, we all love her so much. I hope no one else has our particular problem."
Daughter, Downs syndrome.

Mrs. E. . . . .
"Looking back, things have been better than I expected, but what I expected was sheer hell! At the time, the Spastics Society was running a fund raising advert which said, 'Before she had Tony Mrs A looked like this − now you wouldn't recognize her!' I can still remember it word for word. One has stupid dramatic thoughts when one is alone all day (my husband was out for eleven hours, which seemed an eternity). I was quite convinced that my life and hopes for the future were finished. Life would be just one long nursing job that would never end. Of course, I was ill informed about mental handicap but I knew more than a lot of people − teacher training did cover the broad spectrum of all abilities. Anyway, nothing could have been worse than I expected!"
Son, Downs syndrome.

Mrs. P. . . . .
"Far far better than I expected — I would not change my B for anything in the world."
Son, Downs syndrome.

Mrs. W. . . . . .
"In some respects it has been worse and in others better than I thought, that is, I didn't imagine I would ever love A, and I didn't believe 'mongols are lovable children'. However with knowledge, I now see that they are. They are definitely the 'best' handicap (in my opinion). But, the response, help and understanding has been much worse than expected. You find yourself having to cope with other people's lack of knowledge or embarrassment not your own, which, it is taken for granted, has been overcome."
Son, Downs syndrome.

Mrs. C. . . . .
"After being told my son was brain damaged after meningitis at 8 months it has been worse than I thought it would be."
Son, brain damage.

Mrs. M. . . . .
"I have many times wished that he had never been born and several times in my periods of dark despair have thought how much better we would all have been without him (wicked thoughts). But this week when it was touch and go whether he survived or not I was surprised and pleased to find that I would be horrified if anything happened to him, and all of us agreed that our lives without him would be very miserable indeed. I've never said this to anyone as I'm sure people wouldn't understand and would be shocked by it. No doubt people would say, 'no wonder she had a breakdown saying things like that'. I can't claim much credit for his progress but have come to believe that my breakdown was 'all for the best', and much good has come out of seeming despair and failure."
Son, Downs syndrome.

For all but a few families, the handicapped child was not felt to be a source of intolerable stress. Parents had been willing to make changes and had found untapped levels of patience and understanding in the face of considerable difficulties. Stress in the form of frustration or anger was mentioned more frequently in connection with inadequate or non-existent help and information.

The chance to share their problems with other parents and professionals was considered very valuable — this showed up very clearly in the optimism of those who had support, and the weary sentiments of those who had not.

Progressive disabilities

Sadly, there are a few mental handicap conditions which are accompanied by physical malfunctions, and which shorten the child's life expectancy. In some cases there are defects of major organs which are so severe that the child may not survive more than one or two years. There are other conditions which are caused by the inability of the body to dispose of certain substances, leading to accumulation of harmful substances and damage to major organs. In these cases deterioration is gradual and life expectancy varies according to severity.

Parents in this position have special adjustments to make, and at the beginning at least, their emotions are in chaos. But, all of them who wrote to *In Touch* were glad that they had been told all the facts. Because they had a child who was frail, or likely to suffer recurring illness they were aware that the physical demands would be great. But the knowledge that the task would not go on for ever enabled them to say: –

"His life is likely to be short, so he will stay at home with us, and we will do everything we can to make sure that life is a happy and secure one."

There is of course an ever present dread of the time when the child dies, and the more progress he or she makes, the prospect of losing him seems all the more cruel. Nevertheless mothers have been able to say that there were advantages in being at least partially prepared. They believed it brought them even closer to the child, that it helped them to be more patient and appreciative of his positive qualities.

Mothers who wrote to tell me that their child had died always stressed the amount of love he had given and generated in others, and that his life, though short, had been worthwhile.

Parents in this situation are especially in need of contact with others in the same situation or who had coped with it in the past. Many mothers whose children have died have remained on the *In Touch* list, making themselves available to be contacted by any mother in need of support. They are able to offer a real understanding of the last months of the child's life, when he might need constant attention, and can help the mother through the period of grief after the child has died.

Often those who have lost a child continue to be involved in activities with other handicapped children, perhaps running Toy Libraries or playgroups. They feel that their experience of looking after such a child, coupled with the sudden availability of spare time and energy, should be used as a kind of tribute to their child's life.

When a child is unlikely to reach adulthood, and when during childhood he needs careful medical care, the mental handicap does not assume so much importance. For parents who spend much of their time visiting their child in hospital, making sure he is not exposed to infectious illnesses, working out special diets or giving medication or treatment, the child's slowness of learning is the least of their worries. Often, mothers would say that they would willingly have their child mentally backward if only he could be relieved of his physical suffering and could run about. To them, he is less a mentally handicapped child, more a sick one.

The courage and good sense shown by mothers in these circumstances is amazing. They do not give up their efforts. Some find themselves having to convince doctors that they do not want treatment withdrawn and a few have had to insist on treatment. Many have completely confounded those doctors by achieving progress where none was expected or by extending the child's life expectancy much further than predicted. Several times mothers have been told by consultants that they had 'never known a child with this condition do so well'.

It could seem that extending a life by a year or two was pointless, or that it only prolonged the agony for all concerned. But, knowing the mothers, no one could sustain that view. For them, there is every point. When the child does die they will not be tortured by guilt wondering if they could have done more. They will know, beyond any doubt, that they did everything possible, and more important they will know that their child felt safe, secure and loved to the very end.

In the past, some conditions brought about the death of the child in a matter of weeks or months — and this short life expectancy came to be regarded as inevitable. No child survived long enough to show developmental progress. However, when mothers, with their care and determination, can extend this time, it provides a great deal of information about the condition and its long term effects upon the child. Doctors can now look at children of three and four years old, mapping their progress so far, and hopefully will come a little nearer to helping those affected in the future.

MRS. A. . . . .

"When E was newborn we had great problems to get her 'shunt' inserted (for the hydrocephalus). She was considered inoperable and great pressure was put on us to withhold treatment. It was very wrong because although E's prognosis isn't good she has a very happy life and is doing well considering her poor health. She is now crawling and will pull herself onto her knees now and then and sometimes will pull herself to a sitting position to play. She has six words now, the latest being 'didder' (dinner) and 'ilk' (milk) — all of which is very encouraging. And she is such a joyful and content child. It would have been such a dreadful waste of a happy life to let her die untreated. We are lucky to have her albeit she's a constant headache healthwise. She is certainly not the cabbage forecast by the paediatricians.

I would like the address of Mrs S. whose daughter died from this condition. I'm sure she will be able to give me great strength. E is a very sick child and we are always being told that her prognosis is not good. She has been on the point of dying twice — last time I phoned our parish priest to come over with his little black bag. We realise that it is only a matter of time and accept this now.

It really doesn't hurt us anymore. If E lives as long as Mrs S's daughter we shall have been extremely lucky and privileged. It's wonderful to know that we are not the only parents producing an 'oddball' — forgive me if I sound hard. If I couldn't laugh at E's problems and call her a 'rat bag' when she's a trial I would probably end up in a locked ward of our local mental hospital!"

Daughter, rare chromosome abnormality.

Mrs. R. . . . .
"We know that she may never reach her teens, but we're glad we were told. Obviously we dread losing her – but we are prepared for it. We would hate her to become increasingly disabled and left without us. As it is, we shall probably outlive her and (though perhaps it's awful to say this) we can't help being glad that she won't be left alone. Knowing that her life may be short we can concentrate on making it as happy as possible".
Daughter, metabolic disorder.

Physical handicaps

Useful books (see also Publications)

1 **British Institute of Mental Handicap**
a) Management of the Physically Handicapped Child – guidelines to handling, Rosemary York-Moore (1981).
b) Management of the Physically Handicapped Child – guidelines to carrying, lifting and seating, Rosemary York-Moore (1981).
c) Progress To Standing – for children with severe physical handicap, Katy Hollis (1977).
2 Handling The Young Cerebral Palsied Child At Home (Second Edition), Nancy R. Finnie (1974)
   William Heinemann Medical Books Ltd.
3 More Than Sympathy – The everyday needs of sick and handicapped children and their families.
   Richard Lansdown (1980) **Methuen.**
4 **Souvenir Press**
a) The Wheelchair Child
   Philippa Russell (1978).
b) Insights from The Blind
   Selma Fraiberg (1977)
c) Teaching The Handicapped Child
   Dorothy M. Jeffree, Roy McConkey and Simon Hewson (1977).
5 Help For The Epileptic Child
   Jorge C. Lagos (1974)
   Macdonald and Jane's.

Chapter Eight

COMING TO TERMS

Before they can begin to make plans for their child's future, parents must live through their own present; unravelling chaotic emotions and allowing time for the initial grief to subside. Only then can they begin to make sense of the facts and get them in perspective.

In the sense that handicap means an interruption in the normal pattern of living, parents are, for a while, as handicapped as the child, but in a different way. They are handicapped by shock, lack of knowledge and fear of the future, and often describe their feelings in physical terms, such as 'a slap in the face', 'a life sentence', 'stunned', 'drained' and so on.

The child himself is blissfully unaware of the 'label' pinned on him and the drama that surrounds it. He has no sudden sense of loss, so unlike his parents, has no need for a period of recovery. For all the child knows that is how he (and everybody else) is supposed to be. His parents do the suffering for him. Until they can recover from the way they *feel* they are helpless to act in any constructive way to help their child.

Many parents have described how their attitude to their child was improved once they had recognised certain conflicts in or prejudices in themselves. Once they became aware of negative feelings they could set about disposing of them by 'retraining' their thoughts. Their own emotional turmoil was getting in the way of their recovery, and using up valuable energy.

This change in approach does take time, and some parents were more successful than others.

New parents may feel pessimistic about achieving it at all, and may be quite unable to visualise a time when they can talk about the child with optimism – or even to mention the handicap without physical pain. Most parents of older children would recognise that pessimism, because they experienced it with exactly the same intensity.

Expectations

Parents who have been highly educated, successful at school, university, career and perhaps in 'social standing' have much to offer their handicapped child. They are usually articulate, forward looking and confident in their ability to deal with professionals. They may also be well versed in medical or educational developments, or have training in teaching or child care. They are used to thinking for themselves and have organisational ability which they use in the setting up of self-help groups, toy libraries and so on. It is important to them to find out all they can about their child's handicap and his prospects, and they will be more insistent upon getting answers to their questions.

Sometimes, however, the very fact that they themselves had experienced satisfaction and enjoyment in education makes acceptance of a handicapped child very much harder. It is natural for them to expect their offspring to be intelligent, responsive, alert and interested. Even before their children arrive they anticipate pleasure in helping them with schoolwork or sport. These expectations are not contrived but are simply seen and accepted as the probable course of events, and a good education is a priority in their hopes for their children.

For deep thinking parents the diagnosis of mental handicap can be a great personal disappointment. The loss of intellectual potential seems particularly cruel and sometimes can lead to bitterness and thoughts of rejection. The child is set apart from them by his handicap and sometimes it is very hard to identify with him as their child. Many, in correspondence, say that he seemed to be a stranger or intruder. One or two highly educated mothers described in vivid detail their struggle to accept their child at face value. They analysed their every emotion, testing themselves constantly for their reactions as they handled the baby in the hope that they might feel something for him. They tried to rationalise their fears – 'it's not the baby's fault, he can't help it, he is my child, he needs me'.

The constant effort to force a love for the child only tended to increase their tension and prevent any instinctive feelings from coming through. Every small contact with the child was accompanied by wondering why they felt so bitter and why they could not feel 'maternal'. So handling the child became an even greater ordeal.

One mother spoke about her phobia about deformity and handicap and how ashamed it made her feel. She felt that she should have had the strength of mind to overcome it and see the baby as helpless and innocent, but, as he was the embodiment of all her fears it was extremely hard for her. Sometimes too, parents like these have moved away from their home area, to university or professional careers. They may live in areas where neighbours see little of each other.

The husband's job may be a demanding one involving long hours and trips away from home. Grandparents may live too far away to be of regular support or to get to know the baby as he grows older. If it is her first baby, the mother may have given up a satisfying career to start her family, making the contrast with her earlier life all the greater.

Their main fear is not how they will look after the child in practical terms, but how they will tolerate him as a member of the family. Most do come through this initial conflict, especially if the feelings are not shared by their husbands. If the husband can provide some of the rational thought his wife needs, the issues become more balanced and in perspective.

Mrs. B. . . . .
"P is nine weeks old now, and a dear little thing. My husband has accepted her unreservedly (he has a much nicer nature than me!) I love her, but feel she is really nothing to do with me or us as a family. I'm sure this is because she is so alien-looking, that I don't feel a blood bond — just that I'm looking after someone else's child. At birth she didn't look too different, but now I can see her features setting into a pattern. Our doctor, on his solitary visit to us said, "Of course she will grimace, and loll her tongue out as she develops."

This filled me with horror, and of course, now I'm aware of it every time she puts her tongue out, and it distresses me terribly. For the first time in my life I wish we didn't live in a village, it's a real ordeal to push her out and I cringe whenever anyone looks at her. I dread the time when she will be sitting up, especially if the doctor proves right.
Daughter, Downs syndrome.

If it is the husband who cannot face the implications of the handicap — as sometimes is the case — the mother finds herself taking the more positive line and in the process she usually strengthens her own resolve. If the couple can work through the initial conflicts they can begin to channel their energies into giving the child the benefit of their abilities. When they have come to terms with their personal disappointment, they are 'released' from the worst of their internal struggles to help the child develop to his fullest potential.

Mrs. P. . . . .
"H spent the first three days of his life in an incubator. The paediatrician on his first visit, told me he was an abnormal looking baby.

I must admit he was an ugly looking baby but it hurt dreadfully that a paediatrician should tell us this, just twenty four hours after our first longed for child had been born. Six weeks later he was found to have a hip slightly out of place. At three months he was very ill and was in hospital for five weeks. During the first four months there was no mention to me that H was anything other than a sick baby. As time went by it became obvious that he was not progressing as he should. My husband said this was because he had been so poorly — I wanted to believe this very much. Many tests were carried out, and when he was eighteen months old, we were told that he was very, very backward, and may never walk — only time would tell. Although there have been times when I have been upset about the whole situation, I accepted it almost as if it was natural that our baby should be as he is. My husband found it very hard. He would only talk about it to me, and only when I brought it up. As the baby seemed to get more and more precious he started talking about it more and more. Once we accepted the situation

together, life became less tense and we got on with the job of helping our little boy. We are extremely pleased with the paediatrician he is under now, but we certainly have come across a lack of assistance in the early months.
Son, Smith-Lemi-Opitz syndrome.

Inability to accept the child
For some however the feelings do not change however hard they try. If both husband and wife feel so strongly that they cannot form a relationship with the child, they reinforce the anxieties in each other.

Two mothers wrote to the *In Touch* scheme about this, and they and their husbands were unable to overcome their feelings sufficiently to keep their baby at home. From the beginning they were unable to tolerate the mental handicap, and as such, the child who reminded them of it a hundred times a day. They felt that the unhappiness it brought threatened their marriage and drained them both physically and mentally. The only way they could look after the child at the beginning was to regard him as temporary until he was old enough to go to a residential home or to foster parents.

In both cases, the children were at home until they were about three years old, and the parents tried to have arrangements made, without success, for almost all of that time. Neither couple was prepared to let their child go somewhere they felt to be unsuitable, and were adamant that he should be in a homely atmosphere where he would establish relationships. For some, living with a child for three years would diminish the wish to let him go. But, in these two cases, this did not happen. There had been moments, they said, when they had felt less resentful – even a little warmer towards the child, but for most of the time they looked after his daily needs simply because they had no choice.

These were not unfeeling or cruel people – on the contrary their lives were fraught with feelings of guilt. They wondered why others seemed capable of loving their handicapped child when they could not, and lived a daily conflict of trying to balance their duty against their resentment. The feelings that all parents experience for a time after diagnosis did not, for them, soften with time.

The child did not win them over as a person because the mental handicap clouded everything. They went on feeling as they had in the beginning while trying to appear as if they were coping well.

Both of these mothers had children with Downs syndrome; the same condition which prompted other mothers to say that life had been far better than they could ever have guessed at the beginning. The children had no additional medical problems and were not especially difficult or unresponsive.

Both made good physical progress. Downs children usually show great charm very early and this helps to ease the despair and cement a loving relationship with their parents. Both mothers were more than adequately equipped to deal with day to day care and were likely to produce mildly retarded capable children. Their children went into residential schools at around three years, where they made good progress and were happy. The parents felt they had made the right decision, for themselves and their children. It was the mental handicap with all its implications which they could not endure, and they felt completely unable to accept the baby who personified it.

Mrs. B. . . . .
"When D was born we had been married a year and three months. I was twenty two and had completed my first probationary year of teaching, and we wanted to have our family straight away. My husband had just entered a General Practice partnership in a town new to us.

I was perfectly aware of the birth, and could see D's skinny little legs before the rest of her arrived. Having a breach birth meant that she came rather awkwardly, and grew short of oxygen. She was rushed to the Special Care Baby Unit. I kept asking, "Is she alright?" and was reassured. We were both a little worried about her, but very pleased to have a daughter.

Later on, my husband came back, and told me without preamble, that our daughter was a mongol. All the emotions of childbirth now seemed to be invalidated. The first of our family wasn't at all. A mongol, and imposter placed instead of our baby. A minute genetic mistake. We both cried and cried. All the months of delighted expectation and forgotten hurtful struggle of giving birth, were entirely separate from the resulting infant.

They were real and lovely, and everything to be desired. What happened now was unreal and like a bad dream – but, it was real. The times when I went over things in my head could not be counted. Not least was my overwhelming pity for my husband who had known straight away, despite the reluctance of the obstetrician and paediatrician to agree definitely about the mongolism before tests, and who had gone home and sobbed on the bed before coming to tell me. All alone, and the first tears since childhood.

That night and the following day I wished and wished with all my heart that she would die. A useless life of being kept and looked after, and never self-supporting, was ahead for her. It may as well end before it began. But, she pulled through. In the morning the hospital cleaners and nurses regaled me with "You're a new one, have you had your baby? Girl or Boy?" "Down in Special Care is she, never mind, she'll be up with you here, soon," etc. etc. I answered all with bad grace and as briefly as possible, struggling not to cry. I hated her, I didn't want her, to think about her, and especially not to see her.

In between my coming home, and D coming home, we talked around the subject endlessly. We decided right from the start to regard her as temporary – to look after her until a school could be found. We knew nothing of the residential or special school provisions, but we were determined to put her into a residential school when she was toddling, or as soon as she could be admitted.

We couldn't face the thought of her growing up as part of the family — which was more important than ever. Neither could we resign ourselves to the thought of having a permanent dependent after the other children had grown up and left us."
Daughter, Downs syndrome.

Taking the child as he comes

Those for whom educational achievement is not a priority are still, of course, very distressed to discover that their child will be backward. But because their expectations for their children do not extend to particularly high levels of academic achievement, they do not feel the same kind of personal loss. Such mothers have said, in correspondence, "We accepted him for what he was, he's a baby like any other," "We know he'll never be Prime Minister but it doesn't matter so long as he is happy" or "We'll just do our very best for him and give him lots of love." While they may be saddened by his lack of development, they are not irritated or horrified by it. They don't analyse their relationship or have any pre-conceived ideas about what it should be and seem more able to take each day as it comes and meet problems when they come.

Mothers like these rarely express any thoughts of 'rejection' — in fact they see the child as needing them more than ever because of his special difficulties. They are much more concerned with the everyday practicalities of life than anything else and, as many are unaware of the alternative of residential care, the question of rejection does not even arise.

When the baby is small he is seen to be no greater problem than any other baby so why consider handing him over to someone else? To part with their small baby goes against all their instincts, as for a few others, keeping him goes against all theirs.

'Money doesn't bring happiness but it helps you to be miserable in comfort.'

If there are financial worries already, an extra mouth to feed takes on greater implications. Financial security does not lessen the problems but it does eliminate one worrying aspect of the future. Being able to pay for help in the house and owning a house which has plenty of space and labour saving equipment gives the mother time to recover and get to know her baby. Owning her own car makes hospital visits and shopping easier. Having the money to buy educational toys and play equipment, to pay for playgroup or private short stay care if it becomes necessary provides some assurance for the future.

All parents are entitled to various grants and allowances and to some items of equipment from their local authority. For the better off these are a matter of choice, for others they may be a necessity. A mother who had intended to go back to work when her child was at playgroup or school might not be able to do so after all. She may have to travel long distances on public transport or in taxis for hospital appointments. For her the search for available financial help, making application, filling in forms or being interviewed, all adds to the strain.

Entitlement to financial aid is rarely mentioned at the beginning despite the fact that there are many Government leaflets available to Social Workers. (Chapter 14 gives details of this). Mothers have struggled through shopping with a handicapped child and a baby — pushing one, carrying the other, or have been unable to shop at all unless they could leave one of the children with someone else — all the time unaware that they could get a double lightweight push chair from their Social Services Department.

The mother of an incontinent child washed dozens of nappies a week for seven years before she heard (by accident) that she could have had free disposable nappies delivered to her door from the start. Sometimes a Health Visitor or Social Worker has been as surprised as the mother to find out that these aids could be provided. The wearing routine of an extended babyhood can be lightened by practical means. It would relieve one anxiety at least if all parents were given full details of the available financial help soon after the child's handicap is diagnosed. The offer of free equipment or money is perhaps thought unnecessary or even unseemly at the time of diagnosis. But if parents are armed with the knowledge they do at least have the choice of seeking help or rejecting it — rather than no opportunity at all.

Families should not be made to feel that they are receiving 'handouts'. Rather, they should be helped to see themselves in partnership with the authorities in doing a specialised job, for which there are special requirements.

Grants and allowances are in recognition of the family's extra needs arising from their child's handicap. It is not charity and far less unseemly than needlessly spending seven years up to the elbows in dirty nappies.

Religion

For some, who do not believe in God, the arrival of a handicapped child may reinforce their disbelief, or they may simply accept it as a medical fact without relating it to any philosophical or religious view.

However, other parents have said that prayer played an important part in helping them to come to terms with their child's condition. Not only those who have had a longstanding and deep faith are drawn to prayer but there are others who say, "I'm not really a religious person but I prayed continually for strength."

Some go so far as believing that God has given them this child to challenge them to test their faith, or that they have been chosen because their faith fitted them to provide for the special needs of the child. This firm conviction that God has entrusted them with the care of such a child reinforces their sense of partnership with Him; and in return they are able to put their trust in God to see them through.

Deep religious faith can, however, be a drawback if a mother feels that she is being punished for some imagined fault. Fortunately the improvement in knowledge of the causes of handicap means that most people realise that 'it can happen to anyone'. Nevertheless, in the vulnerable state in which a mother finds herself, a sense of guilt may persist and in such cases the support and reassurance of a minister or a priest is all-important.

Parents who belong to a religious denomination can often discover practical help of which they had not known the existence earlier.

They may be offered baby-sitters, outings with or without their child, and even special services for handicapped children and their families — occasions when their child can make as much noise as he wishes without being regarded as a nuisance.

Mrs. M. . . . .
> "R too, has given us cause to feel proud of him. Last Sunday he took part in some Bible Readings about the Christmas Story, at a special church service for the handicapped which is held every year. He stood there — his nose hardly reaching the lectern, and read his allotted piece just beautifully and I could hardly believe that when he was younger I thought he would never be able to read at all with understanding. I was told afterwards that there was not a dry eye in the church, as he was the youngest ever to take part, and I was pleased that he could show what can be done for children like him, with patience and perseverance. His school teacher is the greatest and much of it is thanks to her."

Son, Downs syndrome.

Mrs. N. . . . .
> "I believe that parents should be taught early on that through early stimulation they can almost always help their child to achieve more in later years. A visit to Lourdes may seem ridiculous to those who are not religious, but seeing the many kinds of disability, and being in such a spiritual atmosphere was very beneficial to us — and we are not Catholics."

Daughter, microcephaly.

Mrs. E. . . . .
> "Saying, or praying 'one day at a time' and determination to prove that something good can come forth. I'm not particularly religious but the parable of the talents has been my motto."

Daughter, Downs syndrome.

Items from the *In Touch* newsletter . . . . .
> "Mrs L feels that the clergy of all religions could be of great help to parents in the various crises which crop up in bringing up a mentally handicapped child. And, she believes that many would be only too willing to assist, if only these problems were brought to their notice. She says, "one of the ways that I think the churches might well do some good is in helping people who are reluctant (in some cases horror stricken) at the thought of sending their children to special schools or at parting with them for weekly boarding, even though this would provide them with the help and relief they need. While social workers etc could help with practical arrangements, they are simply not able to give a great deal of time to helping with emotional problems. Clergymen, nuns and so on, being the sort of

people who can drop in on families in an informal way, might be able to offer support or perhaps might even be able to arrange a meeting with someone else who had faced the same decisions. I feel that the churches, with their many dedicated workers, should at least be alerted to the nature of help that is needed, and also to know who to contact if they come across parents who don't know what to do".

"Mrs L tells me that she was recently approached by a teacher and asked if she would like her mentally handicapped son to go to a local church playgroup. It is a Roman Catholic church, but the playgroup welcomes children of all religions. Her son is collected and brought home by the staff. The church will also baby sit for elderly relatives, regardless of religion. Mrs L wonders if other churches offer this kind of practical help, and thought it worthwhile to pass the information on, so that other parents might like to make enquiries in their own area."

Chapter Nine

ONE DAY AT A TIME

Finding the best approach
It would be possible to give a selection from parents' remarks which implies that, once the initial shock had passed, life with a handicapped child is endlessly rewarding, full of love and laughter. Equally, it would be possible to provide statements which imply that it has been a bitter struggle from the beginning. Both of these impressions would be dishonest and unrealistic.

The truth is that, for most people, life with their child brings a mixture of intense love, pride, achievement and humour, punctuated in varying degrees by weariness, frustration and anger.

Life with any child, handicapped or not, conforms to this pattern. How this affects family life as a whole depends on a whole range of circumstances.

Mothers often say, in correspondence, "Only those who have had a handicapped child themselves can really appreciate the feelings involved." The following advice comes from such people — people who have experienced the same conflicting emotions and the same practical problems.

A number of parents were asked:

"In the light of the knowledge and experience you have gained over the years, what would you consider to be the best mental approach that new parents should try to cultivate to help them adjust and recover more quickly?"

"Accept him for what he is," is a frequent remark, often followed by an apparent contradiction, *"Don't assume that your child will not improve."* In fact the two suggestions are complementary. It was felt to be vital that the child was not compared to others, held responsible for his difficulties, or regarded as of less value than other children. Comparisons were held to be unproductive and a waste of mental energy.

One mother commented,
> "Until you have accepted that you want this child, even with his limitations, you cannot relax and look forward. You may wish that things had been different for him, but if you would rather have him as he is than not have had him at all you are well on the way to recovery."

Accepting the child is acknowledging his place in the family, being able to find pleasure in the characteristics he possesses and the things he can do, rather than concentrating on what he lacks.

It cannot be forced or switched on, but as many parents can testify, it is almost impossible to be in close day-to-day contact with a child who is particularly dependent, without a growing warmth, and with it, acceptance.
Another told me,

> "I found that it helped to 'tell myself off'. I obviously couldn't talk myself into being glad he was handicapped, but I did concentrate on dismissing negative thoughts and feelings like resentment, anger or regret, as being a waste of time and unlikely to help him. I decided I was being self-indulgent and wallowing in my own misfortune so I tried to adopt a more positive — perhaps almost clinical — approach. I think it helped."

'Accepting the child as he is' is very different from accepting a gloomy outlook for him. His parents have responsibility for his future, and that very responsibility results in every effort being made on his behalf to increase his ability and his enjoyment of life. Phrases like "Don't be put off!" and "Leave no stone unturned", crop up time and time again in my correspondence. Moreover they have a special urgency when they come from parents who have felt that they themselves had been too ignorant or apathetic. To find out something which could have helped the child, long after his need for it is passed, is tremendously frustrating.

Parents' comment included further apparent contradictions — *"Take each day as it comes, one at a time, without worrying about future problems,"* But *"Start to make plans for his education as early as possible and investigate good residential facilities before he is in his late teens and the waiting lists are too long."*

Here again it is a case of operating on two levels. It *is* important to consider the various types of education available, the availability of playgroup places, of holiday homes for short term care, of financial provision in the form of an insurance policy, and so on. Then when the time comes for decisions to be made, time is not wasted in casting around for information. This 'policy' planning gives a sense of purpose and direction — knowledge of the paths open for immediate exploration when necessary, provides security.

'Living from day to day' and 'taking each day as it comes' imply a philosophical approach — if yesterday was a good day, why shouldn't today be the same? If it was a bad day, forget it — it is past. 'We didn't manage to get him to feed himself yesterday but we'll have another go today."

Refusing to worry about the possibility of a setback or to become obsessed by achieving a specific goal by a given date seems to take the edge off anxiety. It is the approach which allows for each day's events to be met, dealt with and then put aside, with an inward resolve to meet tomorrow's when they occur and not before.

Those who have learned from the experience of bringing up a handicapped child have a real desire to ease the passage of others who are only at the beginning.

Their suggestions are thoughtfully expressed and their own words give a more personal feeling than any narrative. Before giving a selection of individual viewpoints, it may be useful to summarise them in a way which is easier to memorise and refer to mentally.

> Try to accept the child 'as he is' – someone with his own personality – not as a problem!
>
> Do not expect a miracle cure but be quietly optimistic about his development and press for as much information as you can.
>
> Do not be forever looking back saying "if only" – or forward saying "What if . . . .?" The past cannot be changed and the future fears may never materialise.
>
> What you are doing now is the important thing.
>
> Take one step at a time and be proud of yourself for what you have achieved.

Mrs. M. . . . .
> "If one had to do the best thing for everyone at all times – handicapped child, husband, other children, yourself, one would collapse under the strain. There are times when it is just not possible. It has taken me a long time to realise that there is no shame in a compromise. One can only do the best thing for the majority in a certain set of circumstances. One will never be able to say 'this is best' – it has to be 'this seems the best in the circumstances, at the moment'. This philosophy seems to avoid the raw nerves and guilty feelings we all have at times."

Son, Downs syndrome.

Mr. R. . . . .
> "I believe that new parents of a handicapped child must just accept the reality of the handicap. Then, having done so, they should enjoy their child as he is. I think it is right to be realistic about the nature of one's child's handicap, but never to let it stand in the way of giving him all the experiences of a 'normal' child."

Son, mild retardation.

Mrs. H. . . . .
> "Try to treat the child normally, especially if their are older brothers and sisters – do not forget your spouse too! As the child gets older (if not already) get in touch with Social Services and with a local group. An appointment at the local childrens hospital when my daughter was about six weeks old, followed by an open appointment (I averaged about one visit about every three months) though brief, was emotionally helpful. Be prepared to leave the child for a holiday – at a suitable place though!"

Daughter, Downs syndrome.

Mrs. B. . . . .
"I feel it is impossible for parents to really 'face the facts'. In spite of part of one's brain knowing the facts, a small part of one's emotions just doesn't accept them. I read the baby books as to what ages a baby should smile, laugh, sit up – and if A did something at about the 'right' time, I was convinced he was about to make medical history! I have seen a friend do the same thing, and see myself in her. I am not saying I was completely deluded, but little hopes made the future look brighter.

I feel that the brain interprets what one can take, and rejects what would be lastingly damaging. To force someone to face the facts before they are emotionally ready would be cruel and harmful. The facts are slowly assimilated. One knows, of course, that one's child will never be the same as others, but it seems to be part of that initial misery that one should pretend to oneself that, if things are not right, they might not be too bad. Even knowing precisely how my friend felt, I could do nothing to help her, except tell her what a lovely baby she had, and concentrate on his good points.

Looking back, the only mental approach I cultivated was to pretend. I pretended I loved A just the same (though I wasn't sure), pretended he was going to be much more advanced than deep down I knew he could ever be. I pretended I was sensible and matter of fact and capable. It got me though a bad time and it was better than crying all day. I don't suppose the experts would think much of it – one isn't supposed to pretend any more – but it worked, and so long as one doesn't do it for too long, what harm can it do?"
Son, Downs syndrome.

Accepting help

High on the list of suggestions for new parents was the importance of accepting practical help, in arranging for the child to be left with others when young so that husbands and wives could go out, or just spend a quiet Sunday together. This has a double value, in that it accustoms the child to relating to others rather than making demands on his parents alone. Perhaps it even benefits the friends and relations who wish to help. They feel gratified that they are allowed to become involved and are trusted enough to form a relationship with the child. There are some parents who, because no help was offered, or because they were reluctant to let anyone else look after their child, find, too late, that they have a teenager who refuses to co-operate with anyone but them. He demands their undivided attention because that is what he has been used to receiving.

One couple had not slept together for years because their son had stayed awake for hours on end, night after night, and would only sleep if his mother stayed with him. Eventually in order to get enough sleep to keep up with him in the daytime, she moved a bed into his room. The couple regretted and resented this intrusion into their one remaining time together, but it happened little by little, and in the end became a choice between the breakdown in the mother's health or getting sleep at all costs. What had started off as continuous devotion to their young child, had progressed to the giving up of visits to friends because he didn't like strange places, and ended up with complete domination of their lives.

The couple was not so young when he was born, so by the time he was in his teens, they were in their late fifties. They found themselves increasingly worried about handling their son as they grew older and wondered endlessly how he would adjust to life in a residential community.

Many mothers found it was all to easy to become possessive of their handicapped child, coming to believe that only they could 'understand their little ways'. They were reluctant to allow anyone to baby-sit, partly because they were anxious that the child would be upset by their absence, or unable to understand a explanation of it, and partly because they were worried that the baby-sitter may not have known how to handle the child if he should 'play-up'.

So it was sometimes easier to give up going out than to be unable to relax and enjoy the freedom. In fact, if baby sitting help is offered and accepted while the child is still a baby, none of these worries need arise. If he can be at ease with a familiar friend or neighbour from the outset, the arrangement is beneficial to all concerned. Offers of help are often made at the very beginning but, if they are constantly refused, it will be assumed that the help is not welcomed. Those who allowed others to share their child from his babyhood (and those who did not and regret it) were adamant that it is essential for the continuation of normal family life.

In similar vein, mothers felt moved to remind those with newly diagnosed children that they should not be drawn into such a single-minded devotion to their handicapped child that they have less and less time left for their spouse or other children. They advocate a little "selfishness" and self-indulgence – "If your child is asleep or with someone else, blow the housework, put your feet up and read a book while you can", "Try and arrange a regular outing on your own – to night school or visit a friend, and hold on to it except in the direst emergency – you are entitled to relaxation and freedom and it keeps things in proportion."

More suggestions from parents

Allow others to get to know him and accept help when sincerely offered.

Provide for some activity which will allow you to relax and 'recharge' yourself.

Remember that the child will not be helped by gaining attention to the exclusion of the needs of others in the family. He is an important member of it but not the only one.

Try to ascertain what provision – voluntary and statutory – is available in your area. Join the local society for mentally handicapped children, to gain information and meet other parents.

Mrs. F. . . . .
> "He now goes to a special nursery two afternoons a week, and he loves it. I feel it's done me even more good as I was very possessive

and I wouldn't allow anyone but my husband to feed him or look after him. I thought he would choke, catch cold or pull something down on himself if I wasn't there. I wasn't aware of this until his first afternoon at the nursery. I was very worried that if someone sat N on an ordinary chair he would try to get off and would surely fall. I thought — I hope they don't force him to sit on a potty, he's used his after lunch, and as he saw nothing wrong with wetting his nappy he won't seen why he has to sit on it again, or God, I hope no-one steps on his fingers (he moves around on his bottom), or opens a door without first knocking on it and saying "out of the way N. . . . ." I'd forgotten to tell them that. But of course, he was so happy and cocky when he got home he wouldn't let us close the back door, he kept looking down the drive — we presume to see if he could see the van. When we went next time he got into the van with his head held high and the cocky look on his face! He hasn't many words, but makes us understand what he wants most of the time — when he doesn't, there's trouble, he gets very cross.

Son, Rubenstein-Taybi syndrome.

Mrs. G. . . . .
"The best mental approach is to realise that on the whole, parents are the ones who are going to grieve and suffer — more than the child. They should try to share their despair, to talk together and cry together. Crying in each others arms can be a great comfort, and a great relief. Try to see the child's handicap as part of life, not the whole. Do not allow it to become a religion or a regime. Realise **that after diagnosis is the depths, and that the only way is up.** Life is a voyage of discovery and make the best of it. Accept all the help that is offered. If the help is not needed now, remember to ask for it later, or else for something else that will help you now. Sometimes help offered is the only way people can express their admiration for what you are doing — it is a gift, so do not reject it."

Daughter, tuberous sclerosis.

Mr. S. . . . .
"I think if parents can face up to facts that their child is going to need help, that they are the ones who are going to have to fight to help the child, then by doing something positive, they can also help themselves.

I would urge all parents to leave no stone unturned in their efforts to see that their handicapped child leads as full and normal a life as possible. Accept all help and advice offered, and turn down no opportunities which are open to the child and the parents."

Son, brain damage.

Mrs. O. . . . .
"Don't let the handicap run the family. We enjoy a two week holiday without N, and we feel fresh again to cope with him when we come back. He's noisy and unsociable at the meal table, and we like to dine out, so we take J (his brother) to a restaurant and I get a baby-sitter for N. I feel I'm a person, and as mental handicap is incurable, I mean to start as I go on. I would be a mental wreck if I didn't have interests apart from my child."
Son, retarded.

Mrs. H . . . .
"Do not overprotect your child, especially if he is an only child. Make him as independent as possible and used to being away from home from time to time − if possible, before the age of nine or ten, then as he grows up he will be much more self-reliant. There is nothing more heart rending than seeing ageing parents no longer able to cope with a situation that they could have avoided if they had let go earlier − the handicapped person with help, can grow in maturity and self-sufficiency like any other person."
Son, Downs syndrome.

Mrs. L. . . . .
"Don't look too far ahead − try to accept the situation. Try to cultivate patience (can be very difficult). Have a good weep if you need it but try not to feel too sorry for yourself. Try to find someone else in similar circumstances, or worse, and don't be afraid to talk to them. Join a group of parents with similar problems and 'let your hair down'. Push for help and accept it when offered. Don't try to solve all the problems on your own.

If you can find someone willing to take over for a few hours, let them and get away from it. Keep a sense of humour and think, 'I've coped today, I can cope tomorrow'".
Son, retarded.

Telling others

The mother may have overcome the first shock, may be ready to love and care for her child, and, perhaps, so long as she has her family beside her, the attitudes of other people should not matter.

But to many new parents, especially to the mother, it does matter. Taking one's baby out for the first time, and meeting people who have 'followed' the pregnancy is something to look forward to. Neighbours want to visit the house, or they come up to the pram asking "What did you get − a boy or a girl?"

But, when you have a handicapped baby, do you forestall their looking by announcing that there is something wrong with him? Or, if there is no physical sign of handicap, do you allow them to admire and coo over him, knowing that they may feel embarrassed later when they find out the truth?

If neighbours and friends already know about the handicap do you invite them round to see the baby or wait for them to make the first move? And if they do not come, is it perhaps because they feel uncomfortable?

Perhaps these seem trivial worries; but because this is the first acknowledgement of the handicap (outside home or hospital) it becomes a hurdle. Until now the problem has been aired only within the family or to nurses, with the mother being cushioned by the practical help and concern around her.

But, sooner or later, the father has to go back to his job, parents or in-laws must return home, the midwife's visits stop — and the mother realizes, perhaps with a sense of panic: "This is it." For much of the time from now on she is on her own.

Some mothers remembered how they cut themselves off from people only going shopping when they could leave the baby at home, making excuses to avoid visiting friends with normal babies. All those who reacted like this regretted it later, recognizing how much it increased their isolation and unhappiness. With nothing to divert them they brooded over the whole business from morning till night.

Inevitably they had to go out and meet people eventually, so all they had done was prolong the agony. And, almost always, the actual experience did not turn out to be as harrowing as they had imagined. In fact, most people they met had already heard of the handicap so asked "How are you?" rather than rushing to the pram. Of course it is difficult; people feel uneasy and at a loss for something to say, but if the mother volunteers more information it gives an opening for more specific questions. Most people are genuinely interested in the best sense and are sympathetic, especially if they have children of their own.

Sometimes mothers decide they will tell people simply but frankly because they prefer others to know the facts rather than hear from someone else that the baby is 'not quite right' or 'a bit funny'. They do not want others to think that they are ashamed or embarrassed by their baby nor do they want people to avoid them in case their interest is taken for morbid curiosity.

But it isn't easy to launch into a detailed explanation of mental handicap in a street or a crowded shop. Most mothers simply say that their baby has problems, that he's still under the hospital because they think there is something wrong or, sometimes, "We have been told that he's going to be a bit slow/have difficulties/not develop very quickly." So depending upon the setting and the person they are talking to more details follow or are left until another time.

Talking about the child is harder for some than for others. The sooner the hurdle is overcome the sooner it gets into proportion. Having spoken about it to one person it becomes easier to talk about it to others. It is one step towards acknowledging the problem, involving others and ultimately to coping.

One mother commented,
> "I don't know what I expected people to say but I had a vague idea that they would recoil in horror from the baby or whisper together as I walked past. As it happened it was nothing like that. The first person who asked about him had grown up children. I surprised myself and came right out with the fact that we'd been told he would be mentally backward. She just said, "Oh I'm so sorry, you must be awfully upset." She came out of the shop to look at him, said he was lovely and said I should try not to worry because it might not turn out as bad as they thought. After that she made a point of asking about him and always made a great fuss of him."

Another mother whose baby had Downs Syndrome remembered how she went to a neighbour's house with the baby the day she came home from hospital. The neighbour was a good friend and the mother knew she would be upset by the news and dread coming to see her. By making the first move she helped herself and her friend to feel more comfortable in discussing and handling the baby.

Everyone feels strongly that they don't want pity but what people feel is not necessarily pity in its worst sense. They do feel sympathy, perhaps something even greater than sympathy, but it is because they are affected by seeing a disabled baby, and by imagining what it is like for the mother facing the situation. If a mother is extremely sensitive she may misinterpret every remark and every look. People may be clumsy in expressing their sympathy ("perhaps he'll grow out of it", "you can't take any notice of doctors," "and he looks so normal too".)

Mothers are in agreement that the best way of showing sympathy is to offer it in terms of practical help such as baby-sitting but, of course, not everyone is in a position to do that. People may be taken aback by the news and say whatever comes into their heads, however trite or tactless. There is nothing wrong with genuine sympathy and if it can be accepted in all its forms, it can save a lot of irritation and offence.

An older child can create awkward situations in public places. When a seven year old decides to kick up a fuss in a crowded store his mother is not only faced with handling him but with looks and comments from all around.

If she adopts an outwardly calm attitude as she tries to ignore the outburst, she is likely to be subjected to glances which suggest, 'what he needs in his bottom smacking'. If she gets angry and gives him a slap she draws even more attention to herself. Because a smack would be unlikely to make the child any calmer, it is usually pointless – the mother knows this, the onlookers don't.

Sometimes a stranger talks to a child who either doesn't reply or does so in a way that is hard to understand. Here again the mother has to 'rescue' both the child and the stranger from greater confusion by explaining the situation.

Views from experienced parents frequently contained the same points: –

Do not delay going out with your child because you dread people asking about him.

Most people know something about mental handicap these days and anyone worth knowing will not look at you as though you are unclean.

Tell people what is wrong with the child but don't go to the extreme of talking about nothing else each time you meet.

You will find that most people are genuinely interested in how he's getting on and they will be eager to ask questions once they feel you don't mind talking about him.

Tactless remarks are usually made in ignorance but are usually well meant. Try not to look for offence, or analyse every word.

As soon as you are able, get to know other parents of handicapped children in a local support group. There you will hear the subject discussed constructively and naturally and you will find yourself joining in. Those who lack knowledge and understanding will matter less once you know people with first-hand experience.

If you can convey to others that the child's handicap does not cloud your love for him they will be more likely to be drawn to him too.

You will get many admiring comments: "I don't know how you do it," "You must have tremendous patience" and even "you must be a wonderful person" (and how does one reply to that?) Some of these comments may seem rather ridiculous given that you didn't choose the job anyway but the point is that you *are* coping.

You have had to accept your fair share of disappointments so accept the admiration and praise in the spirit in which it is intended, and let the compliments spur you on.

Mrs. K. . . . .
"M is now nearly eight months old. I have a daughter of three who will be a big help to him. Already they are becoming playmates. I always took my daughter to a toddlers club, a group for children up to three years and for her sake, I kept going when M was born. I found that it helped us all a lot. They have always treated M beautifully and now that A is starting gradually to go to playgroup I shall keep taking M to toddler club and all the other places I went to with A. He has always come out with all the family right from the start, and you soon start forgetting that he's different. I have no mother and the rest of the family are at work, so although I felt very self-conscious at first I had to take him everywhere – and I'm sure it's better to get out and about as soon as possible."
Son, Downs syndrome.

Mrs. M. . . . .
"You can't change the facts. Don't hold out false hopes of a cure. Don't compare your child with another child with a similar handicap. Try to make the best what you've got. Look for all the good points and play these up. Don't keep saying 'why me?' You must convince yourself that it is not your fault or your husbands.

Although you should tell other people don't blurt it out straight away as though apologising for the handicap — saying, 'but we love him just the same'. Other people will base their reactions on your behaviour and will take their cue from you. Don't take as gospel everything you are told by professionals. They don't know it all and children differ so much anyway. Don't be dismayed if you have been told that your child won't live beyond a certain age. It may not be true, but if it is, make the most of him while you have him (our son had two serious virus infections and was at death's door twice, yet recovered). Twice we had braced ourselves for the worst, having been told he would not survive another attack, and I know of other Downs children who have got down to a thread of life yet have recovered. So, never give up hope. It takes courage, but it's worth it."
Son, Downs syndrome.

Listening to others

Mothers who are still very shaky in their acceptance of the handicapped child are very vulnerable to suggestions and 'advice' which seems to come at them from many quarters. Frequently they are told "it isn't really fair on the other children, perhaps he would be better in a place where there are others 'like himself'". It seems to be one of the first things that acquaintances suggest — either openly or in a veiled manner.

The worry is that other children may be held back, embarrassed or teased and will have their lives restricted and overshadowed by the handicapped child's presence. The fear seems to be rooted in something 'odd' or different coming into the family which may be 'caught' by the normal children. The reasons for it are not difficult to understand, but when the child is only weeks or months old, it can plunge the parents into even deeper gloom. The very same thoughts may have crossed their own minds and hearing others reinforce their anxiety seems to make it justified. Some mothers almost decided to come home from hospital without their babies because of this pressure.

Part of them wanted, more than anything, to run away from the problem, but when it came to the point they simply could not do it. As one mother said, "I knew that I would suffer just as much from guilt as I would from looking after the baby. I would always feel I hadn't even tried, that I had chickened out without giving the child a chance. I'd never stop wondering how he was getting on and if I could have done more for him."

Most couples with other children may already have prepared themselves for the fact that the children would have to make some adjustments and give practical help. But the suggestion that the handicap would rub off on them added a more sinister aspect. Fortunately, most mothers were able to see that the child's future relationship with brothers and sisters could not be firmly predicted. So they preferred to wait and see.

One mother, faced with the "put him away for the sake of the children before you become too fond of him" theory when she was at a very low ebb, told how she was nearly persuaded to give him up. Then, left to think it over, she found herself becoming very angry at this assumption that her baby could be so easily dismissed.

> "The friend meant well. She said that she could never look after such a child like that and would have to let him go. Well, I'd have said the same in her position but you don't reckon with the fact that it becomes a very different matter when it is your own child and a living person. In a way it helped me because I felt so insulted on his behalf and became quite aggressive — so I knew then that I must love him! I couldn't see why she thought I'd be incapable of coping. I decided then that I would at least give my other children the opportunity of understanding and co-operating instead of deciding in advance that it would be bad for them."

Another mother made the point that her other children might have been just as badly affected if they had 'sent him away' because there was something wrong with him. "They would probably have felt it was unfair and may have started wondering when it was their turn."

Some parents were forced by others to face a whole lifetime's problems in the space of a few months after diagnosis. Most found it impossible to duck the responsibility for their child's welfare before they had had time to find out just what the problems would be. His place in the family could only be judged by exprience, the effect on brothers and sisters only proved by time. Most parents with handicapped children do bring up other children as well, meeting and overcoming any problems which occur. If the time comes when the handicapped child becomes too difficult to be coped with at home the parents will recognize it and begin to look into alternatives. *In that case it is a considered decision arrived at in the light of their own experience and knowledge.*

Mrs. N. . . . .
"Now J is getting older those who we thought were our friends don't want us to take him into their homes. Mums of children who are alright just seem to think we are dragging him up. I have been given all kinds of advice but you can't just give J a backhander to make him do what you want. Yet they think it should work with him. I told one friend that J had more tidy ways than her nine year old who had a good I.Q. He dropped an ice lolly on my carpet and just stamped on it. J would have picked it up and put it in the sink. He puts all his sweet papers into my shopping bag when we are out or back in his pocket. So I just had to tell her to put her own house in order first. If I could teach a mentally handicapped child to be clean and tidy, it should not be so hard with her son. I would never have said a word but she had just told me it was time I gave him a good smack."

Son, severely retarded.

Mrs. T. . . . .

"We do need an understanding attitude from people. Some parents are embarrassed because people stare at their obviously handicapped children. J looked perfectly normal but was very hyperactive. He had many behaviour problems; kicking over tins in supermarkets, dashing across the road, suddenly giving someone a kick or a thump; so people thought he was a badly behaved child and we were often upset by remarks such as 'he needs a jolly good hiding.' In the early stages conflicting advice from well meaning friends and neighbours presented problems. Well meant but misplaced advice from one vicar to 'put him in a home at the other end of the country and forget about him', or from a specialist to 'go home and have another baby to shower your love on' – they didn't help at all. We were helped by regular visits to a special clinic. We were collected by a Social Worker, and taken there every three months. There we met doctors, Social Workers, other parents and children. It gave us a feeling of security and we felt that help was never too far-away – the next visit being only a few weeks away."

Son, brain damage, autism.

Chapter Ten

HELPING DEVELOPMENT

Parents as teachers
There are many excellent books for parents which set out to give detailed guidance on the teaching of skills to young, handicapped children. (Details of useful books are given at the end of this section.)

The value of these books is immense – written by people who have had experience in teaching handicapped children, they provide general advice, original ideas and a step by step programme covering all the early skills. They are not rigid schedules to be followed slavishly, but flexible and practical suggestions adaptable to the home environment and the child's capabilities. So many parents of older children complained that they were left to find out how to help their child by 'trial and error'. So they made mistakes and valuable time was wasted. It is a great boost to the confidence to know what they are doing with their child is constructive and has been proved effective with other children. The general 'rules' for teaching a handicapped child are the same as those which most parents put into practice quite naturally with their other children. But, because the child may take longer to 'catch on' parents may need to remind themselves of these rules to avoid too much frustration – theirs and the child's.

Suggestions from parents
It can be very tempting to spend too long at one session when it seems that with a bit more effort the aim will be achieved.

Once the child's concentration is flagging (usually easy to pinpoint – his attention wanders, he starts fidgeting and is obviously no longer interested in the task in hand), nothing can be achieved by 'one more try'. The child will become impatient or protest, or will simply make no attempts at cooperation. This in turn makes the mother feel irritated and the whole situation turns from a combined effort into a 'you against me' battle.

Once relaxed co-operation is no longer possible, persistence only succeeds in creating an issue – the mother feels exasperated because she felt success was near, the child senses the exasperation and this is what he will remember next time they attempt the same 'lesson'. His mother's impatience confuses him and he senses that their game is an important matter to her. Because he couldn't do what she wanted him to do, he may begin to dislike the whole idea and shy away from trying again. The secret is to "quit while you are ahead", to stop when the child is being successful − either in a small part of the task, or in beginnning to grasp what is required of him, even if he is not yet able to put it into practice. Then next time the task is attempted the child will remember his mother's pleasure and praise and will be keen to please her again. The first time a new skill is attempted the child's concentration may be held for only a few minutes, but if the task is something which interests him and is within his capabilities his concentration should increase little by little.

The younger the child and the more excitable his temperament, the shorter the time he would be able to focus his attention on one occupation and this has to be taken into account.

Of course, keeping a calm relaxed approach, treating learning as something to be enjoyed, not becoming over anxious, recognizing when to turn to other things, are ideals − and parents would have to be superhuman to maintain such angelic behaviour at all times. Other distractions make it impossible not to show impatience at times but progress is not going to be impaired forever by the occasional lapse. It is very easy to be over ambitious and sometimes a skill is attempted too soon, but if in general the parents aim to keep the relationship friendly and relaxed, it has a beneficial effect all round. There is little advantage in attempting anything new unless the parent feels in the mood − if he or she is tired or tense, it is hard to conceal and is likely to transmit a feeling of intensity to the child. Similarly, if the child is obviously tired or irritable, he is unlikely to co-operate in something new.

One mother remarked that with practice she learned to judge, usually correctly, when the child was ready for introduction for something new. She said: −

"You have to learn to adjust your expectations. If you expect too little of him, you end up doing everything for him, he makes no attempt to learn and becomes lazy. If you expect too much of him, he gets upset because he can't cope. You can only learn what to expect of your child by living with him and by making quite a few mistakes."

Mrs. A. . . . .

"Try to look at all achievements, however small, as deserving of praise. Think − "This is a handicapped child and he is dry at night − good!" Not "This child is only just dry now, and he is four, how slow compared to his brothers and sisters." Set your sights high − but make haste very slowly! If you fail in getting your child to achieve something, leave it for a few months then go back to it later. My theory is that just as subconsciously we wake up in the morning with problems solved, so subconsciously, a child's brain may be working slowly on things. Realise that bringing up any child has problems − this normal child wets at night, another refuses to give up a dummy, bigger children can be impudent, disobedient etc.. Your mentally handicapped child's problems are just different, or more so."

Son, Downs syndrome.

Mrs. P. . . . .
"The past four years has been a nightmare, but gradually, as our daughter grows and develops her own very determined personality we realise just how worthwhile all our efforts have been. P was, and still is, very severely physically and mentally handicapped unable to sit or stand on her own, but with her determined spirit she manages to get downstairs, and feed herself. Her speech is really good now, although we were told she would never speak clearly she is understood by most people. We still have problems at night as she never seems tired and won't sleep for long periods. We've grown used to hearing nursery rhymes being sung at two a.m.. Her uncanny ear for tunes is fantastic. She gets very frustrated at her failing to be able to move forward and gets furious with her legs for not working, I can see we may have many problems with her in years to come, as she is very determined to walk. Our other three children seem very well adjusted to having a handicapped sister and are very gentle and will play with her. I do wonder how they will cope with being a handicapped family as they all grow older. I think it is a subject which needs a lot of thought and I know lots of parents share my thoughts."

Daughter, cerebral palsy.

Mrs. W. . . . .
"In her first year, L was just like a rag doll — couldn't hold, or do anything much. However, the only real problem was that she was anti-social and would go purple, screaming if anyone came into the house, very nervy and terrified of loud noises. Since she started to go to a special school she is now doing really well. She says about five words now, can drink from a cup by herself, but the main thing is — she is happy and enjoys the company of the other children. I fully understand that no matter how much she progresses, she will never be a normal child, yet I thank God each day that I've got her. People annoy me immensely when they offer pity — our children don't need it. They offer us far more than a normal child does. My only wish at present is that L walks or crawls by Christmas!"

Daughter, unspecified retardation.

Mrs. F. . . . .
"D. . . . is now seven years old. I was thirty eight, at the time, having married later in life than most. Every mother's feeling are different. I can honestly say I never felt bitter at this happening to me, — just guilty at not having given my first born a normal life. D did not walk until she was 4½ partly because of jealousy, I think, when her sister was born two years later as she could push the trolley down the lawn or feed herself until she was three. But once she made up her mind there was no mess like her normal sister! She was always very clean and I never had to bother about toilet training. Her normal sister was quite the reverse, but this might have been to get extra attention I feel!

She has always had a independent spirit, and unlike most mongols she has never been affectionate and prefers to play on her own — though playgroup and school have helped enormously to make her more sociable. She has been talking since she was four and since then has been far less frustrated. She is the most sympathetic and appreciative member of the family and has brought us much joy and happiness."

Daughter, Downs syndrome.

Mrs. E. . . . .

"We were, of course, very distressed at first and almost afraid of our daughter but this was before we got to know her, and to realise just how much we could help her. We are also surprised we find her just as much a personality as our other normal children and we have come to love her very much. We have to count our blessings as quite by chance we heard of a small school for mongol children run by someone who firmly believes that these children are capable of being taught many things, if they are taught early enough. P is now four, knows all the colours and numbers up to ten, also the right sound of every letter in the alphabet. She is being taught the elements of reading already. They are shown how to feed themselves, and wash, and many small social graces to help them be accepted into normal life.

I carry on the teaching myself at home and get great pleasure and satisfaction from her slow but steady progress. One finds one is not bashing at a brick wall, but feeding information into a small mind. If one really tries hard that mind soaks up what one is saying — like an ailing plant that needs special feeding, and the results are so very worthwhile."

Daughter, Downs syndrome.

Mrs. P. . . . .

"T is now ten years old and improved beyond recognition. In fact, she loves books and her reading is excellent. She makes straight for the T.V. page of the paper and picks out the programme for the evening — and we all have to agree with her choice! She can sew and loves to help me cook. The latest thing is pouring the tea, though it makes me very nervous! She can dress herself and manage the buttons. Hair care is still a problem but improving. She can amuse herself for hours without making too much mess, post letters for me and crosses the road doing her kerb drill. She is very tall for her age, and I have to buy clothes for a thirteen year old.

She is also beginning to develop a bust so she is growing normally. He confidence is still a little shaky but she makes friends easily. She has a fantastic memory for people. Her latest achievements which has surprised and delighted us is that she has learned to speak a little German! My husband has been teaching her and it started as a joke. Now she can count to ten, knows the part of her face and some animals. She never ceases to amaze us.

One thing is sure, all of us realise how lucky we are to have her. If she wasn't handicapped she would not be nearly so sweet tempered and gentle. When I see how precocious other ten year olds are it makes up for all the heartache."

Daughter, retarded.

Mrs. N. . . . .
"A family with normal children gradually 'weans off' the various stages in their progress. With A he still needs attention when washing and going to the toilet. He cannot bath himself or clean his teeth. He is just beginning to dress himself completely. I have to put his clothes on a chair in the right order, this way he can manage himself. With eating, he's fine. It is not only A who is handicapped, but the whole family. Most things we do circle around A. When planning a holiday or outing we have to choose a place that won't make A feel uncomfortable. Toilets have to be nearby. We are limited as far as baby sitters are concerned — only people who know A and he them are suitable. His work at school is showing progress — he's happy that's the main thing as far as we are concerned. We are able to take him most places with us without upset. He gives himself away when he speaks, he doesn't make conversation, very few sentences.

One does tend to be over protective, but this is not good for the child — he needs just as much discipline at home as at school."

Son, retarded.

The portage system
"The Portage system took over 12 years to develop in the small American town of Portage, Wisconsin and is particularly attractive because it gives 'front line' professionals like health visitors and social workers a very easy way of teaching parents how to teach their own children. The designers of the system claim that it takes only three days to teach these professionals who come into regular contact with mentally handicapped children in their homes how to use the system. The kit is simple, consisting of a check list covering the main developmental and learning stages which would be expected of a normal child of up to about 6 years of age. The list is divided into six main areas: infant stimulation, socialisation, language, self help, cognitive, motor. For each item on the list there is a corresponding information card which has detailed suggestions of how to teach the child to reach that stage. The results in Wessex have been impressive with a very high proportion of the children learning the target activity quickly. Equally important it has given the parents positive and concrete advice on teaching their children and helped them to cope better with the day to day problems that arise." "Accident of Birth" by Fred Heddell. **BBC Publications.**

Many parents of mentally handicapped sons and daughters now in their twenties or thirties are convinced that, had their child been born more recently they would have achieved much more. They speak of their total isolation, the fact that no one attempted to tell them how to set about helping their child, and how they simply taught by trial and error. Now more and more psychologists, teachers and therapists are sharing their expertise with parents. Of course, it is not possible for professionals to include every parent in their teaching or therapy programmes, but the detailed accounts of their methods in books for parents, can be the next best thing to working with them in person.

Mrs. D. . . . .
"My first ten years with my Downs Syndrome son were dreadful because I had not guidance at all in the early years and made many errors – bad for him, bad for me and bad for the family. After that he seemed to change and do more for himself. Maybe it was because I got tired doing so much for him and left him to it."
Adult son, Downs syndrome.

Parents as partners

The Warnock report was published in 1978 after five years of investigation into special education. The report drew attention to the willingness of parents to help professionals in the care and education of their mentally handicapped children. Of course, parents have always wished to play a major part in changing legislation and improving facilities – many of the existing voluntary organisations were set up by parents. But in addition to their involvement in such organisations parents are now frequently to be found working as voluntary assistants in schools, hospitals, toy libraries and so on.

Courses for parents

There are already courses run by the City and Guilds of London Institute which are designed to help teachers and others in their dealings with handicapped students in Further Education. Parents might find the syllabus of interest, and might like to enquire if such a course is available at their local College of Further Education or Technical College.

Syllabus (course 731)
1) Provision for People with Handicaps. Central, local and voluntary provision. This is to include special groups of handicapped who cannot be catered for in the ordinary colleges.
2) Reports and Legislation. An appreciation of relevant reports and legislation affecting the handicapped.
3) Provision at School and Post-School level. Special schools, units, special provision in the ordinary school. Selection of students, levels and types of course. School/College liaison.
4) Different Types of Handicap and their Characteristics.
5) Special Needs of People with Handicaps. Problems of people with handicaps, access, care needs, linguistic, social, cultural difficulties, psychological problems and an examination of the integration/segregation issue. Mobility and communication.

6) Liaison with Outside Agencies and Support Services. Relationship with other agencies in the development of suitable courses and their content and evalution. The need for consultation. An examination of the available support services in the light of the problems identified.
7) Curriculum Development. Curriculum development in the design of courses and work experience for people with handicaps.
8) Teaching Method. Adaptation, development and evaluation of methods of teaching, learning and testing for people with handicaps.

Some universities also run courses for parents, which deal with handicapped children from pre-school age to school age, and with handicapped adults. The Open University now offers similar courses including **Special needs in Education,** and **The Handicapped person in The Community.**

From the description of the course in **Special Needs in Education** –
1) Understanding Special Education. Describes what special education is like, why it is as it is, and what it is like to be part of it.
2) Meeting Special Needs. The course looks at how far needs are met by existing provisions and how special education might better meet these needs.
3) Relating Special Education to the System as Whole. It examines how normal schools meet children's needs, to what degree some children are in special education because normal school can't or won't accommodate them, and how changes in one system affect the other.
4) Integrating Children with Special Needs into Ordinary Schools. The course asks: What are the conditions for successful integration? What are the reasons for segregation and the arguments for integration?

Parents as teachers
Useful books (see also Publications)
1 **Souvenir Press**
a) Teaching the Handicapped Child
   Dorothy Jeffree, Roy McConkey and Simon Hewson (1977)
b) Starting Off
   Chris Keirnan, Rita Jordan and Chris Saunders (1978)
c) Helping your Handicapped Baby
   Cliff Cunningham and Patricia Sloper (1978)
2 **British Institute for Mental Handicap**
   Crossing the Road – a guide to teaching the mentally handicapped
   Peter Taylor, Paul Robinson (1979).

Chapter Eleven

BEHAVIOUR

Psychologists have produced a number of methods of changing a child's behaviour — that is, eliminating aggressive, dangerous, anti-social or obsessive tendencies so that the child is easier to live with, more socially acceptable and more capable of learning. This is usually referred to as behaviour modification.

Parents are well aware of the effects of uncontrolled mis-behaviour within the family, and outside it. They often express determination that their child shouldn't be allowed to "get away with" things that his brothers and sisters are reprimanded for. Yet at the same time, they are also aware of the child's limited understanding, his immaturity, his lack of co-ordination, the need to let him explore and so on.

The questions present themselves — when is bad behaviour the result of conscious rebellion and when is it due to the intellectual and emotional effects of the handicap? How does one get across the notion of "knowing right from wrong"? If a previously incurious and inactive child suddenly pulls a toy to pieces or refuses to do something he's told, is he behaving badly or showing initiative? Most parents solve the problem — or tackle it at least — by finding where 'to draw the line'. The difficulty is that they may find themselves dealing with the stages which all children go through, though delayed, and over a longer period of time.

If a toddler gets the urge to run off in a public place, the mother can catch him, put him under her arm and put him into his pushchair. Not quite so easy with a strong and active six year old. A two year old's tantrum doesn't raise so many eyebrows as one thrown by a child three times that age. An older child may be able to reach the bathroom taps, the shelves in the supermarkets, the cooker or a plugged-in iron — yet he may have the inquisitiveness of a two year old, and the same impulsiveness, with no sense of the possible consequences of his actions.

Such children, because of their ceaseless activity, coupled with a lack of any sense of danger, can be very wearing. Often they are children who were not diagnosed as mentally handicapped in infancy and their unusual behaviour may be one of the first indications that there is something amiss. The mother may have been coping with the difficulties for many months, wondering why she seemed unable to control her child, before seeking help. Sometimes it comes as a great relief to know that there is a reason for his behaviour other than bad handling on her part. While he is under five years old, the behaviour problems are usually containable, the situation is relieved when he goes to school and his mother has time to renew her energy and shop in peace. Where there are playgroup facilities, or special schools which admit children at three years old, the sharing of the problems can begin even earlier. Fortunately children who present severe behaviour problems are in the minority.

The undemanding child

By no means does mental handicap always go hand in hand with lack of conformity or social acceptability. In some children, their mental retardation, by its very nature, results in an unquestioning acceptance of the mother's authority. The child who is 'absolutely no trouble' may be easier on the nerves but a complete lack of conflict is, in itself, abnormal. The child who protests when hungry or cannot get what he wants, who rebels occasionally, and who shows independence of spirit, is much closer to what is considered 'normal' and far more likely to make progress.

If he is able to reason and question enough to make his feelings known, he is equipped to extend his reasoning into learning. It may be hard to be pleased about a three year old discovering he can open the fridge and that eggs are nice to drop on the floor, or to find him unrolling a whole toilet roll and stuffing it into the lavatory, but to know that he is 'into everything' like any non-handicapped toddler makes the extra work worthwhile.

As one mother put it: –

> "He wears me out – he managed to open the garden gate the other day and was half way down the road before I realised it, so we had to fit a latch up where he can't reach. I have to keep one step ahead of him all the time, and keep repeating to myself, it's a good sign, it's a good sign! Maybe I'll convince myself one day."

Generally the handicapped child will behave at a level below that of his actual age. Because he takes longer to 'grow out' of each phase and the development of his understanding and self control lags behind his physical growth, allowances have to be made. But parents of older children make a point of mentioning the importance of starting early in making sure that the child's handicap does not become an excuse for doing just as he likes. "Start as you mean to go on" is a common recommendation.

In the words of another mother: –

> "I didn't see why he shouldn't follow the same 'rules' as my other children to the best of his ability. The others were not expected to hit out at people for no reason, they were made to help to put their toys away, were not allowed to tear books or scribble in them, to touch things in shops or other people's houses and so on. You deal with things as they crop up and relate your handling of them to the age of the child. With B I felt even more conscious of trying to bring him up well-behaved. I thought that he had enough problems to cope with and it was very important that he shouldn't grow up handicapped by anti-social habits as well. Once I went out of the room to get a cup of tea for a visitor we had. When I came back B. was standing on this man's knee, with his hands on his head,

> bouncing up and down! He was only three at the time and was used to rough and tumbles with his father and brother! I grabbed him and put him down firmly on the floor, and said crossly, "No you must not do that". The visitor said, "It's alright, don't shout at him, he doesn't understand". This, to me, was exactly why I should shout at him — so that he would begin to understand that you don't jump on people when you feel like it. It may have been quite cute and amusing in a little boy of three — it wouldn't be so appealing when he was six."

Mrs. T. . . . .
> "We have to be careful not to overcompensate. It is easy to be disappointed because our children cannot read and write, and at the same time, not encourage them to do the things they should learn to do for themselves — such as feeding, dressing etc.. As all mums know, it is easier to do things for our children than to stand and watch them struggle, and yet, this is what we must do if we are to help them towards some degree of independence ultimately. It is important to try to treat the children as normally as possible and not to make unnecessary exceptions because of their handicap — some are essential for the safety of the child, or that of others, of course. The children need to be kept fully occupied — many of them are incapable of amusing themselves, at least while they are young. J. always lays the table, does the drying up, brings in the milk, helps with dusting and vacuuming, and works with his dad in the garden a great deal. This all helps to make him feel useful."

Son, brain damage, autism.

An objective approach

In some cases, the child's hyperactivity and erratic temperament makes response and co-operation difficult. One mother of a child prone to outbursts of noisy activity and who had difficulty in relating to his surroundings, managed to cope with him by adjusting her own approach. Knowing she could not influence him by reasoning or smacking, she adopted a nurse-patient role, which somehow removed her from the emotional effects of his outbursts. By regarding him objectively, as a child in need of help rather than her child doing his best to upset her, she found she could lessen the strain on her nerves. Her attitude was to ignore as far as possible, the noise and the charging around until the energy had subsided and he became calmer. Then she would resume the mother role and play with him or talk to him. In this way she was refusing to acknowledge his 'bad' behaviour and rewarding his good behaviour with her friendly attention. As he got older his outbursts became much less frequent and far less 'physical' when they did occur.

Mrs. H. . . . .
> "Be as detached as possible in your relationship with your child. A possible nurse/patient relationship has helped me to cope with the aggressive outbursts."

Son, brain damage.

Suggestions from parents

Summing up from parents (some of whom speak from the success of their experience, some who feel that they were not firm enough, and thus made their task harder) –

> Don't let the handicap be an excuse for every example of naughtiness or non-conformity.
>
> A handicapped child is no different from other children in that he can try your patience for no other reason than that he feels like it!
>
> Try to distinguish between 'unnecessary' bad behaviour and that which comes from his lack of co-ordination, immaturity, physical slowness or excitability he cannot control. Attempts have to be made to correct anti-social or unnecessary misbehaviour early.
>
> Try to be fair to other children in the family. They will not find it hard to accept that certain allowances have to be made for their handicapped brother but if he is always put first, they may resent it. By not allowing the handicapped child to spoil their special treasures or expecting him to be included in every game with their own friends, they will not feel so overwhelmed by his presence.
>
> Don't expect to be a paragon of patience at all times. You will get angry with him, perhaps unfairly sometimes. There will be clashes of personality and irritations as with any child.
>
> Don't hesitate to seek the help of the child's teachers, the hospital consultant or an educational psychologist (through the G.P.) if you can't handle a specific aspect of your child's behaviour. They may have met the problem before and be able to suggest the right method of approach or reassure you that the phase will pass.
>
> Try to gear your expectations of the child to his age and level of understanding. Then try to be consistent in carrying out the standards you decide upon. The child will only understand what is expected of him if the guidelines are clearly made and kept to. A child who finds it hard to handle his feelings is reassured and calmed when someone steps in and 'draws the line' for him. In important matters of behaviour – (important, that is, in the sense that they are things the parents feel strongly about) – co-operation will be slow in coming if the child is reprimanded for something one day, then allowed to do it the next.
>
> If he indulges in tantrums, pay as little attention to him as possible, until the tantrum subsides, so demonstrating its pointlessness. Reward him with friendly approval when he is behaving calmly – so helping him to connect his mother's attention with his 'good' behaviour, rather than the 'bad'.

If the handicapped child is the only child in the family his parents are able to follow such guidelines fairly consistently. But, where there are other children they may find it much harder to be objective, calm and patient. In theory, losing one's temper with a child is unproductive – in practice only a robot could avoid it at all times. One particular caring and patient mother agonised over the couple of occasions when she had 'felt like murdering' her handicapped son, until she had experienced exactly the same feelings towards her second son. "Then" she said, "I realised that all children can be infuriating. But when my only child was the handicapped one, I thought I'd felt angry with him because he was handicapped." To avoid laying hands on him she had walked out of the room until she calmed down. She was extremely upset by the intensity of her anger and only with hindsight did she realise that instead of feeling guilty, perhaps she had cause to feel proud that she hadn't actually given vent to her anger, or lost control. The emotion had been all the more distressing because it was a rare one – a few moments out of hours and hours of patience.

Relatives and friends may try to 'make up' for the child's difficulties by being over tolerant. This caused slight problems for one mother who made weekly visits to her friends with a normal child of the same age. At home this mother had tried to instill the concept of unselfishness and respect into her child; the sharing of toys, sweets etc. with his sister. The friend, in her efforts to be understanding, encouraged her own child to give in to whatever the handicapped child wanted. So his mother said: –

"He became a real menace when we were there. If he saw P with anything, whether he wanted it or not, it became a point of honour to get it off him – he knew my friend would give way to him. He watched the other boy pick up a toy and immediately went over to grab it off him – if the child would not let go, he stood there looking at my friend waiting for her to tell her child to hand it over! It was so unfair on the other child, who always ended up tense and tearful, and it was unfair to T too, as I wanted him to learn to play with normal children properly – and learn to give and take. So, from then on I insisted that he left the other child alone and physically removed him if he started his grabbing. If he persisted I just put his coat on and took him home. I think my friend thought I was being a bit hard on him – "He can't be expected to understand yet", she said. My answer was that if he could work out how to get what he wanted, he could learn that it wasn't always possible.

Parents have to convey to others the importance of helping the child to be independent, unselfish and to have respect for other people. Extra time and love, even a little 'spoiling' is welcomed, so long as it is complemented by firm guidance when necessary.

Pets

The value of a close relationship between a child and a family pet is well known. Parents speak of the calming effect on a child who rarely sits still, of the stimulating effect on a child's mobility or speech, and of the sense of **responsibility which it instills. A handicapped child who is denied** opportunities of playing with other children can join in play with a puppy or a kitten without being regarded as slow. And the child who is used to being told what to do by everyone around him can take pride in his ability to make his pet come to him or sit at this command. Parents are sometimes surprised at the gentleness of their child's approach to a pet, remarking that there seems to be some inborn sense of protectiveness and even a two way communication. The relationship can relax an excitable child, or increase the confidence of one who is timid.

One mother whose baby had shown no sign of trying to move about found an instant solution when they bought a puppy. The child was so anxious to watch the puppy's every move that he gradually, and naturally, taught himself to 'swim' along the floor.

Some mentally handicapped children are not, of course, able to handle an animal, run about with it, or help to care for it. But they may still benefit a great deal from watching or listening to a pet. Their interest may be aroused by the sight and sound of a caged bird, by a tank of fish, gerbils, or a hamster.

Mr. S. . . . .
"H. used to be a very timid child, often scampering away from an animal with her arms held over her head, perhaps in protection. Nothing would induce her even to look at the dog or cat. This was part of her general timidity and we thought she would never grow out of it. Then, feeling we were taking a great risk, we got a kitten. Before long she was feeding it and after some time actually stroked it. So we got a puppy and before long actually had to restrain H from tugging at it (for the puppy's sake!) Although the dog is now almost as big as her she has not only overcome her timidity but also talks to it and about it. In fact she has become much braver about other things which she previously disliked and shied away from. And, of course, she now helps to exercise the dog — and herself.
Daughter, severely retarded.

Behaviour

Useful Books

1 **British Institute of Mental Handicap**
   Helping The Retarded — a systematic behavioural approach (1980)
   E. A. Perkins, P. D. Taylor, A. C. M. Capie
2 **Souvenir Press**
a) Starting Off
   Chris Keirnan, Rita Jordan and Chris Saunders (1978)
b) Helping Your Handicapped Baby
   Cliff Cunningham and Patricia Sloper (1978)
3 **Royal Society for Mentally Handicapped Children and Adults**
a) Behaviour Modification in Mental Retardation
   W. I. Gardner (1971)
b) Behaviour Modification of the Mentally Retarded
   T. Thompson and J. Grabowski (1972).
c) Take Six Children
   Hilary Cass, Karen Grant,
   Michael Lassman, Sheldon Stone (1978).

Chapter Twelve

TEACHING THE BASIC SKILLS

Toys and play

No mother needs to be told that young children learn through play. Mentally handicapped children may lack an innate curiosity or may be unable to be still long enough to concentrate on any activity for more than a few minutes. So play has a particular value in awakening a retarded child's senses or channelling his energies constructively.

Toy libraries are invaluable because children can use toys which are designed with a particular stage of development in mind, and after getting the maximum value from them, they can be exchanged for something else (see information section). Some children's hospitals have a Play Adviser who would be able to suggest playthings appropriate to a child's needs. The hospital Social Work department would be able to tell parents whether there is an adviser operating in the area. If not, the occupational therapist attached to the hospital may see the child and pass on some activity ideas.

Best of all, entry to a playgroup — not necessarily geared to the handicapped — provides social play as well as a wide range of toys.

A young child does not need to be surrounded by commercially designed toys to be occupied and happy. Mothers often remark that their child played longer with a box than the toy inside it. Babies and young children love to put things in containers and tip them out again, and several unremarkable objects gain a new fascination when they are presented in a box for 'exploration'. Household objects can be used to improve manual skills — threading cotton reels on a shoe lace (dipping about two inches in hard setting glue provides a rigid 'needle' for pushing through), putting dolly pegs (perhaps painted in bright colours) around the edge of a cardboard box or tin, putting large pebbles into egg boxes, rolling a small ball through a cardboard tube and so on.

Games can be played with the mother or father which help the child to use his senses and notice what they tell him — letting him feel the difference between rough (sand paper, scouring pad) and smooth (plate, apple), cold and hot, hard and soft, wet and dry etc. Another idea is to put familiar items into a drawstring bag (a squeaky toy, his cup, a ball), get the child to put his hand in and try to pick them out as they are named or to name them himself if he can. Help him to distinguish loud and soft noises, encouraging him to repeat clapping or tapping rhythmns. Stimulate curiosity in a passive **child by hiding and revealing things under a cloth, putting a few objects on** a tray, removing one and getting the child to indicate which is missing. Get him to use his eyes by looking at books (the Ladybird series starting with the Picture Reading and Talkabout series are ideal).

The 'agitated' or overactive child may be calmed (though his parents may not be!) by toys which produce sounds such as a musical box or the specially sturdy player which a child can wind. He might find sustained interest, when small, in mobiles – which are also helpful in amusing an older child who is unable to sit or hold his head up. There are occasional queries from parents whose children don't seem to be interested in toys, despite endless attempts to find something to occupy their time. Usually they are still very young, or autistic children whose state of withdrawal into their own world limits their interest in anything except those things they are attached to. Toy library organisers and their helpers have helped with this problem on numerous occasions. Not only is there a wide range of toys to be tried but there is the experience and advice of the organiser who may find a way of awakening a spark of interest in the child. Once there is a response, however fleeting, the mother can take advantage of it and seek to reinforce it.

Toys and play

Useful books

1 All literature issued by
   The Toy Libraries Association,
2 **Souvenir Press,**
a) Lets Make Toys
   Dorothy Jeffree and Roy McConkey (1981)
b) Let Me Play
   Dorothy Jeffree, Roy McConkey and Simon Hewson (1977)
c) Helping your Handicapped Child
   Cliff Cunningham and Patricia Sloper (1978)
3 **British Institute of Mental Handicap**
a) Teaching Self Help Skills to the Mentally Handicapped using Behaviour Modification Skills and the Development of Play with Retarded Children
   J. Hattersley and M. W. Jackson (1974)
4 **Voluntary Council for Handicapped Children**
   Fact Sheet No 7, Play and Toys for Handicapped Children.

Feeding

Parents with a young mentally handicapped child often encounter feeding problems – their child may refuse to chew or to have anything but sweet foods. This is likely to be overcome eventually and by the time he is eight or nine, he is usually eating a normal diet and feeding himself, unless prevented by physical handicaps. In Downs children there is tendency for the mouth cavity to be small which means that the tongue takes up a lot of the room in their mouth – that is why some Downs children find it hard to prevent their tongue from sticking out. Because of this, they can find it difficult when young, to deal with lumps of food – and they find it easier to push it out than to struggle with it.

One three year old boy would push out any piece of solid food even before he had tasted it, preferring 'baby food' or jelly which would slide down with no effort at all. His mother decided that until he had attempted to taste the food she would get nowhere. She started with chocolate buttons because they melted quickly, and put one between his back teeth and closed his mouth, gently making a chewing movement. He grimaced and tried to push it out – then he got the taste. Before he could get it to the front of his mouth, it had melted and he was both surprised and delighted! When she had done this on a few occasions, she popped in a small piece of shortbread biscuit, and so progressed to cheese, apples etc. By this time he had realised that it was worth a little effort and was becoming far more co-operative. Soon she was able to teach him to bite with his front teeth and he took over the eating of solid foods himself. He still objected to pieces of meat but would take mince.

One mother got her four year old son feeding himself beautifully for several weeks. Then, suddenly, he refused to pick up his spoon. Thinking he may have been tired and needing encouragement, she picked it up and filled it for him – then realised her mistake! He repeated his refusal at each meal time and she found herself back at square one – except that this time she knew he could do it. As though battling with his own pride (and his hunger) he would pick up his spoon – then remember that he was supposed to be rebelling – look at his mother and put it down again. She realised that she would have to ignore him so that he would discover that he was the only one losing by his refusal to eat. So, next meal time she put his plate in front of him and sat down. He had become used to her hovering around, giving anxious glances in his direction. He began his 'performance' with the spoon, getting madder and madder when he saw no one seemed interested. When she had finished eating his mother reached across, said calmly 'have you finished, good boy' and removed his plate.

She described his face as 'a picture' – he was astounded that she had taken his food away. She went on,

> "It took only a few meals for him to get the message – once he caught me glancing at him just as he was going to put a spoonful in his mouth and that was enough. He slammed it down again. It was so hard to ignore the internal struggle with his own will but suddenly one day it was as though he said – "Oh blow it, I give in" and from them on he never looked back."

Getting a child to feed himself with a spoon can need time and patience. Of course some progress to it as a natural course of events but others find the co-ordination difficult and will object to the extent of refusing to eat. Making a battle out of mealtimes is a mistake – if it becomes a competition between mother and child, the arrival of a meal becomes a signal for testing mother's reactions and making sure of her attention. It is not easy to be casual and unconcerned or to resist feeding the child to get it over with but it is worthwhile.

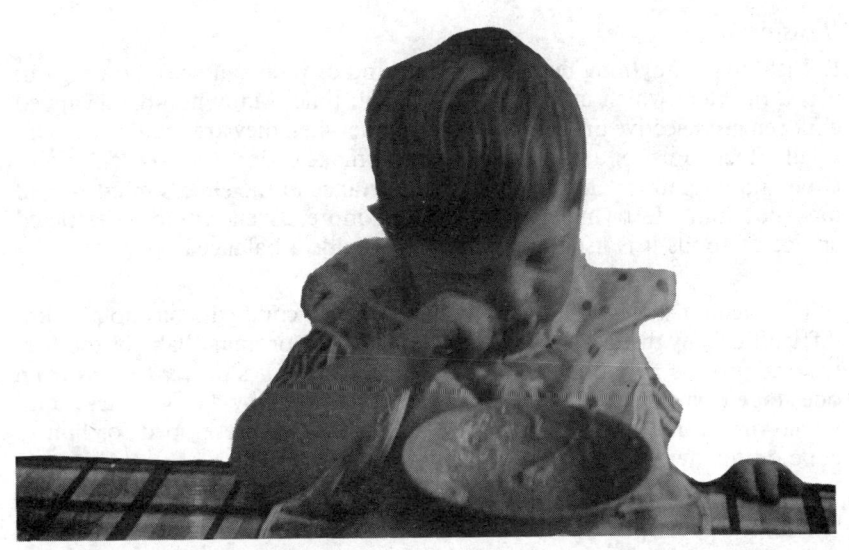

Suggestions from parents

While the child is very young and still being fed, it is a good idea to give him a spoon to hold, bang and experiment with during feeding. When he has become used to it, over a few weeks, hold the hand in which he has the spoon, using it to stir the food from time to time or to scrape food off his chin. From there, go on to using only his spoon guided by your hand, so that in effect he is feeding himself.

Once he starts to take the initiative, filling the occasional spoonful and putting it to his mouth, the help can gradually be withdrawn. Of course the time taken to get to the goal will vary depending on the child, but it will be relatively easy to gauge when to take the next step.

If he refuses to hold the spoon at all in the beginning, insist upon it, if he drops it, pick it up and put it back – perhaps only giving a spoonful of the food when he is holding it.

If possible treat it as a game but be quietly firm about the 'rules'.

It is essential to be in control without raising the voice or losing patience. If the child sees that his refusal is getting his mother rattled, it will interest him and he will decide that the point of the game is to drop the spoon as often as possible to watch his mother's reactions.

Physical difficulties with feeding

A severely physically handicapped child may suffer from spasms or reflex 'gagging' action which can make feeding awkward and time consuming. As each child may differ in his feeding requirements, the best advice would be obtained from a health visitor or the hospital responsible for his medical care. (see suggested reading, at the end of this section.)

'Fussiness'

Refusal to eat anything but a particular kind of food can be frustrating but it is a problem which usually rights itself in time. Many non-handicapped children are selective or seem to eat very little when they are small and suffer no ill effects. Fuss or anxiety only serves to make eating into an even greater issue and it assumes an exaggerated importance in the child's mind – and may put him off trying new foods even more. Even within a restricted choice of foods it is usually possible to provide a balanced diet.

The feeding stages of a mentally handicapped child who has no physical difficulties may differ very little from that of any ordinary baby or toddler. Or, the process may only differ in that the child takes longer to pass from one stage to another. He may need help, or to be shown more often, until his co-ordination and concentration are sufficiently developed for him to cope on his own.

Mrs. B. . . . .

"I was interested in hearing that other mothers experience feeding problems, and I have come to realise since I last wrote in desperation, I am not the only one going through this stage, and that does put things in perspective. Also, its a funny thing, but once I had written down in black and white my terrible panicky feelings when it came to feeding time (sounds like the zoo doesn't it!) I didn't feel half so bad. SO, the old saying, "A trouble shared is a trouble halved" was true in that case. He really has made tremendous strides just lately, in fact I've made a list of his achievements in the last few weeks – can walk in staggering steps for quite a good way, can get down from a chair, can get off a small rocking horse, understands most instructions, can feed himself unaided with a spoon (hooray), can put ten shapes into a Tupperware educational ball and let them out again.

The feeding himself bit is the most rewarding thing that has happened. It came about by accident one day when I was busy (we take summer visitors) and I put his dish and spoon on the table and said "R. . . do it" and walked into the kitchen. The first day he only took two thirds of it and allowed me to scoop up the last bits, the following days, he graduated until he cleared the plate himself. I absented myself from the room, and from his sight. I didn't even peep in at him though it was an awful struggle not to, and just wiped up the mess afterwards without comment. He's pretty good, makes a bit of a mess but no more than some normal children I've had the misfortune to sit at table with."

Son, Downs syndrome.

Feeding

Useful books

1   **Souvenir Press,**
a) Helping your Handicapped Baby
    Cliff Cunningham and Patricia Sloper (1978)
b) Starting Off
    Chris Keirnan, Rita Jordan and Chris Saunders (1978).
2   Feeding Can Be Fun
    Mary Ryan LCST
    The Spastics Society

Speech and language

Many mentally handicapped children have speech difficulties. These are usually part of the wider problem of language disability. Language concerns the understanding of words, and the use of them in the right context — speech is, therefore, only one aspect of language as a whole.

Briefly, a child vocalises when he is able to use his speech organs (tongue, teeth, lips, hard and soft palate and larynx), and when he has something to say. Language development involves the child's intellectual faculties in addition to his ability to utter sounds. To be understood the child needs to put words in the right order and to know how to make a statement, ask a question or make his demands known.

Usually defective, delayed or absent speech is the first sign noticed by parents that their child has a language disability. Because of his slower rate of learning the mentally handicapped child is less likely to use language spontaneously or to understand the language of others. So, it is all the more important for parents to recognize the difficulties as early as possible.

Speech therapy

Parents should ask their family doctor or enquire at the local authority clinic or hospital in their area about the availability of speech therapy. It is helpful to know very early on whether speech therapy can be easily arranged.

A speech therapist would help them to observe their child's development of language and recognize any difficulties. Some parents do not get referred to a speech therapist until the child is well over school age when most of his difficulties are already firmly entrenched. So if speech therapy is not suggested by the time the child is three or four years old, it is worth bringing the subject up. In some areas speech therapists are scarce so the time allotted to each child is limited. But, with advice and instruction, parents can do a great deal as a part of their everyday communcation with the child.

There are several books for parents, written by specialists, which give guidelines for improving speech and language development. It is a good idea for parents to seek the advice of a speech therapist as soon as the mental handicap has been diagnosed — even if the child is very young and speech defects cannot yet be detected. Much can be done during babyhood to prepare for language and speech developments.

Communication by 'signing' (Visual Communication Systems)

Children or adults who do not vocalise need not be denied the opportunity to communicate with others. There is a growing interest in 'signing' systems, originally developed for deaf people, for use with 'non-verbal' mentally handicapped children or adults. These can be learned by parents and teachers in short training courses, and the results are proving very promising. Parents often say that their children understand a great deal, but cannot express themselves, and for these children the signing systems are opening many doors. Some children, previously unable or unwilling to use their vocal organs have begun to vocalise words at the same time as 'signing' them.

Information about signing systems may be obtained from –

1 **British Sign Language and Makaton**
   Royal Association for the Deaf and Dumb.
   7 Armstrong Road, Acton, London, W3.

2 **Paget – Gorman Systems**
   Miss Elma Craig, City Literary Institute
   Keeley House, Keeley Street,
   Kingsway, London WC2.

3 **Blissymbolics Communication Resource Centre (UK)**
   South Glamorgan Institute of Higher Education
   Western Avenue, Llandaff,
   Cardiff, S. Wales.

Speech and language

Useful books

1) **Souvenir Press**
a) Let Me Speak
   Dorothy M. Jeffree and Roy McConkey (1976)
b) Language without Speech
   Ruth M. Deich and Patricia M. Hodges (1977).

2 **Royal Society for Mentally Handicapped Children and Adults**
a) Language Stimulus with Retarded Children
   Mary Le Frenais (1971)
b) Communication and the Withdrawn Child (1977)

3 Feeding Can Be Fun
   (Correct feeding as a preparation for speech development)
   Mary Ryan LCST, **The Spastics Society.**

Mobility

Sitting, crawling, and walking may be acquired at around the expected time for the child's age, or they may be delayed. But, most mentally handicapped children do achieve mobility, unless there are physical disabilities to prevent it.

A mentally handicapped child tends to lack the urge to experiment and discover what his body is capable of. Parents can provide him with the ideas and the stimulus to take the next step. He will not be able to achieve a new skill unless he is physically and mentally ready for it, so parents have to be realistic about their aims. It is of no value to decide 'tomorrow I will teach him to walk' if the child is only able to sit and play. That would only lead to frustration and disappointment. The attitude should be 'let's begin the process that will lead him to walking' and so concentrate on the need for him to discover what his arms and legs are for; to encourage him to reach out, push, kick with his legs and so on. If the parents notice when the child is becoming competent in the skills he has, they can anticipate the next stage and begin working towards that.

Exercising and stimulating movement during play, right from the baby's early weeks, will build up flabby muscles and strengthen the legs. The use of a baby walker encourages the child to move by himself and strengthens his muscles. Progression from one skill to the next may not be automatic. Whereas a non-handicapped child will suddenly crawl or go up the stairs, a handicapped child may need to be 'given the idea' and shown how to set about the next stage. When the child is able to sit up unaided, his parents can begin to invent games which will give him the incentive he needs.

Many of these games can be done naturally as part of normal play – putting a toy slightly out of reach and encouraging him to reach for it, or to move across the floor to get it. If the child chooses to shuffle on his bottom of 'swim' along on his tummy, it has the desired result, and it may not be necessary for him to crawl in the exact sense. But, if he makes no attempt to move it is useful to demonstrate – by moving him along, arms and legs, until he gets the idea and attempts to move himself.

One mother had some lively afternoons trying to teach her two and half year old son to stand up from a sitting position on the floor. He could crawl but seemed to have no idea how to come up from the floor to a standing position. She broke down the process into its component parts – and was surprised how many there were. First she showed him how to put his hand onto the floor and press, while he got onto his knees, then to put his feet on the floor and push. He got this quite quickly, and then stuck with his bottom in the air and his hands on the floor – in an inverted v. It took another two sessions before he could bring his hands off the floor, and straighten his back. To begin with he fell back onto his bottom every time but eventually he learned to straighten his legs and distribute his weight upwards. She went on to standing him up, at first with support, coaxing him to walk towards her holding both his hands and 'walking him'.

One inventive couple rigged up their own contraption to encourage their daughter to walk steadily. They sat on stools facing each other, with a broom handle on either side of them making rails. They put the child inside and took turns to call her towards them while she held onto the 'rails' on each side. This turned out to be popular game and she became so confident that she invented her own 'trick' – pretending to walk towards one parent then turning round midstream, changing over hands, and walking instead to the other.

Another mother had a child who enjoyed being on his feet but needed support. She encouraged him by putting his playpen in the hall then dangling or rattling colourful toys from the landing bannister. At first she stayed upstairs herself calling down to him, encouraging him to look up, and jiggling the toys on the string. At first he had no idea what she was getting at, so she showed him how to hold on to the play pen and pull himself up so he could hit at the toys and make them swing. There was an added advantage in the fact that he was at the centre of the house where he could see his mother in whichever room she was, and she could talk to him and watch his play. Once he had got used to this, she moved the strings further apart so that there was more space between the toys. This encouraged him to move sideways to get at the toys. Soon he began to move around the walls of the playpen for the pleasure of it. From there she showed him how he could pull himself up onto the settee, until gradually, it became automatic for him.

Physiotherapy

When a child has additional physical handicaps, physiotherapy is usually recommended by the hospital and parents are taught how to exercise and stimulate their child. There are a number of physiotherapy methods, some recommended and carried out by hospitals, others which are based on programmes developed by individual therapists. The latter are usually privately run outside the Health Service, and a fee is charged.

Parents can also establish whether their child is suitable for a specific type of programme by making preliminary enquiries, to the Chartered Society of Physiotherapists, who have a list of physiotherapists in private practice. (See Information Section).

Mrs. V. . . . .
> "The greatest thrill came last Christmas when K finally realised his feet were made to walk on. He staggered three paces and promptly flopped down. At 3½ years he was mobile. Now, he never stops and has turned into a great footballer, as his shoes bear witness to! We discovered last autumn that he needed glasses as he was found to be extremely long-sighted. Soon after wearing his glasses he took his first step, and the doctor feels it was the improvement in vision which gave him the confidence to walk. I would strongly recommend swimming. J. has become a veritable water baby, his constant bronchitis has disappeared and he swims as naturally as a young frog!"

Son, Downs syndrome.

Mobility

Useful books

1   Making Movement Fun
    Frederick Mortimore (1977)
    RSMHCA Books.

2   **Souvenir Press**
a) Helping Your Handicapped Baby
   Cliff Cunningham and Patricia Sloper (1978)
b) Starting Off
   Chris Keirnan, Rita Jordan and Patricia Sloper (1978)

3   **British Institute of Mental Handicap**
a) Progress to Standing
   (for children with severe mental and physical handicap)
   Katy Hollis (1980)
b) Progress to improved movement
   (for handicapped children and adults with poor posture)
   Katy Hollis (1980)

Mrs. W. . . . .
> "A. . . needs constant attention, toys don't interest him, he needs someone with him talking to him all his waking hours. I know all babies and children are like this to a certain extent, but watching friends' children makes me realise that A is far worse. Toys just don't hold his attention. Luckily my husband and I both come from close families and I escape to work a couple of afternoons a week whilst grandmothers take over and other people keep me company when they can. His present condition is, in general, behind that of his age group – he doesn't seem to have caught up on that initial poor start. On his last check up, the doctor thought that at 21 months, his mental age was about 16 months, and motor development was 11 months. His attitude to people is very good, although he is suspicious of strangers (too many hospitals I think). He has had one operation to straighten his legs, and is awaiting another – he can't walk yet, but started to crawl last week! His feet impede him since they are small as well as deformed, and he is still rather floppy. I would never have thought it possible to love a child so much. This goes for my husband too.
> A. . . is utterly adored by all his relations and really by everyone who knows him. He is extremely affectionate and very lively and amusing. He is curious, wants to know the names of things and generally investigate life. He understands a lot of what is said to him, and is trying to talk. I'm pleased about that as one of the symptoms of Möbius Syndrome is speech disorders, inability to feed, and dribbling. A. . .s feeding is particularly good and he only dribbles when teething. He tends to accept life as interesting but puzzling!"

Son, Möbius syndrome.

Toilet training
Probably the most tedious aspect of the care of young children is the washing and drying of nappies, guarding against sore bottoms, and carrying **potty, creams, and plastic pants around when travelling. As with all the**

other basic skills, the mentally handicapped child may – though not always – take longer to become clean and dry. Sometimes he may be able to anticipate his needs only in the daytime; but even if he still wears protection at night, or needs to be lifted, the work and the problems are more than halved.

Usually, the more generally responsive and aware the child is the sooner he learns to recognize the need to empty his bowels and bladder. It may take some time for him to recognize the feeling in time to express it in words or to show it in his face early enough to 'catch' him. But if his mother learns to recognize the signs and can toilet him before he has finished the child will gradually learn to control himself long enough to be able to get to the lavatory.

Apart from the work involved in keeping an incontinent child comfortable and clean there is a social consideration. It is embarrassing if a non-handicapped toddler dirties himself or makes a puddle in public; but it is something which most mothers have had to cope with at some time. Parents of older mentally handicapped children dread this kind of accident because it may not be understood by onlookers.

Excitable and over-active children often take much longer to become toilet-trained than those of a more stable temperament. Children with severe spasticity or other physical handicaps may not be able to control bladder or bowel function or indicate their needs at all.

Where there are no additional emotional or physical barriers, the child will, in time, become able to wait for longer periods between being taken to the lavatory. At first he may only indicate that he's soiled or wet only after he has done it; but that in itself is a sign that he is becoming aware of the sensations involved and is trying to communicate them.

One mother reported that her child, though unable to speak, had learned to fetch his potty when he wanted to use it. His mother always kept it in the same place; and even when she was training him to use the lavatory he would use the bringing of the potty as his way of telling her. Eventually he told her by taking her hand and indicating "Upstairs!"

Even after a child has become able and willing to co-operate there will be occasional accidents. Scolding only serves to create anxiety, and anxiety will be more likely to increase the risk of accidents. On the other hand, praise when he has used the lavatory, or remained dry for a considerable period, will encourage him to repeat his success.

For those with severely handicapped children, perhaps with physical disability, the problem is not so much one of training but of management. Ordinary nappies become inefficient for a child beyond the age of two or three years if he is of average size. If there seems to be no likelihood of the child becoming dry and clean in the immediate future, it makes sense to seek assistance with the practical problems. Health visitors can arrange for free disposable nappies to be delivered regularly, and items such as rubber sheets, drawsheets, plastic pants and mattress covers can also be supplied. (See Information Section).

Many non-handicapped children go on wetting at night long after they are able to cope with toileting during the day. Mentally handicapped children may continue to wet during sleep for a number of years, or they may start staying dry as a natural progression from learning control during the day. If a child wets at all, it is likely to be just as he is beginning to wake up in the mornings and even 'lifting' at the parents' bedtime may not prevent this entirely.

Mrs. W. . . . .
"M who is eight, is still in nappies at night. The problem is not so much that he wets or soils himself during the day but that he does so immediately he wakes — which can be at any time between 3 am and 7 am. He stays reasonably clean and dry during the day as long as someone is there to help and encourage him, but, of course, in the early hours there is no-one around.

And, therefore, I have to avoid any mess by putting him in nappies. The situation hasn't changed much in the last couple of years and I am frightened of reaching a deadlock situation where he goes on wetting and soiling because he can't remove his own nappy when, and if, he can eventually cope by himself. When we are on holiday and sleeping in the same room, I often 'catch' him in time. Can any other parent suggest a way out of the situation we find ourselves in?"

(Three months later)
"Success! We set about getting M out of nappies as soon as possible, bought a waterproof cover and nylon sheets, and set our alarm for 6 am, so we could wake before him. We also left the doors open so we could hear him easily. We soon got used to waking when he woke and then had no need of the alarm. After three weeks of 'catching' him in this way, we put him to bed in pyjamas for the first time. Since then he had not worn a nappy and, after a few accidents at first, we now rarely have a wet bed. We have made his bedtime later, so that he sleeps soundly all night and wakes at a more reasonable time. We can hardly believe what we have achieved in so short a time and thank everyone for their suggestions."
Son, hypercalcaemia.

Mrs. I. . . . .
"P's nightime incontinence was one of my biggest nightmares, as he had no idea of getting up in the night or even first thing in the morning. Needless to say, I had tried everything I could think of to cope with this, but nothing was effective. I had two dripping wet sheets every night — he absolutely refused to wear disposable pads. After 16 years this was becoming very trying. However for the last four months, P has been dry at night, and we have no idea why! He has been coming in to me during the night if he needed to go to the toilet, and in the morning he gets up, and comes in with his legs crossed! Isn't that marvellous news? I wish I could put it down to my persistence in trying various methods, but really I can't claim

the credit as I don't know what to put it down to! I hope it is because he has at last realised that he can control his bladder. It can happen even at this late stage − long after one would expect it could, so perhaps other parents will be encouraged not to give up hope if they seem to be getting nowhere with nightime wetting."

Son, chromosome abnormality.

Mrs. D. . . . .
"I always used to use hand towels for R as nappies as he wet his bed until he was 18. I also used good parts of old flannelette sheets (you need 4 or 5 thicknesses). I fastened them with safety pins at the side, and bought the adult size plastic pants. I used a draw sheet as well, as sometimes the pants etc. didn't hold it all! I thinks pads can cause soreness. I know of two mothers whose babies had nappy rash till they started to boil the nappies. If you use hand towels or pieces of folded sheet you can wash them without half the road speculating about it like they do if you use big size nappies. Hang them out if it's raining too, as I think it helps purify them."

Son, retarded.

Toilet training
Useful books
1   **Souvenir Press**
a) Starting Off
    Chris Keirnan, Rita Jordan and Chris Saunders (1978)
b) Helping Your Handicapped Baby
    Cliff Cunningham and Patricia Sloper (1978)

For details of manufacturers of toileting aids, and advice on incontinence see Information Section (Aids and Equipment).

Chapter Thirteen

EDUCATION (SCHOOL, CENTRE AND COLLEGE)

Mentally handicapped children were excluded from the education system until the early 1970's. Previously, they were catered for by the health authorities. The Royal Society for Mentally Handicapped Children and Adults fought a tireless campaign for many years to change the law. They argued that, because mental handicap by its very nature was a learning disability, those affected by it were entitled to a proper education; that mentally handicapped people were not ill and therefore should not be referred to as patients.

Finally their efforts bore fruit in 1968 when the Prime Minister, Mr Harold Wilson, announced the transfer of responsibility for the mentally handicapped from the Department of Health and Social Security to the Department of Education and Science. Eighteen months later the transfer was provided for by the Education (Handicapped Children) Act. In an article for Parents Voice (the journal of the Royal Society for Mentally Handicapped Children and Adults) in April 1971 the then Secretary of State for Education, Mrs Margaret Thatcher wrote:

> "Over 400 new special schools have been formed out of Training Centres and hospital provision. This represents the addition of about two fifths of the total of 1000 special schools and nearly one third of the number of 10,000 handicapped children already in special schools. I am determined that these children shall take their rightful place in the education system and receive their fair share of the resources available."

So, more than two hundred years since the first tiny step was made towards recognition of the mentally disordered by regulation of 'madhouse procedures' in 1744, they had finally been officially acknowledged as deserving of a worthwhile and satisfying existence.

Mentally handicapped children no longer attend training centres; they now attend schools, designated by the terms ESN(M) and ESN(S); educationally subnormal (mild) and educational subnormal (severe). For a number of years children and adults had been described as 'subnormal' and 'severely subnormal' and many people found this term objectionable. The phrase 'educationally subnormal' was generally accepted as a more accurate term because it describes a limitation of only one aspect of the individual's make-up: *it does not imply that he is a subnormal person.*

Children who are 'slow' or mildly retarded, without any serious additional disability are catered for by the ESN(M) schools. Previously these children may have floundered in a large class in an ordinary school, unable to keep up and losing all incentive to learn. Or they may have been excluded from their local primary school, placed in Training Centres for more severely retarded children, because no other alternative was available.

The more severely retarded, perhaps with additional problems such as epilepsy, can now be given teaching in accordance with their ability in the ESN(S) schools. Children who are so grievously handicapped physically and mentally that learning in the accepted sense is almost impossible (though many have shown definite progress in a social sense, within an ESN(S) school) are cared for in Special Care Units where they are given as much stimulation, personal contact and teaching as possible.

Pre school education

The value of nursery education for handicapped children is becoming increasingly recognized. The benefits are obvious – they learn to mix and play with other children, to relate to other adults, and get used to being away from home and mother for short periods.

They have access to a wide range of educational toys and large play equipment – sand trays, slides, bicycles and so on. Physically and mentally it allows them to grow. Many playgroups will take a handicapped child as part of their intake of non-handicapped children. This is beneficial to the handicapped child in terms of observing skills and listening to normally developing speech. Some parents feel very strongly that their child should be part of the social life of non-handicapped children from as early an age as possible. However, others prefer to have their child attend a playgroup which caters especially for handicapped children. If their child is severely handicapped, or an ordinary playgroup place is not available, a specialist group may be the answer. Many local societies for mentally handicapped children run day care centres, creches or playgroups. If they do not, parents should ask at the Education Department or Social Services Department about facilities in the area. The Pre-School Playgroups Association (see Information Section) is interested and concerned about the early education of handicapped children and would be able to answer enquiries about playgroup facilities.

If provision for very young children is very poor, it does not mean that a child will automatically be deprived of pre-school education. Most schools for mentally handicapped children are now accepting children from the age of three years. Local Education Departments will advise if this applies in their area. It is worth making enquiries well in advance as it is very reassuring for the mother of a handicapped baby to know that education will be available to her child at three years old.

Through assessment and consultation with school medical and psychological departments, the local authority decides whether a child is unsuitable for an ordinary school and would benefit from attending a special school. Children may be referred to local authorities for assessment by hospitals, educational psychologists, audiologists or other specialists, or by the family health centres. The school medical officer arranges a medical examination at which all available reports on the child are taken into account. Parents are entitled to be present at this examination.

Ordinary schools

An increasing number of mildly retarded children are being admitted to ordinary (i.e. not 'special') schools at the age of five if it is considered that they would benefit from education with non-handicapped children. Some mildly retarded children are able to cope in an ordinary school throughout their school life, with co-operative staff and remedial teaching. Others may be able to benefit up to the age of seven or eight then transfer to an ESN(M) school, more suited to their stage of development and maturity.

Residential schools

If a child has a specific disability in addition to mental handicap, such as epilepsy, severe spasticity, deafness or blindness etc., parents may feel that a residential school specialising in the handling of that disability would be more beneficial to their child than a school which catered for mental handicap alone. Local Education Departments should be able to provide details of these schools and if they agree that it would be the best education for the child, they would probably pay any fees charged. This is not to say that children with such additional disabilities are only catered for in residential schools. They are also accepted in ESN(S) day schools.

Further education

Mentally handicapped people over the age of sixteen (sometimes nineteen) are the responsibility of the Social Services Department. Twenty years ago, Adult Training Centres were a much welcomed innovation. But now that all areas provide such Centres parents are looking more critically at what the Centres can offer. These parents are used to thinking in terms of education rather than mere occupation. Some are beginning to question the accepted policy of transferring all mentally handicapped sixteen year olds to Social Education Centres (previously called Adult Training Centres). Many are concerned that their sons or daughters are just beginning to grasp basic concepts at the time they are due to leave their ESN school.

Parents are now using the argument that all children are legally entitled to stay on at school over the age of sixteen if they can benefit from extended education. As an alternative most would be satisfied with provision of good further academic teaching within Social Education Centres (ATC's). This is available in some areas, but Centres vary greatly in their educational provision – depending upon the availability of trained staff and financial resources. Most worrying of all for parents is the fact that many Training Centres are now overcrowded and sometimes have to refuse new applicants. Most trainees remain in the Centres for the rest of their working life and the number leaving to go to outside employment, or to live in another area, does not equate with the number needing places each year. Cut backs in public spending often hit the Social Services severely – with the result that Social Education Centres (ATC's), training schemes and hostels are not being provided as quickly as they are needed.

Parents are finding themselves with their teenage son or daughter at home all day with them, growing lethargic, bored and perhaps troublesome, as a result. It is a repetition of the situation twenty years ago, where young adults trailed after their mothers or watched television for most of the time. But it is a more tragic situation, because these are young people who have been used to going to school since the age of five, in the company of other children. In this they differ from the adults of twenty years ago, who may have known nothing else but home, and the company of their immediate families.

Better services – but when?

In 1975 The National Development Group for the Mentally Handicapped (an independent body set up by the Secretary of State for Social Services) published a detailed report giving recommendations for improvement of services in day provision for mentally handicapped adults.

The report recommended that Adult Training Centres should be renamed Social Education Centres and the designation 'trainee' should be replaced by 'student'. They made detailed suggestions for the organisation of these Centres; that they should have four main 'tiers'.

> **An admission and assessment section** which would encourage maturity, provide further basic education and generally prepare the young person for more formal work.

A development and activity section which would give a continuation of the process of learning basic academic skills with an emphasis on social competence and independence. This section would cater for those who are unable to progress quickly to the advanced work section and work similar to that done in Adult Centres at present would be provided.

An advanced work section which would provide a realistic work experience with increased demands and expectations, to give its more capable members a meaningful and satisfying occupation.

A special care section which would cater mainly for the severely mentally handicapped and those with additional physical handicaps, a fully integrated part of the Centre as a whole and not isolated as a separate facility.

The Education Act 1981, which updated the law for the education of children with special educational needs and gave new rights to their parents, received the Royal Assent in October 1981. The Act amended the law broadly in line with the concept of special educational needs proposed by the Warnock Committee on the education of handicapped children and young people. The Act defined 'special educational needs' as covering all learning difficulties except those arising solely because of a difference of language between a child's home and his school. It covered children with relatively minor and transient problems as well as those with severe and complex learning difficulties who had in the past been termed handicapped children.

These brief summaries of proposals and changes in legislation demonstrate the positive approach which now prevails. When these ideal conditions will be provided, or whether they will be provided at all, remains to be seen – economy may interfere with rapid progress.

But it is unlikely that parents, professionals, or the voluntary organisations will allow them to sink without trace.

Chapter Fourteen
FINDING OUT MORE

In the 1971 questionnaire, *In Touch* members were asked **'What do you think parents need most in the early years?'** The majority (63 parents) felt that reassurance, professional advice and information were of primary importance, followed by contact with parents in the same situation (61 parents). Practical help came third (22 parents) and financial help was considered of least importance (7 parents).

Finding out more about the handicap
Usually parents want to know why their child is handicapped, how the condition arose, whether it is hereditary or likely to occur again. They are plagued more than anything by what? why? and how? If they do not receive an explanation which satisfies them, they will go to great lengths to seek out the information themselves − which may involve ploughing through huge volumes on mental handicap to find two or three lines on their child's condition. In some cases, no cause can be found, but if a specific condition is diagnosed, parents feel that they are entitled to know what it is. But as we have seen, it is not enough to throw a medical name into the conversation and leave it at that. There need not be a detailed lecture; it is enough to know that the cause is either a chromosome abnormality, chemical imbalance, an infection in pregnancy and so on. Not only does it help the couple if they're given a reason for the handicap, it helps if they have a simple explanation to give to others.

Ignorance of the thing they are coping with does not bring peace of mind. It has the opposite effect. Once the condition is understood, the wondering can stop. A mother who discovered the name of her son's handicap after thirteen years felt very bitter that only then could she join up with other parents of children with the same condition. There were other families in the *In Touch* scheme with whom she could have been sharing ideas and experiences for several years. Instead, she had presumed her son to be a 'one-off' throughout the whole of his early childhood.

"Your child's condition has a long medical name which you needn't bother about," said one doctor, as he pronounced diagnosis. The mother remarked later that she almost expected him to pat her on the head and tell her to 'run along and don't worry your little head about it.' In fact, the name of the condition bothered her very much − she spent the rest of the interview trying to read the doctor's notes upside down as he spoke, picked out the name of the syndrome and repeated it to herself all the way to the reference library.

Another mother found out by accident — a nurse let the name slip — that her son had an uncommon syndrome, when he was thirteen years old. When she asked why she had not been told as soon as it was identified, she was told that it was decided she would gain nothing by knowing. Because the syndrome presented very characteristic facial 'differences' the mother had always felt that there was more to her son's handicap than 'unspecified brain damage'. What is more, he had a condition which could repeat itself in subsequent children, and she had gone on to have another child — even then, she had not been advised of the risk or told about the condition. Fortunately her second child was unaffected but it might have been very different.

Such secrecy only increases the feeling that the truth is being hidden and there is something sinister which parents shouldn't know. This is rarely the case. Refusal to discuss it with the parents may lead them to seek it out themselves — with much more risk of misinterpretation. One mother who told a nurse that she was going to get some information about microcephaly was told, "That would be a silly thing to do." It didn't stop her from seeking the information.

Most parents are very glad to be given a full explanation; they feel that as they are the ones who have to deal with the child daily they should be in possession of all the facts. If they discover after several years that everyone concerned with the child, except themselves, knew what was wrong with him they feel deceived and angry.

A mother who finally succeeded in getting her doctor to tell her that her ten year old son had Klinefelter's syndrome summed up her feelings: —

> "He implied that it was unnecessary for me to know the name for D's handicap; I wondered why — and made it my business to learn all I could about it. Far from disturbing me, it made so many things more clear. His behaviour was becoming erratic and I had thought I was losing my grip. When I discovered that behaviour of this kind was one of the characteristics of his condition I was tremendously relieved. Knowing that it wasn't due to my own inadequacy, or to flagrant disobedience on his part, I had a whole new approach to it — and as a result both his behaviour and my patience improved. Now I know I can weather the teenage years and deal with his problems with more understanding.
>
> Why they decided it was unnecessary for me to know about the possible effects of the syndrome, I don't know. I'd say it was vital if I was to be able to cope with it."

Mrs. G. . . . .
> "I have found it a great help trying to find out all there is to know about the condition — it cannot change the situation, but it helps me to understand it more (I find at present it is easier to accept things by only thinking forward for one year not trying to rush his

development) coping day to day – get sleep when you can, not too many late nights. Try to keep every day worries to a minimum – a silly example of this is, that I now have an insurance plan on our central heating so that if it breaks down, it gets fixed within 24-hours free."
Son, hypochondroplasia.

If the parents have been given a name for the type of handicap affecting their child they may be able to obtain information about it by contacting The British Institute For Mental Handicap, The Royal Society for Mentally Handicapped Children, or the *In Touch* scheme. If they would also like to find other parents whose children are affected by the same condition the *In Touch* scheme might be able to help. Or, they could ask for contacts by writing a letter to The RSMHCA's magazine, Parents Voice.

Forward planning

There is a vast difference between creating imaginary problems for the future – which may never present themselves – and gathering information for use in the future. It might be useful to make a list of what the immediate needs are going to be. The child has been diagnosed as mentally handicapped – so what is this likely to mean? He will take longer to learn basic skills than he would otherwise have done so it may be necessary to make some provisions to lighten the load. As far as possible parents should get to know Social Workers, Health Visitors, members of local organisations for the mentally handicapped. It is also worth their spending time looking at the relevant directories of services, local and national, in the reference library. Then when a specific query arises they will be able to go more directly to the source of advice.

Organisations

If a diagnosis of mental handicap has been given it makes good sense to consult a national organisation which devotes all its energies to keeping track of developments, determining needs, and providing services for the mentally handicapped and their families.

Information services

(Details are given in the Information Section)

There are several information services which maintain up to date lists of organizations catering for all kinds of disability including mental handicap. These services which include, Help for Health, Line 81, and *In Touch,* are available for the use of parents, professionals and volunteers and can be contacted by telephone.

Organisations such as the British Institute for Mental Handicap (BIMH) and the Royal Society for Mentally Handicapped Children and Adults (RSMHCA) produce literature on all aspects of mental handicap, and provide an advisory service. Even if parents are unwilling or unable to join a local branch of RSMHC there is still tremendous value in subscribing to their national Headquarters. A subscription will guarantee regular copies of their magazine 'Parents Voice' which reports current issues as well as giving information about services and facilities.

Some organisations are concerned with the welfare of children with specific types of handicap, such as the Downs Children's Association, The National Society for Autistic Children, and the National Society for Brain-Damaged Children.

Uncommon conditions

For parents of children affected by uncommon types of mental handicap the sense of isolation can be particularly acute. Increasingly, self help groups are being set up by parents in this situation – for example, The Tuberous Sclerosis Association, the Prader-Willi Association and the Infantile Hypercalcaemia Foundation.

Major organisations catering for mental handicap

The Royal Society for Mentally Handicapped Children and Adults
('Mencap' formerly the National Society for Mentally Handicapped Children)

The RSMHC is the major organisation for parents of mentally handicapped children and adults. It was founded as The National Association for Parents of Backward Children in 1946 and has a network of local branches throughout Great Britain and links with similar organisations in many overseas countries. It offers continuous support for mentally handicapped people and their families, supports research and provides a wide ranging information service. It produces books and literature, organises courses and conferences and is an effective pressure group working for the improvement in services for mentally handicapped people. A number of services are provided by the Society itself, including holiday homes and schemes, residential training courses for the mentally handicapped, a Trusteeship scheme, and a scheme which places handicapped people in jobs in industry.

The British Institute of Mental Handicap

A national charity, set up in 1972 to raise standards of treatment, care and management of the mentally handicapped both in hospital and the community. It provides up to date information to staff working in professions for the mentally handicapped, education and training for parents and relatives through workshops and conferences, the production of books and journals and the provision of specialised services such as toy libraries, social training for long term hospital residents and language unit facilities for children with communication difficulties. They conduct and report research and have established an Information and Resources Centre to answer specific queries on problems associated with mental handicap.

The Downs Children's Association

The Downs Children's Association has demonstrated the wide range of abilities of children affected by Downs syndrome, and has made an invaluable contribution to the understanding of the condition.

The Association provides an assessment and information service for parents of young children, promotes contacts among parents and professionals, supports research and produces advisory publications. There are branches in many areas of Britain.

Barnardo's

Barnardo's, founded over a hundred years ago, is the largest child care agency in Britain and provides a network of residential homes providing services of all kinds. With the development of the Welfare State and its provision of child care and family services, Barnardo's adapted its structure to provide child care services of a specialised kind, especially in areas of the greatest need. Now, a good deal of its resources are directed towards the care of mentally handicapped children. There are residential services, providing holidays, short term and long term care in London, Leicester, Salford, Liverpool, Kendal, Ripon, Belfast, Edinburgh and Skelmersdale.

Their aim is always to provide handicapped children with an environment which is closest to normal family life, either in small group homes or by placing children with families willing to foster or adopt them. The Barnardo's New Families project is specifically aimed at the placing of handicapped children.

Campaign For The Mentally Handicapped

A pressure group, which collects information on local services and uses this to raise specific issues with local and central Health and Social Service authorities. It hold regular meetings and conferences, and produces reports and enquiry papers and these are sold to health and local authorities, parents groups, libraries and individuals. CMH is neither a parent organisation nor a professional body, and its aims are to promote the integration of mentally handicapped people into the community using existing general services whenever possible.

National Elfrida Rathbone Society

A voluntary organisation promoting social welfare work with the educationally handicapped and their families. It works to develop all forms of social work with the educationally handicapped, including club activities for children and young adults, play groups, holiday schemes, family casework, local hostel accommodation, unemployment schemes and training workshops.

MIND

A national mental health charity with 160 local groups. Though much of their work is in the field of mental illness, they are also concerned with the rights of mentally handicapped people and their families. The organisation runs group homes, hostels, day centres, promotes research, runs a casework and information service, organises courses and conferences and provides a legal and welfare rights service.

The Spastics Society (Castle Priory College)

The college offers periods of study for both professional and voluntary helpers working both in the services of the Spastics Society and in comparative fields elsewhere. They organise courses on a very wide range of subjects relating to mental handicap, physical handicap and multiple handicap.

Local Sources

More and more local authorities and organisations are providing handbooks and directories which list the facilities available to parents. A useful starting point in the quest for local information is the Community Health Council. They will at least be able to tell parents what information should be available. It is unfortunately not always the case that parents receive this information from a family doctor, a health visitor or a social worker. So they would be well advised to make enquiries by telephoning organisations such as the Citizen's Advice Bureau, Social Services Departments, Health Clinics and the Education Department. *The more parents enquire about support services the more the need for them (and the need for publicising them) will be recognized.*

Aids and Equipment

Increasingly, modern technology is being applied to the provision of aids or equipment to make daily living easier for disabled people. Designers and engineers, including computer specialists are co-operating with physiotherapists, occupational therapists and others working with handicapped people, and there is a growing application of electronics for aids or teaching equipment. To enable parents and professionals to view items, and to try them out, aids centres in most parts of the country maintain an exhibition and advice service.

(Details of organisations concerned with aids and equipment, and a list of Aids Centres will be found in the Information Section).

Local Authority Provision

Parents of a child who is of the age beyond which he would normally be fully toilet trained, yet still needs nappies, need not go on replacing and washing them. The Health Service makes provision for the supply of disposable nappies, waterproof pants, rubber sheeting etc. Enquiries should be made at the local Health Clinic or through the local doctor or Social Worker.

Other Aids and Equipment

Items such as double push chairs (for a handicapped child who cannot walk, plus another child), wheelchairs, feeding or specially designed supporting chairs, liquidisers for a child who cannot eat solid food etc. can also be obtained free from the National Health Service.

Where there is a problem arising out of the child's handicap which would be eased by special equipment, parents should contact their doctor, Social Worker or Health Visitor. Most Health Departments will assist with items which are too expensive or which are directly relevant to the child's needs.

Toy Libraries

Play is an essential part of learning and toys which awaken all the senses and arouse interest are of particular value to a mentally handicapped child. Toy libraries have seen a rapid expansion in recent years, and most areas now have at least one. They may be run by local societies for the handicapped, attached to paediatric hospitals or started by a group of mothers. For a small weekly fee, children with any type of handicap can borrow from a wide range of toys and brothers and sisters can also use the facilities. Thus, expensive educational toys need not be bought and are not wasted if the child is not ready for them. The Toy Library also provides a meeting place where children can play together in a group and parents can meet others. Advice on suitable toys, equipment and learning aids is also given. Parents should contact their local Society for Mentally Handicapped Children who should know of the existence of a library even if they do not organise it. Alternatively, they can ask the local lending or reference library or write to the Toy Libraries Association for their list of area libraries and details of their literature. They also publish a useful ABC of TOYS and a lively newsletter. If there is no library in the area, the Association will give detailed guidance on how to start one off. It needs only a few people to get together to start in a small way and the benefits are enormous.

Hobbies and Sports, Leisure and Social Life

The value of challenging and satisfying leisure pursuits for handicapped children and adults is being increasingly acknowledged in the growth of riding, swimming, music and art clubs specially geared to their needs. In addition, many Brownie and Cub groups welcome a handicapped member provided they are able to participate in the activities even if only at a modest level. A number of children have great fulfillment in dancing classes, as have others in swimming and riding. Awards are given for endeavour and for skills attained by most of these clubs.

Gateway Clubs are Youth Clubs in which mentally handicapped and non-handicapped young people get together for dancing, record playing, sports and other social activities. They were established by the Royal Society for Mentally Handicapped Children and Adults who will give details of local clubs on request. Gateway Clubs come together for competitions, sports meetings and team matches and they usually admit children from thirteen years old. Some areas now have junior Gateway Clubs for young children.

Useful books

1) **Souvenir Press**
  a) Art Activities for The Handicapped
     Sally M. Atack (1980)
  b) Puppetry for the Mentally Handicapped
     Caroline Astell Burt (1981)
  c) Out of Doors with the Handicapped
     Mike Cotton (1981)
  d) Horticultural Therapy
     Audry Cloet and Chris Underhill (1981/1982)
  e) Yoga for the Handicapped
     Barbara Brosnan (1981/1982)
2) **Royal Society for Mentally Handicapped Children and Adults**
  a) Drama Games for Mentally Handicapped People
     Bernie Warren
  b) A Philosophy of Leisure in Relation to the Retarded
     Kenneth Solly (1975)
  c) Recreation for the Retarded
     Charles H. Jackson (1975)

Short Term Residential Provision

In areas where there is a 'hospital open door' policy for handicapped children diagnosed there, parents 'grow up' with the availability of an occasional break while their child is cared for in a trusted environment. These are not mental subnormality hospitals but general or children's hospitals dealing with diagnosis, assessment and treatment. They do not offer hospital care as such but provide a playgroup or nursery setting in children's units. These facilities are not provided by all hospitals by any means but because hand in hand with the willingness to share the care of the child, goes real support – such a hospital is going to be prepared to talk over problems with parents as a natural extension of their practical interest and positive help.

In the case of a mother's illness, where there is no-one else to look after the child, the local authority will always be able to take responsibility for the child in one of their council homes, with foster parents or in a hospital for the mentally handicapped. Usually there is a relative who can take over in the case of illness but if emergency care is the only solution it is reassuring if the parents can ask a social worker, or a friend to visit the child while he's away.

Fostering and Care Schemes

The importance of providing care for handicapped people within their own local area is now being realised. Many local authorities are setting up care schemes in which volunteers are recruited by the social services department, to provide foster care for handicapped children. Volunteer families are trained and are paid by the local authority.

This kind of fostering scheme is beneficial both to families, who are able to leave their handicapped child with people they know and trust at short notice if necessary, and it is beneficial to the local authority who have a readily available emergency and short stay facility. The search for places in residential homes or hospitals in emergencies poses great difficulties for Social Workers. Fostering or day care schemes relieve this considerably.

Because they are proving so effective, these schemes are likely to increase in number, especially if parents themselves stress the need to their Social Worker or Health Visitor.

Short Term Fostering Schemes

Leeds Social Services Department, in conjunction with parents have established a short term fostering scheme which is now being keenly copied in other areas. In Leeds in 1976 six families were recruited to provide short term foster care for mentally handicapped children. A realistic fee was paid and careful training given, in which the parents of handicapped children were involved. This is now a permanent part of the Department's provision, with 23 substitute families currently offering short term care and over 90 families with handicapped children making use of the facility from time to time.

Crossroads Care Attendant Scheme

Following a three year pilot study in Rugby this scheme became a national organisation in 1977. The primary objective is to relieve stress in the families of disabled people and to avoid admission to hospital or residential care should an emergency arise. Attendants act as 'substitute' relatives, and care is provided on a flexible basis. The scheme is intended to supplement, not to replace, existing statutory services, and schemes are now operating in a number of areas of Britain.

Holiday Accommodation

There is a variety of holiday provision for handicapped children and adults. It includes holiday homes for children without their parents, group or adventure holidays, hotel or self catering accommodation for whole families in which there is a handicapped member.

(Details of organisations providing holiday facilities, and lists of holiday accommodation for handicapped children will be found in the Information Section.)

Other forms of help

The Family Fund

The fund is run by the Joseph Rowntree Memorial Trust, financed by the Government. It exists to help families caring for a severely handicapped child up to the age of sixteen years. Until 1978 help had been given to some 28,000 families in the form of grants to cover items such as washing machines, holidays, car hire or home extensions where these are relevant to the child's disability.

The Fund is discretionary, working within general guidelines, in agreement with the Government. It is not means tested but the social and economic circumstances of the family are considered. There is no set list of items to apply for, parents are encouraged to ask for whatever they most need to make life easier. The Fund's purpose is to complement the help available from local authorities and it will sometimes give a grant for items which the local authority will provide. (For address see Information Section).

Attendance Allowance

Parents whose handicapped child is over two years old and who needs a great deal of attention by day, or night, or both, can apply for the attendance allowance. This can also be applied for by parents whose child is living in a residential school and, if it is granted, will be paid for the times when he/she is at home, i.e. at weekends and holidays. Foster parents of a handicapped child can also claim this allowance.

Mobility Allowance

If a handicapped child is over five years old and unable to walk, parents can claim the Mobility Allowance. It can also be claimed if the child is in residential care.

Invalid Care Allowance

If a man or single woman, of working age, is caring for a handicapped child, they may be eligible for this allowance. The child must be receiving the Attendance Allowance before receiving Invalid Care Allowance. Married women can only claim if they are neither living with nor supported by their husbands.

Supplementary Benefit

If there is no full time wage earner in the family and supplementary benefit is being received, parents may be eligible for extra allowances if they have a handicapped child. Help with the cost of heating and laundry, clothing and shoes can be given.

Exceptional Needs Payment

A lump sum or single grant paid at the discretion of the Supplementary Benefits Commission. There is no legal limit to the amount paid or how often a payment is made, but the need must be considered to be exceptional and essential. For example, a washing machine (probably a reconditioned one) may be given if the family has an incontinent member. If parents have savings of over £2,000 they may be expected to meet the need themselves unless it would reduce their savings to below that amount. Exceptional Needs Payments are usually given to cover clothing and footwear, bedding and household equipment, such as floor coverings and furniture. Grants are given if a family does not have these essential items or they are worn out. Exceptional Needs Payments are not restricted to people receiving Supplementary Benefit. If there is no member of the family in employment (i.e. if receiving Invalid Benefit) an Exceptional Needs Payment may be claimed. If a payment is refused, an appeal may be made against the decision.

OTHER BENEFITS

Family Income Supplement
Where a husband's wage is low or a parent is bringing up a handicapped child alone, they may be eligible for Family Income Supplement.

Free Milk
Parents whose handicapped child is of school age but does not attend school can receive milk for him. If he attends school part time free milk can be given for the days when he is at home.

Hospital Fares
Parents who are on a low income and have a handicapped child may be able to get help with fares to hospital. Those who are receiving Supplementary Benefit can have their fares refunded if they show their order book to the hospital Social Worker when they take their child for treatment. Those who are not on Supplementary Benefit but are on low income may still be able to get a refund if they ask the advice of the Hospital Social Worker.

Housing Adaptations
Local authorities are empowered to pay for part or all of the cost of adapting a house for a handicapped child or adult, and may also provide special equipment and furniture. Provision varies throughout the country and parents in some areas may be asked to contribute towards the cost of the work done according to income.

Tax Exemptions
If a child is unable, or virtually unable to walk, is not receiving the Mobility Allowance but is receiving the Attendance Allowance, his parents may be eligible for exemption from Vehicle Excise Duty (Road Tax). Parents in these circumstances may also be entitled to rate exemption on their garage.

Transport

If your child is blind or has severe walking difficulties, you can obtain an Orange Badge to display in your car. These badges give parking concessions, allowing cars to be parked as near to a destination as possible, thus reducing walking distance. In this case, Mobility Allowance should also be claimed.

Provision for care after the death of the parents

The Trusteeship Scheme – Run by the Royal Society for Mentally Handicapped Children and Adults.

The scheme was designed to alleviate one of the most frequently voiced anxieties – what will happen to our child after we are gone? The scheme provides a personal welfare service for the mentally handicapped after the death of their parents, through appointed Welfare Visitors. They make regular visits to the beneficiaries wherever they may be living. Parents can provide for Trusteeship by means of arranged instalments during their lifetime or by setting aside a lump sum for the purpose in their Will. (see also p.190).

Making A Will

A mentally handicapped person has the same rights as his or her brothers and sisters, but special arrangements have to made on his or her behalf. This may mean formal application to the Court of Protection. It can mean that his or her right to Supplementary Benefit will cease but not if the parents have already made their Will. If the child owns more than £2,000 (current rate) and lives in Local Authority Part 3 accommodation, excess of £2,000 may be used by the local authority for payment of fees. If a handicapped person has a Trust created for them, with assets in excess of £2,000 this too can result in cancellation of Supplementary Benefit and its possible use for payment of fees.

It is very sensible to seek advice from a solicitor and to make a Will, as soon as possible.

Chapter Fifteen

SHALL WE LET GO?

Lurking in the backs of parents' minds is the knowledge that one day their son or daughter will probably have to go into residential care – either during their lifetime or after they are dead. Most parents are adamant that their other children should not be pressurised into taking over the care of their handicapped brother or sister, so wish to make other provisions to avoid it. Of course, there are cases where a sister or brother does take the responsibility, and does so willingly, but it is usually considered by parents to be unfair to expect it. The problem is, should a young adult go into a residential setting before the parents become too old, so that when they become elderly or die he will not have to be uprooted into a strange environment on top of the loss of his parents? Or, should his parents keep him with them until the end of their lives so as not to deprive him of their care any longer than necessary?

The decision is hardest for those whose child does not present them with undue stress and whose personality is pleasant. There seems no reason to 'send him away' and because he is so much a part of their lives, his parents recoil at the thought of parting with him. So, a great many retarded adults are still living with one parent or both, well into their twenties and thirties. In itself this makes the future more of a worry as their son or daughter are set in their ways – firmly settled in an unchanging routine and a seemingly permanent security.

The Difficult Child

Some couples, however, have the decision forced upon them long before the child reaches adulthood. A severely hyperactive child who never seems to need more than two hours sleep, has obsessional habits, who needs constant watching if he is to be prevented from running off, or who generally imposes great stress on the members of his family, can sometimes not be kept at home once he reaches late childhood. Parents with this type of child may find, when he reaches the age of ten or twelve years old, that his size and strength make it impossible to handle him as they once could.

It is at this time too, that other children in the family are growing up. Homework may begin to suffer, and they may become sensitive about bringing friends home. They may begin to protest about not being able to go out as a family, but always leaving one parent at home to look after their brother or sister. These factors all come together to start parents considering residential care for the handicapped child.

The Child with Potential

Others, whose child presents no particular problems and who would have no qualms about his remaining at home indefinitely, come to the decision in another way.

Because their child is alert and capable of progress, they feel that he should be given every opportunity to widen his educational and social horizons. They may know of residential schools which have the reputation for combining specialised education with the encouragement of independence and social capability, so they make the very difficult decision to seek a place for their child as a preparation for his future. In this case, the decision is made in the conviction that it is for the child's benefit and is in no way brought about by his inability to fit in with life at home.

The Adult as Companion

Some elderly parents, perhaps on their own, perhaps in failing health, have often gone on too long to consider parting with their retarded son or daughter. In fact, if they are widowed, many parents come to depend on their child as much as he depends on them. For some, the child is their only and their closest companion, and they are never apart. The more able adult can be of practical help in the house, the less able provides company and affection and perhaps most of all give the parent the assurance that he or she is still needed and important. But the cloud on the horizon is the constant concern about the child's future — "how will he manage when I have gone, how will he understand, what if I am taken suddenly ill and can't look after him?" and so on. The parent dreads the thought of her child going into a hospital for the mentally handicapped yet feels it to be inevitable.

Feelings of Guilt

It the decision has to be made, at whatever time in the child's life, it is reached only after a great deal of heart searching. Even if, because of the stress the child imposes, the decision is unavoidable, the only choice and the best for all concerned, parents are still inclined to feel guilty. They feel they should cope no matter what and wonder if they are being selfish in seeking to hand over the responsibility. After years of adjusting their lives to help their child in any way they could, they feel they are giving up, even 'failing him'. When the child has gone they not only worry about how he is settling but also feel guilty about having peaceful nights, and freedom to do what they want in the evenings — half enjoying the break, half hating it! The change is so dramatic that it takes time to adjust to it. Only when they are sure that the child is happy and settling down can they begin to relax. Once they can see him go back happy after an outing or a visit home the worst is over. They are reassured that they did make the right decision — for him, too — which was where the doubt lay. Having come through the initial break, one mother was able to say that she now looked forward to her son coming home at weekends. Because she knew he was getting so much more from the school than she could give him, she could devote herself wholeheartedly to his enjoyment at weekends, and was completely relaxed during the week.

Many wealthy families send their normal healthy children to boarding school – sometimes from as young as seven years old. Then it is seen as an educational privilege, a preparation for the future in the child's best interests. Guilt plays no part as it is decided in a conscious effort to give the child a special and superior education. If the child has special educational needs, because of a mental handicap, he is also entitled to a 'privileged' education. Of course, the difference is that the child's extra dependence, his inability to communicate well and his immaturity make his leaving home seem like launching him out to sea inadequately equipped.

The fears lie in the fact that he can't be included in the decision to send him to a residential school. The benefits can't be explained to him nor can he be asked his opinion. So, it feels as though the plans are being made behind his back – a kind of 'betrayal'. Anxiety that others may not understand what he wants or that he cannot protest if he is unhappy throws doubts into the decision. Only when parents can feel sure that the people caring for their child are doing so because they have affection for mentally handicapped children, and have enough experience and understanding to cope with them, do these anxieties disappear.

Each parent feels as though their child is the first to go into residential care and that his difficulties are exclusive to him. In fact, those difficulties will have been met with and dealt with many times by experienced staff.

Mrs. S. . . . .
> "D went to a boarding school last September after much heart searching on all our parts. But, the others are grown up and he was getting so bored alone with me all the time, although the school he attended was extremely good. I found I hadn't the stamina to keep patient with him any more. I was having to cope three quarters of the time on my own as my husband goes away a lot. I still feel a certain guilt and always will, and I'll always feel I've failed him. While it is marvellous to be able to pursue my nursing part time and enjoy hobbies to the full, I miss him like hell – I even now have a little weep at his empty room, or some little incident at home that he would have enjoyed. And yet, when it is time for him to come home, again, I am filled with dread. Overall he is cared for very well, and is happy. It's the little things that upset me, like his dandruff problem. I know I must get things in proportion and one can't have perfection, but as a mother I feel wicked at times, as well as relieved – is this the experience of others, I wonder?"

Son, Downs syndrome.

Holidays

If a handicapped child has been used to the occasional holiday away from the family from an early age, he will grow up with the ability to form relationships with other adults than his parents. It will prepare him, to some extent for being looked after by someone else in the case of his mother's illness, and if he has been away from her before, it will make the job easier for whoever has stepped in.

The first time the child goes away for an organised holiday or with his school, the mother is often frantic with worry about him. Yet, if her normal ten year old daughter announces that she would like to go to guide camp, her mother usually feels pleased and regards it as beneficial for the child to have an interesting holiday and learn to be a little independent.

Community Provision

For the majority of parents, the reality of residential care need not arise until the child is well into his teens or twenties. It need not be contemplated even then if there is local hostel accommodation into which their son or daughter could graduate if ever it became necessary. If community provision continues as it should, a young mentally handicapped child should be able to go from his special school, to a training centre or sheltered workshop, while remaining in the familiar surroundings of the locality. This is an ideal not yet realised in all areas, but if parents of young mentally handicapped children are prepared to 'listen out' to developments of provision in their area and to join others in trying to fill the gaps, they will be providing an insurance for much more peace of mind when their child reaches adulthood. If, when children reach the age at which they would normally be expected to leave the family home, they can move in with their workmates in a hostel, they can have the same relationship with their parents as any grown up son or daughter. They will be living independently but seeing each other whenever they wish. Certainly the very best compromise is one in which the child or young person can 'live-in' for part of the time, coming home each week-end. When it works well, this arrangement can solve very many problems.

Short Term Care

The decision to find permanent residential care for a child or an adult would need to be taken far less often if there were sufficient short-stay facilities for all families to use regularly, or when the need arose. In a Utopian situation each area would have its own accommodation with places to take any child, at any time, for periods varying from a few days to a few months.

By no means all parents want or need to be relieved of their children from time to time; many never even consider it in their scheme of things. But, when the handicap is first discovered no-one has any way of knowing how much their lives will be affected by the child or by other circumstances. The assurance that an occasional break is possible and the security of something to fall back on takes the edge off that initial uncertainty.

Mrs. K. . . . .
"Our first child, S now eleven years old, is a spastic. I know how difficult, lonely and heartbreaking it is, but we also know a joy and happiness as well. Unfortunately S is now in a residential home for the mentally handicapped and he has settled down happily. But, this too, brought its heartache at the time — this is the most difficult decision one can face.

> But, because S was growing so quickly, becoming more and more heavy to carry, we had to make the decision. I had to do everything for him — feed him, carry him, give him drinks. I was unable to toilet train him, so I had to administer suppositories and clean up afterwards. We had ten years of this, so I feel perhaps I could help someone somewhere with some of their problems. I would never presume to tell anyone what to do or not do, but I could at least share their experiences."

Son, cerebral palsy.

While it is true to say that a great deal more help is being provided, parents in many areas still have to search around for addresses of short stay and holiday homes, then write to several before they find a vacancy. It isn't always possible to find out beforehand just how good the place is — which adds to the doubts. The first time parents decide to let their child spend a week away from them while they have a separate holiday they naturally feel very apprehensive. Some seem almost surprised that they have actually gone through with the arrangements at all. The first time, it is usually done in fairness to the other children who may only have had local holidays or those restricted by facilities which will suit the handicapped child.

Parents are very torn between reluctance to have their child looked after by strangers and the need of the rest of the family to have a holiday in which both parents can be active.

All too often one parent may have had to stay on the sidelines looking after the handicapped child. Yet, leaving the child behind to go off and enjoy themselves (or at least try to enjoy themselves!) without him does not seem the 'right' and or normal thing to do. Only when they come home and find that he has had a whale of a time without them, do they feel able to make it a yearly event.

Because so many families find short stay care beneficial, it does not mean that parents with a newly diagnosed child should feel that it is 'obligatory', and that it is an essential part of bringing up their child well. It is marvellous if the child is responsive enough to enjoy family activities, physically sound enough to join in with them and co-operative enough to cause no disruption.

But if, for whatever reason, it seems a good idea, it should not be a never ending struggle to arrange it. The benefits of short term care are being recognised by many local authorities, hospitals and private organisations. There are some 'open door' centres which take a child for one night or more, or just for the day, simply on request. Holiday schemes provide a wide range of activities on a daily basis in school holidays and there are community based homes which provide rotating care. For a mother with a wearing child this can be a lifeline. The care is truly shared; a period at home alternating with a period at the Home on a regular basis. It is far easier to cope for a pre-arranged period, knowing that someone will take over for a while at the end of it. Yet, because the child will be home again, it hasn't the same finality as permanent care.

There are sometimes a few problems at the beginning while the child gets used to alternating between two environments, but once the surroundings of the Home and the staff become as familiar as home, parents find that it can work tremendously well for all concerned.

Mrs. T. . . . .
"Outings and holidays can be difficult, and where behaviour problems are present having visitors becomes increasingly difficult. Now, after 13 years of comings and goings, for our son we are able to accept it without too much sadness. J first went away when I had to go into hospital, and having once taken the plunge, he went quite frequently in the most difficult years. This made it easier for me, and hopefully for him to accept his going away to hospital on a semi-permanent basis, then later to a residential school in Scotland where he spent 4½ years. He is now in his second year of a training course. He comes and goes without any problems. The decision to send your child away and to accept that someone else can do more for him than you can, is very hard to reach. J has made progress and is already far in advance of what we were originally told to hope for — so I am sure it was right for us.

We can only hope that one day it may enable him to live a useful life back in the community. Over the past few years, many people have been praying regularly for him, and each time he comes home, life is a little easier and more normal than before."
Son, retarded, autistic.

Independence

Sometimes parents feel it is important to accustom their child to being away from them occasionally because, unlike his normal brothers and sisters, he will not have the natural urge to 'fly the nest' as he gets older. While non-handicapped teenagers would want to go on separate holidays, and eventually live away from home, the mentally handicapped child, by his very nature, remains dependent. Many parents feel that they must actively 'force' a measure of independence upon their son or daughter so that if permanent care was to become necessary it would not be his or her first and only experience of leaving them.

However much advice comes from outside the family, no-one but the parents can make the decision. If and when the time comes for residential care to be considered they will know. If they begin to see a coming necessity for sharing the care of the child, it is an indication that circumstances demand it. No one sends their child to live away from them without endless deliberation, and if the decision is to let go, then there are sound reasons for it. It is the right decision only when the parents feel it is right — and even if they have misgivings about it or feel guilty, it can still be right in practical terms. Life may become easier in physical terms and both the child and his family may benefit, but that in itself does not make the initial decision simple. It requires the balancing of a multitude of factors and often a great deal of courage too.

Preparing for Adult Life
(see also Chapter 16)

School leaving age is the time when many parents decide to find a residential home, or community environment to provide their child with a permanent base for the future. These establishments are growing but there are still too few, resulting in long waiting lists. The time to start considering a place in a private residential home is well before the child reaches school leaving age, so that there may be as little delay as possible when the need for the place arises.

Long Stay Hospitals

Still widely regarded with dread as 'institutions' — a last resort. Facilities do vary; the staff ratio is often less than it should be and in some hospitals the accommodation is outdated. Unfortunately lack of money seems to affect mental handicap hospitals particularly badly; whenever economies are made improvement plans have to be shelved. But many hospitals are 'fighting back' — they are putting on pressure to get the financial help they need to provide a better quality of life for their residents. And, in the meantime, they are doing everything they can to improve the facilities they have got.

Some hospitals provide a really excellent standard of care and the existence for the residents is by no means as Dickensian as some people imagine. Obviously some concessions have to be made to the numbers being catered for and it isn't like living in a small house with a family of four. The lack of the everyday 'niceties' troubles parents who may have spent many years providing for every like and dislike. The mother of a seventeen year old boy who entered a hospital because of her ill-health, spent several unhappy months on his behalf.

> "Then, I realised that of course it couldn't be exactly like home — but I was worrying more about that than he was. It seemed awful to me that he was sleeping in a room with several others and that they queued up for their food and so on. But when I though about it, it was no different from a Youth Hostel or the Forces!.
>
> Actually the food seemed quite good — he always told me what they'd had for dinner and he liked the company of the other boys at night (they used to have a laugh he said and the charge nurse was always kidding them, or they played tricks on him!) What *he* thought important was the Youth Club every Friday, that they could go to see a film or that they played football against another villa or another hospital. He obviously didn't mind about all the things I was worrying about. I had had the feeling that they would be wearing any old clothes which came to hand rather than keeping their own but on one visit I saw a woman sewing name tapes on dozens of underpants — that really bucked me up because they obviously took that much care. The hospital has lots of open days; my son goes on holiday twice a year; he's taken down to the town for shopping and anyone is welcome to come in in the evenings and talk to the residents, play games with them and so on. They really do seem to be doing all they can with the limited resources available."

Other people's experiences of hospital care are less happy — though in some cases it may have been because they did not find it quite as easy to rationalize it. When there are complaints or doubts, they are likely to be about lack of occupation, stimulation, of attention to the details of personal care.

There will always be severely retarded people, especially those needing medical attention, who will have to be cared for in a residential setting. But the present policy is to get as many of the residents of hospitals as possible out into hostels, sheltered accommodation or even houses of their own. Already in some areas, groups of retarded adults are living on their own in houses in the community, with the support of social workers and voluntary organisations.

Many older residents were placed into hospitals many years ago because there were no alternatives. Many of these would certainly not have been admitted with today's provisions. For some it is now too late — the only world they can remember is that of the hospital and they would be incapable of coping with today's 'outside world'. But there are many who could be re-absorbed into society with the right kind of support. In theory this should reduce the numbers and improve the care of those who must be looked after in hospital.

It is pretty certain that this policy would be enthusiastically carried out by hospital administrators if they were not so limited by finance. At the moment, it is an uphill climb.

If parents feel that they may soon have to consider a hospital placing for their child, they should contact the Superintendent and ask to have a talk with him so that they can try to judge the overall approach to care. It is not always possible to judge a hospital by the building it is housed in. The local and regional societies for mentally handicapped children and adults are almost certain to know a great deal about hospitals in their area and their reputation. They may even be able to introduce the parents to others who have a child there.

Mrs. B. . . . .
"Things are so much easier now that G is in a local subnormality home. Her progress is slow but sure. She can now walk, run, feed herself, and is at last trying to communicate with us — not verbally, but by taking our hands and pushing them onto door handles or the fridge door, etc. It seemed like a miracle at first, as we rarely had eye to eye contact with her before. We had a sign at least that she does understand, and 'think' in a very limited way. We have her home for the day as often as we can, and the other two children welcome her. My eldest boy, now seven, who had all the bowel trouble and behaviour difficulties, has settled down a great deal, although I fear he will always be a difficult child, and would have been, no matter what family he had been born into. The youngest daughter, now three, is as easy to manage as the other two were difficult, and we now lead a relatively normal, happy life! I have no doubts at all that we made the correct decision for us all, yet even G

is far better off with all the physiotherapy, special schooling, and far more medical attention than our doctors here would ever put themselves out for."

Daughter, rare chromosome abnormality.

Residential Training Courses

These are being set up to meet the needs of mildly retarded able-bodied young people, who would benefit from a period of further education and training to enable them to live and work in the community. They are usually of two years duration and provide not only work training but encourage social independence and maturity. (Usually privately run). N.B. Where homes charge a fee the local authority in the parent's area may pay some or all of the cost. Contact the Social Services Department or Education Department in the first instance.

Rural and Community Homes

These are usually privately run. They offer long term care and training for retarded adults to that they can work in crafts, farming, domestic work etc. along with non-handicapped people who live in the community. Because places in these communities are highly regarded, waiting lists are usually long − so an early enquiry is advisable.

The Royal Society for Mentally Handicapped Children and Adults maintain several courses; organisations such as the Home Farm Trust, CARE (Cottage and Rural Enterprises), the Camphill Village Trust and L'Arche have established communities or villages in a number of areas.

Mr. T. . . . .
"The Royal National Institute for the Blind have an excellent deaf/blind unit in Shropshire, and the sooner training begins, the better. It was awfully hard parting with R. but he now loves school so much, he just longs to go back. Our next hurdle is − What after training? − for in spite of all the progress R has made, he will never be self-supporting. What has really happened is that he has become manageable and very lovable. I am sure we are all aware of some of the short-comings of some hospitals for the mentally retarded. We are terrified of R ending up in some outdated, understaffed establishment, living and competing with chronically handicapped cases. I am sure that the state of some of our establishments is due to the apathy of the unaffected, and weakness through division, of we parents. Somehow, we have got to get together, and by our concerted efforts, obtain an improvement."

Son, blind and retarded.

Residential Homes, Short and Long-Term Care

Some of these are local authority run and may be on an 'open-door' basis. There are many private organisations such as the Royal Society for Mentally Handicapped Children and Adults and Barnardo's which run holiday homes and provide short stay or long term care.

Barnardo's have a policy of introducing handicapped children into their ordinary homes, whenever possible, to integrate them in a family setting with non-handicapped children.
(See Information Section for details of homes and directories of accommodation.)

Mrs. B. . . . .
"J, my handicapped daughter just cried all day long, every outing was a disaster and every night I was up about five times. Looking back, I wonder how I managed to stay sane, but one has to get on with it as every other mother has done. Eventually I began to crack up, because I couldn't give the other children the attention they needed, because I was coping with J. The doctor persuaded me to put her in a children's home — what a decision — I felt so guilty and cried non-stop for about a week. The place she went to is a small home, 45 children, and only 4 mentally handicapped children. Well, after 3 months she had made some improvement.

The doctor told me she needed constant stimulation, which I just could not give her at home, so they would keep her and see how she improved. She has physiotherapy every day and it really has made her stronger. They even have her in calipers now — in one of those boxes on wheels, they call it a chariot. They have great hopes that she will eventually walk, although they doubt whether she will ever talk or improve mentally — but one always has hope. I never dreamed that they could have done so much for her — what a change in a child (after 2 years now). She chuckles and laughs all day and rarely cries. She comes home every second weekend and gets taken out whenever any member of the family is in town, near the home. I still feel guilty at having given up the struggle myself when I read about all the people who keep struggling on, but we all do feel now that we did the right thing in letting her stay there, and if they get her walking, what a difference it will make to her life."
Daughter, brain damage.

Chapter Sixteen

ADOLESCENCE AND ADULTHOOD

If there is one thing that worries parents more than being told that they have a mentally handicapped child, it is the prospect of having a mentally handicapped adult. People may be upset by seeing a young handicapped child but may be positively frightened of a retarded adult. After all, a child is *supposed* to be childish, enthusiastic, noisy and naive. He may be demanding or awkward but he is also small — and is therefore no real threat. Most people have had experience of talking to children so they can base their approach on that. If the child is slow or physically impaired he brings out sympathetic and protective feelings. But faced with a child-like mind in a grown up body they do not know how to react. Old misconceptions can sometimes die hard, and there is often the uneasy conviction that a backward adult will not 'know his own strength', and is almost bound to be aggressive or violent if crossed.

Perhaps this feeling arises from a belief that, being childlike, he will not have acquired 'self-control' which 'proper' adults are supposed to possess. So if he wants something, what will he do to get it? If he is upset or angry, how will he express it? If his speech is limited or indistinct it adds to the fearsome image — an image perpetuated in literature or film when the six foot man, created by a master who has given him phenomenal strength but a limited brain, breaks out to create havoc and terrorise the population.

Even in supposedly factual material, printed or broadcast, mental handicap is frequently confused with mental illness. Hospitals for the mentally handicapped are called 'psychiatric hospitals', those living there referred to as 'mental patients'. If attempts are being made to set up a hostel in a residential area, there is usually a quotation from a spokesman for the inevitable protest group. "Will our children be safe? What about our property" (Will its value go down?) "What about the noise?" The statement is usually qualified by "Of course we sympathise with these people but *this* is not the area for them." Again, the retardation is being equated with derangement; the unsophisticated brain with the seriously disturbed brain. It is not only unfair to the retarded but also to the mentally ill who are equally maligned by public opinion of this sort. The residents themselves cannot be blamed entirely; they have genuine fears based on what they know — which may be very little.

A Lifelong Responsibility

Almost as soon as their baby or young child is diagnosed parents are asking themselves "What kind of adult are we going to be responsible for?" They realise that their responsibility will last for the whole of their lives whether the child remains at home or goes into residential care. What is certain is that he will be unlikely to make his own way in the world, leaving home for a career and marriage as a natural process, voluntarily and with their blessing. It is impossible not to wonder what it will be like.

By the time a couple have brought their mentally handicapped child through childhood and teenage, they have amassed a great deal of knowledge; not only about their own child but about the mentally handicapped in general. Usually they have seen children and young people with varying degrees of backwardness and of different temperaments through their child's school, local societies, youth clubs and so on. Their other children have grown up or are becoming less dependent and the retarded son/daughter is so much a part of the family that they never doubt their love and say that they couldn't imagine life without him. They almost always find a philosophical approach: "We know of children far more handicapped than . . . ." "He could have been a lot worse." Even those whose children are frankly as retarded as it is possible to be, surprise one by saying how lucky they are that he is so pleasant, that he has good physical health or isn't deformed. Having come so far, having coped with the problems they dreaded so much in the beginnning and brought up their other children too, they have at least dispensed with many of their initial uncertainties. Their main concern is for the child's future and they are now too involved with practicalities to agonise over why it happened in the first place. Time, events and familiarity with their child have rearranged their priorities.

The Adult At Home

The fact that they have not been driven to find residential care for their child suggests that any behaviour problems he presented were containable, or that they diminished as he grew older. That is not to say that there were not times when it was considered very seriously, but because they weathered the problems or they could not find the kind of residential care which they felt would be right, the decision was never taken.

Mrs. N. . . . .
> "I feel that those brain damaged children like mine, who are not in the severely subnormal category, yet are not normal, are the most neglected section of society. They don't fit into 'severely subnormal', so there are no clubs for them, and the 'normal' people don't want to know them either. These young people know they are different, and know they are neglected by society, because they are intelligent enough. It's more of a strain for the parents too, because their children are more aware, and if they look normal but behave badly or immaturely people don't understand as they would

with a handicap that arouses sympathy — ie, not walking, blindness, mongolism. And we don't get the same financial allowances either. It is difficult taking 'bad behaviour' children out on public transport, yet we have no mobility allowance or even concessions of a percentage of the cost of a new car, as the disabled do. I feel that if you are a family with a mentally handicapped child at home, you get little help or support. I get the feeling that some people think you should put them in a home with others like themselves. I think I want to give my son the right of a home life as long as I can.

After all, he will go residential when we die, won't he? So, why not let him enjoy the benefit of home love and comforts while he can? He is deprived in many ways already, so why deprive him of home and loving care?"

Son, mildly retarded.

Mrs. D. . . . .
"From the time P was five weeks old he started being sick — and hasn't stopped since! When he was eight it was discovered that both he and his father had a hiatus hernia. But, now, he can be sick at will. I, doctors' psychiatrists — everyone has tried everything to stop it, but so far, no good. He is epileptic, slightly spastic, incontinent and doesn't talk. Despite all this, P is a very happy boy and very loving. He attends a local hospital by day and I have him home each night. He sleeps in on a Saturday to give me a break and to try to get him used to being away from me, as otherwise its impossible as he pines so much — this aggravates his sickness and he refuses to eat. Therefore I often refuse a holiday as I hate to leave him, but I know one day he will have to be hospitalised for good. I intend to cope for as long as I can.

Ten years ago my husband walked out on us, so I am coping alone. Anyway, I coped, and I know other mothers do. Love works wonders and this child has had double love right from the time he was born. He is a real treasure, and he helped me through my broken marriage, as without him, I am sure I could not have gone on each day. But, as he needed me so badly, I did.

Before my mother died three years ago (at nearly 83) she and P had a marvellous relationship/affinity together. There was always a special sort of love between them; they adored each other, and P had no eyes for me when Nana was staying here. Although P can't say anything, I am sure he still misses her and remembers her. If he sees anyone walking past the house who looks the remotest bit like his Nana, he concentrates very hard, and then looks crestfallen when the person walks past the house."

Son, brain damage, epilepsy.

A couple whose normal children have grown up and left home will still find their lives restricted by the constant presence of a young person who cannot be left on his own, who may need help or supervision with personal management and escorting to and from outside activities. Often their outings are limited to events connected with mental handicap – local society meetings or social events. Many parents become increasingly involved with local society work as their own family responsibilities decrease; they work to assist other, younger families. Even if their leisure time is tied up with mental handicap it does not mean that it is reluctantly done from a sense of duty – in fact friendships develop quite apart from the shared interest in mental handicap and many parents find a new talent for organisation or even public speaking. A mother of a seventeen year old retarded son described the satisfaction and pleasure she got from her local society.

"We were at a social committee meeting getting things ready for the children's party. I don't think we talked about mental handicap as such all evening – though we talked about our children in the usual way. One of the mothers said suddenly, 'Have you ever wondered what you would be doing with your spare time if you hadn't got all this to do?' They all decided that they might have gone to nightschool or taken up a hobby but agreed that it wouldn't have given the same feeling of purpose. We all really enjoy doing what we can. I suppose it's a sort of thanksgiving that we've all managed to come through sane and able-bodied."

Continuing Education

The provision of further education, vocational assessment and training for a mentally handicapped school leaver will vary with the area and the severity of the handicap. Discussion with the child's school and a Careers' Officer should result in the right kind of advice for the child's future. Sometimes there are specialist Careers Officers who can help to assess the child's potential, and who will discuss the possibility of further training or education, or the finding of a job where possible. It is worth finding out what the possible alternatives are before the child is of school leaving age. It is usual for the more severely retarded to go to an Adult Training Centre where adults are employed in simple work contracted to the Centre. Often mildly retarded adults, where there are no suitable alternatives available, attend ATCs but can still find it rewarding if they are given challenging work and social responsibility in the Centre. Since the publication of the Warnock Report, Colleges of Further Education have accepted more mentally handicapped students, some for half a day a week, some for several years of fulltime 'study'. These facilities are not widely publicised but they do exist. In fact, research carried out in 1980 in the north of England revealed that most Technical Colleges and Colleges of F.E. accept handicapped students. Interested parents should write to either The Registrar, Bolton College of Education (Technical), Chadwick Street, Bolton, or to Registrar, Huddersfield Polytechnic, Holly Bank Road, Huddersfield.

(It should be noted that neither of these colleges accept mentally handicapped students but they do have up to date lists of Further Education Colleges which do.)

Just as the Further Education Colleges see their role as changing so do the ATCs. Following the recommendations of the National Development Group they are being renamed 'Social Education Centres' and, more important, they now put greater emphasis on helping young mentally handicapped people to cope with everyday living rather than with **preparation for paid employment.**

Finally, just as the Colleges of F.E. and ATCs are changing their policies so are many special schools. Some are now able to send their pupils to the local College of F.E. for a half or full day each week on what are called 'link courses'. Some allow their pupils to stay at the Special School until they are nineteen years of age. As in so many other decisions, parents would be well advised to discuss these options with the head of the Special School or with the Education Department of their local authority.

Mrs. C. . . . .
"A teacher I know feels that at 16 years, a mentally handicapped child is just starting to grasp and show an interest in learning some things. She also feels that they are mentally very young and an extra two years at the special school would be a great benefit to them. She would like to see the school leaving age raised to 18 years, and feels that all parents with children at special schools should get together and do something about it. She says one of the things that worries her most is the position of the girls. They are taken from her care at 16, very immature, then put into a Senior Centre where

there are not only very much older retarded adults, but neither are they taught more school work. There are very few further education classes so really they are just put in a work centre and forgotten. The normal person can leave school now at 16, but they can stay on till 18 if they want to. Should the same thing not apply to the mentally handicapped, being backward in the first place?

We feel she is right, as our daughter at 13 years is just starting to pick out words. She is just starting what she should have done at 5 years. The teacher says she knows of cases where the child is so bewildered by this change that she can't cope, goes into her shell, and all the work they have done trying to teach them something, is wasted. She feels sure the extra two years would allow them to mature enough to face the world."

Daughter microcephaly

Mrs. R. . . . .

"I would like to see the school leaving age for the mentally handicapped raised — for my daughter it was the happiest time of her life. Mentally she was not ready for the Adult Training Centre. Let's face it, a normal child can stay on. My own daughter lacks concentration and at the centre they stay at boring jobs for 1-2 hours at a time — absolutely frustrating, hence her epileptic fits and bouts of temper. Another problem — short term holiday care, I am still looking around, Not for me so much — I have learned to live with the noise and non-stop music — but my other two girls need the break desperately. If my husband could find a residential home for her, he would be off, but I won't part with her, Holiday breaks yes, but she is my problem. I have worked, worried and cried myself to sleep over her and no-one is putting her away like an old toy which is now a nuisance."

Daughter, retarded, epileptic.

The Mildly Retarded Adult

It is usually the most severely handicapped who evoke the greatest sympathy but the position of the mildly retarded is often more complex. There is little question that a severely retarded school leaver will go on to an Adult Training Centre (S.E.C.) or that it will be suited to his needs. The sixteen year old who is classified as 'backward' presents a more difficult problem. He may be able to read and write to a degree, to travel alone on familiar routes and to care for himself, but may be immature and lacking in confidence. Naturally, his parents feel that he has the ability to do a useful job within the community, earning a reasonable wage and a measure of independence. But with unemployment presenting problems in so many areas, it may be almost impossible to find work for a young person with limited intellect. Usually 'odd-jobbing' in factories, parks and gardens or supermarkets are considered — but in practice it needs an understanding employer who is willing to release other staff to give training or to supervise work.

One young man has worked successfully for years collecting and replacing trolleys in supermarkets, another is a general helper at a hotel near his home. Once the work is understood these young people can usually be relied upon to do it in the way it has been taught, reliably and willingly. One couple sold their house and bought a grocer's shop in a small village when their mildly retarded son was only ten years old – an example of real forward thinking. He has a job waiting for him in the family business the day he leaves school.

Work

Because of the difficulty of getting suitable work many mildly retarded young people go into a Social Education Centre. Parents are sometimes distressed by this, feeling it to be a retrograde step for him to spend his time with others more handicapped than himself. But when the only alternative has the teenager sitting aimlessly at home, losing motivation and becoming awkward because of loneliness and frustration, the Centre can meet some of his needs. One Centre manager said that about one third of his trainees were of ESN(M) level but he felt that they benefitted because they were able to regard themselves as the 'best workers'. They could be given fairly complicated instructions, left to get on with the job, and use initiative when necessary. They were given positions of responsibility working with the staff in sorting and fetching materials, delivering messages and so on. They were useful in the centre and highly regarded.

Vulnerability and the risk of exploitation

The mildly retarded person has the disadvantage of enough intelligence to be aware of his shortcomings. He knows that he cannot do many of the things his younger brother can do and he knows when he is being unfairly treated or teased. Perhaps it is preferable to be so intellectually limited that comparisons with others are impossible and unnecessary. It never occurs to a severely retarded child that everyone around him can read, write or drive a car – he lets them all get on with it and does his own thing.

It seems unfair that the sight of spastic limbs should provoke sympathy and understanding while a retarded adult is dismissed as 'simple' or 'a bit funny'.

Because the mildly retarded adult is more likely to go out unaccompanied or may work amongst normal people, he is much more vulnerable to exploitation. Fortunately most people are humane enough to treat them kindly and any teasing may be of the gentle or affectionate kind – which the young person can take or even enjoy. It is one of the things, however, that parents worry about – particularly if their child is a girl and vulnerable in a sexual sense too. Because the severely retarded adult is usually accompanied by an adult or works in a sheltered environment, exploitation is less likely, and if it does happen, may cause more distress to those caring for him than the young person himself.

One incident involved a young man over six feet tall and weighing fourteen stones. He used to stand at his gate meeting a crowd of youths walking past. Each day he went in to tell his centre staff about his 'mates' who 'told him jokes and gave him cigarettes'. Not until he showed cigarette burns on his palm was it realised just how 'friendly' this gang had been. The young man could have floored all of them with a blow but it hadn't crossed his mind. Had he done so, no doubt he would have been instantly labelled as 'dangerous' and aggressive, and would probably have been assumed to have made the burns himself. He still talked of them as his pals and was disappointed when they no longer passed (having been warned off.) The real motivation for their interest had completely escaped him. He had laughed with them and had so relished being accepted (as he thought) into the group that any attention had been worth it.

Mrs. B. . . . .

"I don't even know what label my daughter goes under. I know she isn't a mongol – just that she is mentally handicapped. I feel much more is being done for the mentally handicapped now than twenty or even fifteen years ago, yet one aspect worries me. That is, the intention to try to get these people out and into normal society. In our village we have a home for twenty women, some of whom are capable of work. Even those who are not capable of work are allowed to go out unaccompanied. Some of them attend our chapel and are welcomed at all our social events, yet by the very nature of their affliction, they always remain apart. Their conversation is so limited, even the people willing to talk to them cannot converse for more than ten minutes, and not everyone is willing to spend time with them. I didn't like to say this but I know of one house where two of them were made welcome, but they wore that welcome out. These are the less severely handicapped of course, but if my B ever came to be placed in this home (which is a beautiful house) it is this very freedom which could be her undoing. Until my illness I always took her out, now she goes out alone two days a week, and I am very grateful. Our area does try to help those in need, but borderline cases don't seem to fit in anywhere.

Unfortunately, ours has never been a happy home. My husband lived with his mother and grandmother from the age of eleven. He is genuinely incapable of thinking about anyone else, yet he gives the impression that he is very concerned about me. If this was so, he would try to understand B better – Now I'm just moaning – sorry!"

Daughter, mildly retarded.

Moods

Common problems are stubborness, bouts of temperamental behaviour or awkwardness – in other words, the adolescent swings of mood experienced by all growing children. In the mentally handicapped these moods may show themselves at a later chronological age and are expressed in the only way the child knows. They are subject to the same physical changes as their bodies mature, so inevitably feel the same effects. Sometimes an otherwise placid young person may be upset by a change to a new environment, a different department in a Training Centre or a change of staff. As they get older and more 'set in their ways' they tend to need continuity even more, and are happiest with the situations and people they are used to. Familiarity gives security in a confusing world and dealing with new surroundings is unnerving if you are not very sure of yourself to begin with.

Mrs. S. . . . .
"I am an 'older' mum — I'll be 60 this year. I have two 'girls' — 35 years and 37 years, both State Registered nurses, one married. Just after the last war we adopted a son, because I was advised not to have any more children for health reasons. Then, I found myself pregnant when I was 40, and gave birth to another girl. She had whooping cough at six weeks which her brother passed on to her. When she only crawled at 15 months, no one was concerned — the whooping cough would have held her back. She said words at the normal age, but would repeat them hundreds and hundreds of times, especially when I put her to bed. It used to drive me almost mad — I even contemplated smothering her with a pillow. She didn't walk till two years old, but I was assured there was nothing to worry about. Bed wetting was never any problem, she became clean quite quickly. She began to read and spell the same as any other child of her age, but as time went on we found that money and figures baffled her (still do). She will soon be twenty years old. She used to do some weird things like twisting herself round for what seemed like hours, but never got dizzy. She always argued about things, and having started on a subject, nothing, encouragement, annoyance, even ignoring her, made any difference.

If you walked out on her (and I've done that many times to save losing patience), even half an hour later she will insist on discussing the subject. She went to a council school, a private school, and later a special school. Three years ago she left, and has been working in a factory where they make electric light bulbs. She goes to a local club here most evenings, where they play records and dance. The young people are very tolerant of her as she can be very charming. She has crushes on certain types of men and boys but isn't interested sexually — she draws them, and gets others to draw for her. Her bedroom wall is full of these pictures, and pop stars. She has her own electric organ and can play quite a lot by ear. She likes to feel secure and dreads any change. She won't even go on holiday since the last two years. I feel now that she is growing up, she feels her frustrations more and gives vent on us more and more at home. She apparently works quite well, but being a monotonous job, she has her bad days. This 'in-between' situation is hard to deal with."

Daughter, brain damage.

Menstruation and Pre Menstrual Tension (PMT)

Most often, it is parents of girls in their late teens or early twenties who report a particularly noticeable change in behaviour. A girl who has always been reasonably placid and tractable may start to show aggression, 'moodiness', bouts of temper. In some young women at least, these changes of mood are almost certainly brought on by pre-menstrual tension. Because the girl is unable to understand the reasons for these powerful feelings and cannot herself take steps to prevent or ease them, she shows them in a physical way.

Mrs. J. . . . .
> "S is a 'head banger' and for the week before her period she is like someone completely deranged. Pots are thrown, she nips and pulls her hair to an increased degree. Her breasts become rock hard and unbearably tender. It is only the fact that I suffer from pre-menstrual tension and know how she is feeling, that stops me flipping my lid."

Daughter, unspecified retardation.

After repeated visits to her doctor, insisting that these moods were connected to her menstrual cycle, Mrs J sought out the details of one of the few clinics in the country which specialises in treatment of PMT. Investigations are now being done, and a series of treatments being given.

Mrs. H. . . . .
> "We had quite a problem with S about six months ago when she suddenly began to assert herself and wouldn't do what we wanted her to do. She also became a bit aggressive which just wasn't like her. It got so bad that the teachers couldn't cope with her at school and we could barely cope with her at home, so she went into hospital for a few days. They couldn't find anything wrong with her and she is a bit better now, though she rarely does as she is told. We think perhaps her age has something to do with her behaviour although she hasn't started her periods yet. I wonder if other parents have had this problem, and how they dealt with it?"

Daughter, severely retarded.

It is a source of sadness to many mothers that their daughters, too retarded to bring up a family of their own, should have to cope with monthly periods and all that goes with them. For some, it emphasises the fact that their daughter is becoming a physically mature young woman and yet will miss the satisfaction of marrying and having children. Because of her slowness the child seems such a little girl and it can be quite an emotional experience.

Mildly retarded girls are usually able to accept a simple explanation, which reassures them that what is happening is normal and nothing to worry about, without going into the biological reasons. If they have learned to wash and dress themselves, they will probably be able to handle the practical side of their periods with a little help or training. There is a booklet, 'Growing Up Young' which will help with the explanation. (See list of useful books at the end of this chapter).

A few severely retarded girls, who are also over-active, present particular problems. They may simply refuse to wear any protection and will remove it if it is put on. A girl with this degree of handicap may also be incontinent so keeping her clean and comfortable is a very real problem. It is a problem of lack of co-operation more than backwardness. Most girls will accept belts and pads and will not interfere with them.

Inhibiting Menstruation

In cases where there is a real difficulty, a doctor may prescribe the contraceptive pill or injection to inhibit menstruation. This has been normal practice for some time where no other alternatives can be found. Mothers do feel concerned about the possiblity of risks or side effects from continuous dosage, so it is wise to take medical advice about the possibility of other solutions first. After discussion with a doctor or Family Planning Clinic the mother will be in a better position to weigh the advantages against the disadvantages.

From Mrs. E. – (a regional officer of the Royal Society for Mentally Handicapped Children and Adults.)

> "It is possible to suppress menstruation but it is unwise to suppress it entirely. So after 9 months, a withdrawal is allowed for and the course is then started again. Of course this must be done under strict medical supervision. Many nurses and parents believe this is the best method for those severely retarded women who could not be trained to cope with menstrual hygiene."

The sterilisation of retarded girls has long been a controversial issue. Some parents feel very strongly that it should be done but usually find it difficult to arrange. An American mother found it impossible to find a doctor in her area who would consider the operation for her fourteen year old daughter, but she was so convinced it was right that she came to England and paid to have it done privately. Others are equally strongly against, seeing it as an infringement of the girl's rights and an interference into something about which she cannot voice her own opinion. Mothers who want it to be done do so, not because their daughter is promiscuous, but for the opposite reason. Because of her sexual ignorance, affectionate and trusting nature, they feel she is more at risk than normal girls from men who perhaps would have no scruples about taking advantage of her. Knowing that pregnancy and childbirth would be traumatic – the child just might be handicapped too – and that the girl would be unable to keep the child anyway, some parents feel strongly that, rather than risk conception and abortion, they would prefer to have a sterilisation done.

Mrs. G. (from the U.S.A.) . . . . .
"Right now I am trying to get A sterilized. My doctor agrees with me and wants to do it. The lawyers cannot find a law against it but the doctors want to be protected in case of law suits. Can you see a Downs Syndrome girl going through pregnancy and childbirth? — I cannot. There would be a chance of the baby being retarded, and who would look after it? — we mothers that's who. Some mothers are in their early 50's like me, are grandmothers, and their health is not good. Someone told me that I had no right to deprive A of motherhood. Am I completely on the wrong track or is everyone else right and I wrong? I honestly cannot change my opinions about this and I feel I am right in wanting to prevent A from ever becoming pregnant. Am I an unfeeling mother, or am I being selfish and thinking only of myself? I have raised five children, one of them will always stay a child, and I honestly need a rest."
Daughter, Downs syndrome.

Masturbation

Masturbation is only a social problem when it is done constantly and obsessively in public.

One mother found her mentally handicapped son only did it when he 'didn't know what to do with his hands' so whenever they went out together she got him to carry or hold something for her.

If the masturbation is persistent and public it is best to see a doctor who may recommend the help of a psychologist.

When it is considered that the mentally handicapped experience all the sexual drives and sensations felt by all young people of their age, it is easier to understand the urge to use masturbation. After all, they are denied the understanding and expression of their feelings in any other way. It may be that mentally handicapped young people do not indulge in it any more frequently or fervently than many young people but, because they are totally unaware of its sexual connotations, they see no reason to do it in secret. They are probably less inhibited and certainly see no reason to be ashamed.

The fact is, though, that masturbation is not acceptable behaviour in company; people are disgusted or frightened by it — it also tends to reinforce their prejudices that a young man is sexually dangerous.

If it is a problem, it is necessary to try to instil a 'sense of place' (it is like going to the toilet, we don't have people watching us), or reduce the habit to a controlled minimum by providing some kind of distraction.

At the same time it helps if parents understand that masturbation is part of growing up, will probably diminish and that the feelings the young person is trying to cope with are not unnatural. It occurs in young people of normal ability too, but while they have the awareness to restrict it to a limited period in private and can read about it, so that they can understand what is happening to them, the retarded youngster may need the guidance and co-operation of his parents. If masturbation is not allowed to become so obsessive that the young person wants to do nothing else, and he or she is provided with plenty of interesting activity, the situation should not get out of proportion.

Mrs. W. . . . .
"I would very much like advice on how to deal with masturbation in my son who is retarded, and 18 years old. I wonder if it is a phase which he will come out of, or if I should set about trying to teach him to control it."
Son, severely retarded.

Mrs. N. . . . .
"I have a nineteen year old son with mild cerebral palsy, classified as E.S.N. As his masturbation has recently become evident I feel it is time to give him some simple sex education. I and my married daughter would like advice on the best way to approach this, as we find it hard to discover how much he knows already. I am a widow so have no man in the house to help to deal with it."
Son, cerebral palsy.

The subject of masturbation is dealt with in detail in **Teaching the Moderately and Severely Handicapped (Vol II), by Michael Bender and Peter Valletutti.** University Park Press, Baltimore (U.S.A.).

Extract from "Learning to Cope" by Edward Whelan and Barbara Speake, (Souvenir Press) . . . .

"Point out that the changes during adolescence are signs of becoming an adult, and that this brings with it both greater opportunities and greater responsibilities. Give examples of ways in which you yourself have come to expect more from your son/daughter since he/she has achieved adulthood.

Discuss the significance of displays of affection and how these differ between children and adults. Discuss how one should behave when with friends of either sex and appropriate/inappropriate displays of affection.

We suggest that you discuss these matters with parents of other handicapped people of a similar age and also with professionals who may be working with them on a daily basis. Should your son/daughter form a close and long-term relationship, beyond merely having a girlfriend/boyfriend, discussion on the feasibility of marriage will inevitably arise. Review your son's/daughter's progress and ability to cope, and consider his/her strengths and dependences in the context of those of the prospective partner. With help and support many mentally handicapped individuals have shown themselves to be capable of stable and satisfying marriages and long term friendships, and your son/daughter may be one who could achieve this with your support and that of appropriate professionals. We feel that you would want to explore this matter as fully as possible."

Adulthood and Adolescence

Useful Books

Learning To Cope **(Souvenir Press)**
Edward Whelan and Barbara Speake

Getting To Work **(Souvenir Press)**
Edward Whelan and Barbara Speake

A Home of Their Own **(Souvenir Press)**
Victoria Shennan

We Can Speak for Ourselves **(Souvenir Press)**
Paul Williams and Bonnie Shoulz

Like Normal People **(Souvenir Press)**
Robert Meyers

Housing for Mentally Handicapped People **(Royal Society for Mentally Handicapped Children and Adults)**
Chris Heginbotham

Guide for Handicapped Adolescents and Those Working with Them **(Voluntary Council for Handicapped Children)**

The Sexual Needs of Handicapped Young People **(Voluntary Council for Handicapped Children)**

How We Grow Up **(Health Education Council)**

Sex and Social Training in an Adult Training Centre **(RSMCH)**
Lindsay Lowes

Sex Education and the Mentally Retarded **(Royal Society for Mentally Handicapped Children and Adults)**
George W. Lee

Help Your Child To Understand Sex **(Royal Society for Mentally Handicapped Children and Adults)**
Victoria Shennan

The Sexual Rights of the Retarded **(Royal Society for Mentally Handicapped Children and Adults)**
George W. Lee

Growing Up Young **(Kimberley Clark Ltd)**
Mary Abbot

Chapter Seventeen

REWARDS

People who presume that the mentally handicapped never grow up have obviously never seen a young man or woman helping to serve supper to visitors, or playing with a baby. Their intellectual limitations do not prevent them from acquiring dignity and self respect, and it is not hard to see why their parents are so proud of them. The more outgoing individual may still greet people with noisy enthusiasm, as though he is his long lost brother, and it can be a little overwhelming for those who don't know him well. But because he regards everyone as his 'pal', there are usually few people in the neighbourhood who don't know him, are used to him and know how to respond.

One of the things parents value most is their child's continuing appreciation of them and of the simplest of pleasures. If they have experienced the 'off-hand' and uncommunicative phase in the teenage years of their normal children this is particularly refreshing. One sixteen year old never failed to notice if her mother had had her hair done or something in the house had changed, remarking "That's nice"! She was delighted with any present she was given and had no reservations about showing it. She carried her birthday cards around for months, bringing them out to look at or to show other people, re-living her birthday. She had retained the child-like quality of expressing all her emotions without guile or self-consciousness. It is the kind of quality which prompts parents to say that their child had taught them far more than they had taught the child, in terms of real appreciation of what they had, lack of competition or jealousy, and about enjoying life for its own sake.

One mother joked: –

> "Sometimes I wonder if she isn't really very clever and is having us all on! After all, she has no real worries – no curriculum to cover or exams to sit, no worries about earning enough to keep herself. She doesn't know about politics, starvation in India or cancer. She never questions our love for her or her own for us. We are the centre of her world and if she had been normal I wonder if she would be the same gentle girl we know."

Even those with physically disabled adults are able to find this quality. Innocence, trust, and contentment are as appealing whatever the size of the individual. Parents with this kind of child face enormous practical difficulties every day of their lives, yet their only complaint tends to be "He's getting a bit heavy to lift now."

An inexperienced person would also be very surprised to discover how much fun a mentally handicapped person can be (yet would not deny that one can have a great deal of fun with a non-handicapped child and can laugh at their antics or sayings without feeling 'cruel'). The sharing of a joke cements relationships and in any group of retarded adults one gets the characters who know they are popular and amusing, and enjoy it.

Parents of a newly diagnosed child who may be wondering what the next few years will bring, may be reassured to know that there are many families who speak with great pride of the bearing and behaviour of their adult sons and daughters. They were not always people who had had 'easy' children – some had had years of hyperactive or even aggressive behaviour and many difficult periods as they worked to bring up their children. But for them, the effort and the perseverance paid dividends. Not only was their handicapped child a credit to them, their other children had grown into well adjusted adults in successful careers or with families of their own.

There had been problems but they had tackled and overcome them. A mother with a family of teenagers remarked: –

> "If my normal children were half as nice to have around as L. . . . it would be marvellous. The other girls are at that stage where they know it all, want to stay out late at night, criticize me, and swing between being angels and devils! L. . . is content to potter around and play her records and thinks her mum and dad are great. She helps round the house, always willingly, and is so affectionate and gentle. She doesn't think she knows it all and doesn't care either. I can take her anywhere and know she'll behave beautifully. I never thought I'd actually be grateful for my handicapped daughter but there's something very comforting in her lack of sophistication and her unwavering devotion to us."

Mrs. H. . . . .
> "Our daughter – the second – is now 23 years old, and at 6 months a dour Scottish doctor told us – to quote his words, "She will never walk or talk, in fact she will not live to be much more than four or five as these children suffer so much from heart and chest complaints." However, from the very first realisation of our difficulties, we have treated her as a full member of our family. We never accepted that she could not do for herself what our other children could do, or be taught everything in the way of washing, dressing, taking meals at the table with everyone else, and so on. Years of patience were called for – it would have been easier to continue with a bottle or spoon feeding for example, but we put up with the 'messy stages' until she could eventually cope. At a relatively early age she could be taken into any hotel and be relied on to act well. Naturally, she has never attended school – for a short while she went to an Occupation Centre, but when we moved,

we agreed that if there was no centre nearby, we should not worry, but allow her to make herself a useful member of a farming family. She is quite capable of performing any household task (except cooking), she is scrupulously clean in her personal habits, and keeps her room impeccably tidy. You will gather we are extremely proud of her.

When she celebrated her 21st birthday and we had a party for her, an old friend proposed a toast – quite spontaneously she made her thank you speech to the guests for coming and bringing her presents, to her mummy and daddy for giving her the party – I thought of that doctor and all his speculations so many years ago! The medical profession has always taken a keen interest in K. . . and say of course, that she is a high grade mongol. I maintain that many could be of a higher grade if they (the medicals) refrained from assuming that they know what each individual child is capable of. I feel they often hinder progress as parents sometimes accept all the limitations they imply as inevitable. In my opinion because 99% of mongols look and react the same, that is not to say that number 100 may not be capable of greater achievement, given certain circumstances."

Daughter, Downs syndrome.

Mrs. E. . . . .

In the middle of December, K went in for a sponsored swim to raise money for a local Youth Club. I was very dubious at first as though she swims widths quite well, she wasn't usually too happy in the deep end. But, safety regulations were good and we agreed that she should try for a maximum of two lengths. In fact she only managed one length as she was talking to herself all the time and wasting her breath! But, she made over £30,000 from those who sponsored her. It wasn't just the money which meant so much, it was that she had been so *useful*. After being told one's child would be a 'lovable cabbage' I watched her swim and wanted to shout that even one small talent can achieve something, and that our children can give something back however small".

Daughter, Downs syndrome.

Appendix 1

THE "IN TOUCH" SCHEME

Most parents like to talk about their children. In particular, mothers of young children feel a real need to get together with others to share the ups and downs of life with their children.

Non-handicapped children differ in their rate of development but each stage *is* reached within a certain period of time, without special teaching from their parents. But, for the mother who has been told she has a mentally handicapped child, those differences take on a much greater significance. 'When he is walking' becomes 'Will he walk?', 'When he grows up' becomes 'What will he be like?'. Seeing other children progress effortlessly from one skill to another can be painful. Having the one 'different' child in a group − however welcoming − can emphasise her isolation and enlarge the problem.

The *In Touch* scheme was started to provide a means of informal contact for parents of mentally handicapped children and adults, so that they could discuss their experiences with others who had a similarly affected child.

The apparent need for this kind of personal contact had been demonstrated to me after I left my job in a special school, and began to foster mentally handicapped children. Several times, I was contacted by parents of newly diagnosed children, who knew of my interest, and asked if I would talk to them. Despite the fact that there was a lively local branch of the Royal Society for Mentally Handicapped Children in the area, none of them had been told about it. They felt that until they had been able to talk to someone personally, they could not join an organised society, and in addition, they did not feel ready enough to accept that the handicap was 'official'. Once it was explained to them that the RSMHC was an organisation composed mainly of parents, who would willingly talk to them, rather than a faceless body of people arranging Garden Fetes or appeals, they made enquiries, and later became members themselves.

Talking to these parents made me wonder if this need for personal and private contact was a general one and, if so, whether the need could be filled by a simple pen friend scheme. I wrote to a national newspaper offering to link up parents of mentally handicapped children. But I was not prepared for the size and enthusiasm of the response − up to a dozen letters a day for three weeks, all pouncing upon the idea as though it was a revolutionary discovery!

Once the letters had been carefully read, however, it was possible to 'match' all of them with two or three others. I did not expect the parents to enter a correspondence with me, but asked that they wrote me one letter, to let me know how successful their contacts had been.

Even those who were active in local organisations for the mentally handicapped seemed to find some value in writing to others. As one mother said,

"When your child has been driving you mad with frustration all day, you want to say it NOW, not next time you meet someone. So, you write it all down and feel better straight away, because you know they'll understand exactly how you feel. Its the same if your child suddenly does something you've been waiting for – you can't just stand up in a meeting and announce it for no apparent reason".

Some parents wrote long and frank letters, saying that it was the first time they had spoken to anyone outside their family in this way. The writing in itself seemed to be therapeutic; many ended their letters by saying they 'felt better already'. It began to appear that the scheme had more complex functions and greater benefits than I had realised.

The parents who first contacted me did not just write one letter to let me know how they were getting on; most of them began to write at regular intervals, giving me news of their child, ideas they had found useful, and asking about particular problems. As this 'feedback' increased it seemed logical to find a way of making the information available to all. So, the first newsletter appeared.

The first newsletter, for October 1968, covered one foolscap sheet – they now cover ten or twelve sides. There was never any need to publicise *In Touch*. As time went on, other parents joined because they had heard about it from someone else, magazines offered to publish items or articles about it, and radio and television programmes asked if they could mention it.

There are now approximately thirteen hundred names on the newsletter mailing list; four hundred and fifty of these receive their copies through the Royal Society for Mentally Handicapped Children and Adults Communications pack.

Newsletters are sent out three times a year, but any parent, or professional on behalf of parents, can contact me between newsletters if they think I can help. This 'casework' now constitutes most of the work of *In Touch*.

The most surprising development has been the interest of professionals; teachers, paediatricians, psychologists, social workers, health visitors and national organisations concerned with mental handicap and allied conditions. About a third of the *In Touch* membership is made up of 'non parent' members.

The most personally satisfying development is the role *In Touch* plays in 'finding' contacts for parents who have a child with a rare disability. Parents like these are unlikely to meet anyone in their own area who has a child with exactly the same condition, but because *In Touch* is national and international it is often possible to provide parents with addresses of another family – in some cases, several. Many have been told that their child's condition is so uncommon that there are no other known cases in the country; their delight when they *are* given the name of someone else is very rewarding.

In several cases *In Touch* has been able to help to form new organisations for specific rare conditions. They started with two mothers linked together, and as others contacted *In Touch* a small group has been formed. From there, the mothers went further afield, using newspapers, writing to hospitals or schools to find others coping with the same condition.

As the newsletters go into many hospitals, clinics, social work departments and Toy Libraries it means that they are seen by many more people than those on the mailing list. This network of potential helpers is the essence of the scheme. Often, a new and unusual query is 'fed' into the membership, and a reply will come from an entirely new source.

A mother wrote about her son who had a rare neurological disability – though he was not mentally handicapped. She knew only that the condition had been identified in the United States. As I was about to write to a member in America, who ran a home for mentally handicapped young men, I asked if he could try to find a reference to this condition. Two months later his reply arrived, bursting with photocopied material, and including the address of the American parents' support group. He had, he said, gone to a meeting the day he received my letter and mentioned the condition to a doctor there. Two days later, the information arrived on his doorstep. That mother has now found several more cases in Britain, and we have since discovered a newly formed group in England.

A young lady wrote from Malta, to say that her nineteen year old sister had been brain damaged in an accident, and she was anxious to help her learn to walk and talk again. Again, this was not really a mental handicap, but her request for help was included in the next newsletter. A few weeks later, I had a leter from someone I had not heard from before. She was an Occupational Therapist, and told me that one of her colleagues was soon going to live and work in Malta and would be happy to contact the young lady and to help in any way she could

Despite the growth of *In Touch* I have been determined not to lose its informality, and it is run in exactly the same way as it always was – except that it is no longer possible to run it as a spare time activity. It appears to be its 'ordinariness' which parents welcome, and it is constantly surprising to me that so many should have found it a 'lifeline'.

A mother in South Africa asked for information about her son's handicap. The condition is progressive and severe in its effects. I gave her the address of a mother in England whose child had the same condition and they began to correspond. I am often told by members that they have found close friendships through *In Touch,* but these two mothers sent me the letters they had received from each other, to show how much they had gained from them. This was the first time I had actually seen the development of a relationship between members. It brought home just what it could mean. The South African mother, a single parent, has now found three other families in her own country, and shares her letters from England with them. In her last letter to me she wrote . . .

"I am so fortunate to have my 'experience' and friendship with A in England, to assist me in trying to be a comfort to P. She was quite oblivious of the implications of the disease, but all the time had an awful feeling that the doctors were keeping things from her. Now that she has seen my son, S, and has learned all my news, her husband says she is a different person — which just goes to show how important it is that we all 'get together' with our problem. Of course, P is still shattered but she has a far more realistic and calm approach. It is so lovely having the letters from A to look forward to. Myself, and the three mothers I know here are so grateful for her honesty and optimism. It's really hard to explain how we all feel about each other. It is a real bond, which I hope will never be broken".

The parents' comments contained in this book were collated early in 1980, and describe events during the period 1968-1980.

It would be interesting to find out if current mental handicap services are producing more effective early support for parents.

The author would be pleased to hear from parents of recently diagnosed children, about their own experience, and how it compares with those described by In Touch members.

Letters (which may be anonymous if preferred) would be welcomed, and should be sent to . . .

In Touch,
10, Norman Rd.,
Sale,
Cheshire, M33 3DF.

Appendix 2

INFORMATION SECTION

Organisations

Action for the Disabled
26, Barker Walk, Mt. Ephraim Rd., London SW16. Tel. 01-677 1276.

Adoption and Fostering
(see Parents for Children, National Fostercare Association, Barnardo's New Families Project)

Adoption and Fostering, British Agencies for,
11 Southwark Street, London SE11

Adoption Society, Independent
160, Peckham Rye, London WC1. Tel. 01-837 0496.

Autistic Children, National Society for
1A, Golder's Green Rd., London N7. Tel. 01-458 4375.
Advice, information and support through regional groups. Publications and assistance for parents.

Autists, Research Group for
Mrs. G. McCarthy, 49, Orchard Avenue, Shirley, Croydon, Surrey CR0 7NE. Tel. 01-777 0095.
Aims – to encourage research into the causes of autism, provide members with information on recent medical findings, to raise funds for research into understanding the mechanisms which may be involved in autism.

Barnardo's
Tanner's Lane, Barkingside, Ilford, Essex. Tel. 01-550 8822.
(see Adoption, Residential Accommodation, Fostering)

Barnardo's New Families Project (fostering and adoption)
Lindsay Smith, Warman House, 12, St. Botolph's St, Colchester, Essex. Tel. Colchester 62438/9.
Aims – to find families for children who may otherwise grow up in childrens' homes, to offer support for adopters and foster parents and to help with any difficulties arising in the initial settling in period.
   Scheme operates in N & E London, South Wales, Glasgow, Leeds, Newcastle.

Broadcasting Support Services (see Line 81)
252, Western Avenue, London W3 6XT. Tel. 01-992 5522.
Run in conjunction with the BBC Literacy programmes (ie On The Move) Produces relevant publications, and runs an advice service on all aspects of disability.

Blind, National Library for the
Cromwell Rd., Bredbury, Stockport, Cheshire SK6 2SG. Tel. 061-494 0217/9.

Blind, Royal National Institute for the
224, Great Portland St., London W1N 6AA. Tel. 01-388 1266
(see also Partially Sighted, Optical Information Centre)

Blind Society, Jewish
1, Craven Hill, London W2 3EW. Tel. 01-262 3111.

Brain Damaged Children, National Society for
35, Larchmere Drive, Hall Green, Birmingham 28.
Provides information on organisations which promote assessment and evaluation by the Doman-Delacato method of treatment.

Brain Injured Children, British Institute for
Knowle Hall, Knowle, Bridgwater, Somerset.
Assessment and treatment programmes.

Brain Research Trust
Institute of Neurology, 64/65, Guildford Street, London WC1 1DD.

Charities Aid Foundation
48, Pembury Rd., Tonbridge, Kent TN9 2JD. Tel. 0732 356323.
Advisory service on all aspects of charity registration.

Cheshire Foundation
Leonard Cheshire House, 26-29, Maunsel St, London SW1P 2QN. Tel. 01-282 1822.

Chest, Heart and Stroke Association
Tavistock House North, Tavistock Square, London WC1H 9JE. Tel. 01-387 3012.

Child Psychology and Psychiatry, Association for
Adam House, 1, Fitzroy Square, London W1. Tel. 01-387 4263.

Children's Bureau, National
8, Wakley St., London EC1V 7QE. Tel. 01-278 9441.
Provides a wide ranging information service and publications on all aspects of childhood disability.
(see Voluntary Council for Handicapped Children).

Children in Hospital, National Association for the Welfare of
Exton House, 7, Exton St., London SE1 8VE. Tel. 01-261 1738.
Campaigns for recognition of the right for mothers to be with their children in hospital, promotes play in hospital etc.

Children's Research Fund
6, Castle St., Liverpool, Lancs L2 0NA. Tel. 051-236 2844.

Church of England Children's Society
Old Town Hall, Kennington, London SE11 4QP. Tel. 01-735 2441.

Citizens Advice Bureaux, National Association of
110, Drury Lane, London WC2B 5SW. Tel. 01-836 9231.

Cleft Lip and Palate Association (CLAPA)
34, Villiers St., Surbiton, Surrey. Tel. 01-399 4665.

Compassion
120, Salisbury Walk, Magdala Ave., London N19 5DY. Tel. 01-263 1252.
Committee of parents against substandard institutions of nursing.

Compassionate Friends
2, Norden Rd., Blandford, Dorset. Tel. 0258 52760.
Help and support for families who have lost children.

Community Transport
30, Poland St., Manchester M4 6AZ. Tel. 061-205 2226.
Transport for people, furniture, etc. Advice on mobility problems.

Cope
28, London Rd., Elephant and Castle, London SE1. Tel. 01-281 1946.
For people suffering from emotional stress.

Council for Children's Welfare
183–189 Finchley Rd., London NW3.

Crossroads Care Attendant Scheme
11, Whitehall Rd., Rugby, Warks CV21 3AQ. Tel. 0788 61536.
'Sitting-in' service for disabled relatives. Schemes operating nationally.

Crossroads Care Attendant Scheme, Scottish
4th Floor, 24, George Square, Glasgow G4. Tel. 041-226 3793.

Cruse
126, Sheen Rd., Richmond, Surrey TW9 1VR. Tel. 01-940 4818.
Organisation for widows and their dependents.

Deafness – Breakthrough Trust
Charles W. Gillett Centre, Selly Oak Colleges, Birmingham B29 6LE. Tel. 021-472 6447.
For the deaf and hard of hearing.

Deaf/Blind and Rubella Handicapped Children, National Association for
86, Cleveland Rd., Ealing, London W13. Tel. 01-991 0513.
Caters for children with hearing, sight or learning problems as a result of rubella (german measles) in pregnancy.

Deaf/Blind Helpers League, National
18, Rainbow Court, Paston Ridings, Peterborough, Cambs. PE4 6UP. Tel. 0733 73511.

Deaf Children's Society, National
45, Hereford Rd., London W2 5AH. Tel. 01-229 9272.
Parents organisation covering all aspects of deaf and hard of hearing children's development. Register of all other organisations catering for the deaf.

Deaf, Royal National Institute for
105, Gower St., London WC1 6AH. Tel. 01-387 8033.
(see also Hard of hearing).

Dental Council, General
37, Wimpole St., London W1H 8D9. Tel. 01-486 2171.

Dental Health Foundation, British
Mrs E. Elliott, 26, Ravensdale Ave., London N12 9HS. Tel. 01-445 5547.

Disability Alliance, The
1, Cambridge Terrace, London NW1 4JL. Tel. 01-935 4992.
Publications, advice and information service on grants and allowances, and other sources of financial help for disabled people.

Disablement Income Group
Attlee House, 28, Commercial St., London E1 6LR. Tel. 01-247 2128.
Advice on financial matters for the disabled and their families. Many publications, guides to benefits etc.

Disabled Living Foundation
346, Kensington High St., London W14 8NS. Tel. 01-602 2491.
Covers all aspects of handicap apart from purely medical ones. Support, research projects, literature, advice service.

Downs Childrens' Association
L. Cordukes, Quinborne Community Centre, Quinborne, Birmingham. Tel. 021-427 1374.
Assessment of children with Downs syndrome from as early an age as possible. Training and advice for parents, publications, conferences, research. Local groups in many areas.

Education and Science, Department of
Elizabeth House, 39, York Rd., London SE17 PH. Tel. 01-928 9222.

Educational Subnormality (mild)
National Elfrida Rathbone Association, 11, Whitworth St, Manchester M1. Tel. 061-236 5358/9.
Research and information concerning mildly retarded children. Clubs, centres, activity and hobby groups.

Employment, Department of
Caxton House, Tothill St., London SW1N 9NA. Tel. 01-213 3000.

Environment, Department of
2, Marsham St., London SW1. Tel. 01-212 3434.

Epilepsy Association, The British
Crowthorne House, Bigshotte, New Wokingham Rd., Wokingham, Berks. Tel. 03446 3122.

Epileptics, National Society for
Chalfont Centre, Chalfont St Peter, Bucks. Tel. 0240 73991.

Epileptics, Scottish Society for
48, Govan Rd., Glasgow G51 1JL. Tel. 041-427 4911.

Family Fund, The
Joseph Rowntree Memorial Trust, Beverley House, Skipton Rd., York YO3 6RB.

Family Welfare Association
501-505 Kingsland Rd., Dalston, Liverpool, London E8 4AU. Tel. 01-254 6251.
Casework service to offer practical help and support to families with a handicapped member.

Fostercare Association, National
Francis House, Francis St., London SW1P 1D5. Tel. 01-828 6266/7.

Foresight (Association for the promotion of pre-conceptual care)
Woodhurst, Hydestile, Godalming, Surrey GU8 4AY.
Aims — to promote optimal health and nutritional status in prospective parents, prior to conception. To aid research into identification and removal of potential health hazards to foetal development. Also working to alleviate epilepsy, hyperactivity, migraine and other conditions by combating allergies and adjusting diet.

Gingerbread
35, Wellington St., London WC2. Tel. 01-240 0953.
For one parent families.

Handicapped Children, Association of Parents of
77, Rugby Rd., Cubbington, Leamington Spa. Tel. 0926 22537.

Handicapped Childrens' Aid Committee
c/o Templars Drive, Harrow Weald, Middlesex. Tel. 01-421 1222.

Handicapped, British Red Cross Services for the
9, Grosvenor Square, London SW1.
Advice on aids, equipment, holidays, transport, wheelchairs etc.

Handicapped Childrens' Fellowship, Catholic
2, The Villas, Hare Lane, Stanley, Co. Durham. DM9 8DQ. Tel. 0207 34379.
Branches in other areas.

Handicapped Children, Voluntary Council for
8, Wakley St., London EC1V 7QE. Tel. 01-278 9441.
Run by the National Childrens' Bureau. Wide range of publications, and advisory service on all aspects of childhood disability.

Handicaps, Friends Service Council
Friends House, Euston Rd., London NW1. Tel. 01-387 3601.

Head Injuries Trust
Birmingham Accident Hospital, Bath Row, Birmingham B15 1NA.
Social Work Dept — 021-643 7041.

Headway — The National Head Injuries Association
17/21, Clumber Ave., Sherwood Rise, Nottingham NG5 1AG. Tel. 0602 622382.
To help people who have suffered head injuries in accidents, and their families.

Health and Social Security, Department of
Alexander Fleming House, Elephant & Castle, London SE1 6BY. Tel. 01-407 5522.

Heart Disorders, Association for Children With,
11, Milthorn Ave., Clitheroe, Lancs. Tel. 0200 2652.

Heart Foundation, British
57, Gloucester Place, London W1H 4DH. Tel. 01-985 0185.

Help For Health
Wessex Regional Library Unit, South Academic Block, Southampton General Hospital, Southampton, Hants. SO9 4XY. Tel. 0703 777222, ext. 3753.
Probably the most up to date and comprehensive list of organisations and information for all disabilities. Anyone may telephone and ask for information about support groups, organisations etc.

Hester Adrian Research Centre
The University, Manchester.
Research into all aspects of mental handicap. Conferences, courses for parents, parents' workshops, library, many publications.

Homeopathic Association, British
27A, Devonshire St., London W1N 1RJ. Tel. 01-935 2163.

Hyperactive Childrens' Support Group
Mrs. Sally Bunday, 59, Meadowside, Angmering, West Sussex.
Newsletters, diet sheets, support for parents with a hyperactive child (see also Foresight).

Infantile Hypercalcaemia Foundation
Lady Cynthia Cooper, 37, Mulberry Green, Old Harlow, Essex. Tel. 0279 27214.

Inherited Metabolic Diseases – Research Trust for Children with
Mrs. L. Greene, 9, Gerard Drive, Nantwich, Cheshire CW5 5JR. Tel. 0270 626834.

In Touch (see Mentally Handicapped)

Invalid Childrens Aid Association
126, Buckingham Palace Rd., London SW1W 9SB. Tel. 01-730 9891.

Kidney Research Fund
138B, Station Rd., Harrow, Middlesex HA1 2RH. Tel. 01-863 4469.

King's Fund Centre
126, Albert St., London NW1 7NF. Tel. 01-267 6111.
Library, publications, guides, conferences, courses.

Line 81
252, Western Ave., London W3 6XJ. Tel. 01-992 5522.
Organised by B.B.C. Support Services. Advice bureau, phone-in information service, publications.

Maternity Services, Association for Improvement in
67, Lennard Rd., Penge, London SE20 FLY. Tel. 01-778 0175.

Mental Health Foundation
8, Hallam St., London. Tel. 01-636 7161.

Mental Handicap, British Institute of
Wolverhampton Rd., Kidderminster, Worcs. DY10 3PP. Tel. 0562 850251.
Conferences and courses for parents and professionals in the mental handicap field. Library and information service. Publications.

Mental Handicap – One to One
National Projects Office, 76, Cambridge Rd., Kingston on Thames, Surrey KT1 3LB.
Work with long stay mentally handicapped people in hospitals, encourages community participation. Games, activities etc., organised with residents.

Mentally Handicapped, Brothers and Sisters of (see Publications)

Mentally Handicapped, Campaign for the
96, Portland Place, London W1N LEX. Tel. 01-636 5020.
Pressure group. Aims to improve existing services and facilities for the mentally handicapped. Publications, reports of projects, investigations etc.

Mentally Handicapped Children and Adults-contacts for parents
In Touch, Mrs. A. P. Worthington, 10, Norman Rd., Sale, Cheshire M33 3DF. Tel. 061-962 4441.
Contacts and information service, newsletter.

Mentally Handicapped, Centre for the
Sunley House, Gunthorpe St., London EC1. Tel. 01-247 1416.

Mentally Handicapped, Jewish Society for the
140, Wembley Hill, Wembley, Middlesex. Tel. 01-904 7717.

Mental Handicap-Exodus
12, Park Crescent, London W1. Tel. 01-636 5020.
A group of mental handicap organisations campaigning to bring mentally handicapped people out of hospitals, into the community.

Mentally Handicapped, Association of Professionals for the
Kings Fund Centre, 126, Albert Place, London NW1 7NF.

Mentally Handicapped Children and Adults, Royal Society for (MENCAP)
117, Golden Lane, London EC1Y 0RT. Tel. 01-253 9433.
Over 400 affiliated local societies. The major organisations for parents of mentally handicapped children and adults. Information and advice, support in local groups, holiday and short stay homes, further education and training courses, research, quarterly, magazine.

Mentally Handicapped Children and Adults, Scottish Society for
13, Elm Bank St., Glasgow, G2 4QA. Tel. 041-556 3882.

Mental Subnormality, British Society for the Study of
Moneyhill Hospital, Birmingham B30 3QB. Tel. 021-444 2271.

Mind – National Association for Mental Health
22, Harley St., London W1N 2ED. Tel. 01-637 0741.

Mind – Scottish Branch
67, York Place, Edinburgh EH2 3JD. Tel. 031-556 3062.

Mind – Northern Ireland
Beacon House, University St., Belfast BT7 7HE. Tel. 0232 28474/5

Mongolism (see Down's Children's Association)

Mucopolysacchiridosis (MPS) Society, Inc.
Mary Majura, President, 552 Central Avenue, Bethpage, New York 11714. USA.
Support group for parents of children suffering from one of the MPS conditions, including those associated with mental handicap ie, Hurler's syndrome, Hunter's syndrome, San Fillipo syndrome. There is no equivalent organisation in Britain at present, but the Trust for Children with Inherited Metabolic Diseases is an umbrella group for these conditions. It is likely that parents would find others who have children affected by Hurler's syndrome, Hunter's syndrome, or San Fillipo syndrome, by contacting the Trust (see under Inherited Metabolic Diseases). Contact with parents of children with the above conditions can be provided by the In Touch scheme.

Optical Information Council
418 – 422 Strand, London WC2R 0PB. Tel. 01-836 2323.

Partially Sighted, Association for the Education and Welfare of the
Mr. E. Dugmore, East Anglian School, Church Rd., Gorleston-on-Sea, Great Yarmouth, Norfolk. Tel. 0493 61788/62399.

Patients Protection Law Committee
59, Hackworth Point, Rainhill Way, Bow, London E3.
Aims – to protect patients from human medical experimentation and to establish firmly their rights by law.

Parents for Children
222, Camden High St., London NW1 8QR. Tel. 01-485 7548.
Arranges fostering and adoption for children considered 'hard to place'.

Patients Association, The
11, Dartmouth St., London SW1 H9BN. Tel. 01-222 4992.
Represents and furthers the interests of people in hospital. Publishes a directory of organisations catering for all types of disease and handicap.

Phenylketonuria and Allied Disorders, National Society for
6, Rawdon Close, Palace Fields, Runcorn, Cheshire WH7 2QQ. Tel. 0928 714444 ext. 248.

Pre-School Playgroups Association, National
Alford House, Aveline St., London SE1. Tel. 01-582 8871.

Post Help
Dave Watkin, 42, White Farm Rd., Sutton Coldfield, Warks.
Action group helping to fight for the rights and improved opportunities of mentally handicapped people living at home.

Prader – Willi Association
Mrs. Janet Williams, 30 Follett Drive, Abbots Langley, Herts.
Information and contact for parents of children affected by P – W.

R.A.D.A.R. (Royal Association for Disability and Rehabilitation)
25 Mortimer Street, London W1N 8AB. Tel. 01-637 5400.
Information service, publications on all aspects of disability.

Restricted Growth, Association for Research into
2, Mount Court, 81 Central Hill, London SE19 1BS. Tel. 01-670 2984.
Provides information, supports research into conditions in which restricted growth is a factor.

Retarded, British Association for the
117, Golden Lane, London EC1Y 0RT. Tel. 01-253 9433.

Rubenstein Taybi Syndrome
Mrs. Ann Ferry, 8, Parkside, Tynemouth, North Shields, Tyne and Wear NE30 4JN.
Parents of children who have this condition are invited to write to the above address if they would like to be put in touch with other parents.

San Fillipo Syndrome (see also mucopolysacchidosis, Inherited Metabolic Diseases)
Mrs. Linda Matthews, The Gables, Rock Lane, Standon, Stafford, Staffs, ST21 6QZ.
This is not an organised association, but anyone whose child has this condition, and would like contact with others, should write to the above address.

Skin Camouflage, Society of
Wester Pitmenzies, Auchtermuchty, Fife, Scotland.

Sexual and Personal Relationships of the Disabled
The Diorama, 14, Peto Place, London NW1 4DT. Tel. 01-486 9823/4.
Advice and publications on all aspects of sexual and personal issues as they affect disabled or handicapped people.

Spastics Society, The
12, Park Crescent, London W1N 4EQ. Tel. 01-387 9571.
Wide range of activities, publications, homes, holiday accommodation and support for anyone who is spastic or has a spastic relative.

Spastics, Scottish Council for
22, Corstorphine Rd., Edinburgh, EH12 6HP. Tel. 031-337 2809.

Sitting in service (see Crossroads Care Attendant Scheme)

Voluntary Organisations, National Council for
26, Bedford Square, London, WC1B 3HU. Tel. 01-636 4066.
Keeps a register of community and local Councils for Voluntary Service, and will put people in touch with their local branch. Wide range of publications.

Speech Therapists, College of
Harold Foster House, 6 Lechmere Road, London NW2 5BH. Tel. 01-459 8521

Speech Therapy, National Research Trust for
Park Manse, New Road, Mistley, Essex CO11 2AG.

Spina Bifida and Hydrocephalus Association (ASBAH)
Tavistock House North, Tavistock Square, London WC1. Tel. 01-388 1382.
Mutual help through local organisations.

Spina Bifida Association, Scottish
190, Queensferry Road, Edinburgh, Scotland. Tel. 031-332 0743.

Steroid Aid Group
Mrs. L. Wilding, 35, Landowne Road, Seven Kings, Ilford, Essex, IG3 8NF. Tel. 01-597 0823.
Aims — to put people having steroid therapy in touch with one another to monitor effects.

Toy Libraries Association
Seabrook House, Wyllyotts Manor, Darkes Lane, Potters Bar, Herts, EN6 2HL.

Tuberous Sclerosis Association
11 Deveron Road, Bearsden, Glasgow, Scotland.

Vaccine Damaged Children, Association for
Mrs. R. Fox, 2, Church St., Shipston-on-Stour, Worcestershire.

AIDS, EQUIPMENT AND CLOTHING

There are several organisations which publish extensive lists or catalogues of aids and equipment, with addresses of manufacturers and suppliers. Some have a continuous information service; issuing lists of aids with new items added, and previous lists brought up to date. These are sent at regular intervals on payment of a yearly subscription.

Equipment for the Disabled
2, Foredown Rd., Portslade, Sussex BN4 2BB. Tel. 0273 419327.
Publishes a series of A4 size books on all aspects of disabled living, including, Clothing and Dressing for Adults, Disabled Child.

Disabled Living Foundation
346, Kensington High St., London W14 8NS. Tel. 01-602 2491.
Aids Centre, information service, publications. Bi-monthly sheets giving details of new equipment and aids.

British Red Cross Society
9, Grosvenor Square, London SW1X 7EJ. Tel. 01-235 5454.
Publishes details of aids, nursing items. Will sometimes loan items.

Active
Seabrook House, Wyllyotts Manor, Drakes Lane, Potters Bar, Herts EN6 2HL. Tel. 0707 44571.
Collects practical information about adaptations and designs for toys, games, aids, and equipment. Advisory service, including details of electronic aids.

Scottish Information Service for the Disabled
18-19, Claremont Crescent, Edinburgh EH7 4QD. Tel. 031-556 3882.

R.A.D.A.R.
25, Mortimer St., London W1N 8AB. Tel. 01-637 5400.
Advises on all aspects of disabled living.

The Spastics Society
12, Park Crescent, London W1N 4EQ. Tel. 01-636 5020.
Aids, adaptations and equipment.

Handicapped Advisory Service Committee
c/o Biological Engineering Dept., Faculty of Medical Sciences, University College, Gower St., London WC1.
Advice on aids, equipment, adaptations, mobility.

Rehabilitation Engineering Movement Advisory Panels (REMAP)
Mr. N. Brearley, Thames House North, Millbank, London SW1P 4QG. Tel. 01-834 4444 ext. 4112.
Panels of designers, engineers etc, who work together to make aids equipment and adaptations for the disabled. Will advise and assist individuals with specific requirements. Panels throughout the country.

Disabled Motorists Federation
Copthorne Community Hall, Shelton Rd., Shrewsbury, Shropshire.
Privides a list of a large selection of accessories and adaptations on receipt of a stamped addressed envelope.

AIDS CENTRES
Glasgow (covering the whole of the Strathclyde area)
Florence St. Health Clinic, Glasgow, Scotland.

Newcastle upon Tyne
Council for the Disabled Aids Centre, Mea House, Ellison Place, Newcastle upon Tyne NE 8XS. Tel. Newcastle 23617.

Merseyside
Merseyside Aids Centre, Youens Way, East Prescott Rd., Liverpool, Lancs. Tel. 051-228 9221.

Cheshire
Aids/Assessment Unit, Stepping Hill Hospital, Stockport, Cheshire. Tel. 061-483 1010.

Manchester
C.H.S. for the Disabled, 26, Blackfriars St., Manchester 3. Tel. 061-832 3678.

Durham
c/o Salvation Army Hall, Saddler St., Durham DH1 3NU. Tel. 0385 49445.

Leicester
Medical Aids Department, British Red Cross Society, 76, Clarendon Park Rd., Leicester, Leics. Tel. 0533 700747.

London
Disabled Living Foundation, 346, Kensington High St., London W14 8NS. Tel. 01-602 2491.

Hampshire
AHA Aids Centre, c/o OT Department, Southampton General Hospital, Southampton, Hants SO9 4XY. Tel. 0703 777222 ext. 3414.
Sheffield
Aids Centre for the Disabled, 87, The Wicker, Sheffield 3, Yorks. Tel. 0742 737025.
Wakefield
National Demonstration Centre, Pinderfields General Hospital, Aberford Rd., Wakefield, Yorkshire WF1 4DG. Tel. 0924 75217.
Wales
Wales Council for the Disabled
Crescent Rd., Caerphilly, Mid Glamorgan, S. Wales, CF8 1XL. Tel. 0222 869224.
Warwickshire
Disabled Living Centre, 84, Suffolk St., Birmingham. Tel. 021643 0980.

LOCAL AUTHORITY PROVISION
Area Health Authorities are empowered to provide aids and equipment for those who are caring for a sick or disabled relative at home. Not all the services are available everywhere and some authorities are more aware than others of the range of items they can provide. Contact a Social Worker, Health Visitor to arrange for the provision of, or loan of specific aids or equipment.

Items and services which can be provided . . .
Disposable nappies, commodes, incontinence pads, protective or plastic pants.
Drawsheets, rubber sheets, bedpans
Wheelchairs, special prams, special chairs, walking aids, bath aids
Kitchen equipment (i.e. blenders, scales, etc.) where a special diet is necessary
Bus or train fares, especially for hospital visits.
Home Helps
Residential Accommodation, long and short term
Holidays, transport for holidays, financial assistance for holidays
Day Centres
Nurseries and Playgroups
Special Schools
Physiotherapy, speech therapy, dental service, child psychology service etc. (via G.P., hospital or school)
Telephone installation
Home adaptations, i.e. handrails, ramps, downstairs bathroom etc.
Laundry Service – usually run in conjunction with the Home Help Service.

SELECTION OF AIDS, EQUIPMENT AND CLOTHING

There are many more items available than those listed here. It is a good idea to write to the manufacturers, asking for catalogues or leaflets on their full range of products.

Apron ('Jiffy – tensile plus')
Covers front and sides from shoulder to knee, slips over head, Velcro fastening.
Philip & Tacey Ltd.

Baby Slings, Carrying Seats
The Chaucer Co. Ltd.
Mothercare

'Trans-Sit Seat'
Nylon carrying seat with shoulder straps worn by the attendant. Seat folds. Weighs only 2 lbs. 2 widths – 13 inches, 15 inches.
Ellis, Son & Paramore, Ltd.

Bathmats, Towel Cloaks
Mothercare
Boots

Baths (see Showers and/or Baths)

Bath Seats (see also CHAIR, INFLATABLE)
J. & A. Carter Ltd.
Homecraft Supplies
The Spastics Society

Beakers and Mugs (Adapted)
Antiference
Bickipegs
Boots
Martin Russell Ltd.
Selfridges Ltd.
Sherrards Centre
The Spastics Society

Beds
Horatio Myer & Co. Ltd.

Bed Warning System
Care-Call, Tubiton House, Medlock St., Oldham, Lancs OL1 2HS.
Emits a warning if bed is vacated.

Bedding – Quilts, Sheets, Pillows, Mattresses, Pads
Mothercare and Mothercare by Post
Heal and Sons Ltd.
Henleys of Hornsey
John Lewis Partnership
Robinsons of Chesterfield
Smith and Nephew
Talley Surgical Instruments Ltd.
Price Bros. & Co. Ltd.

'Kylie' Absorbent Bed Sheets
Nicholas Laboratories, 225 Bath Road, Slough, Berks. SL1 4AU.
Single bed sheets, with absorbent rayon layer which retains urine even under pressure, with a brushed nylon top which provides a dry surface to lie on. Tucks in to hold firmly in place. Washable.

Waterproof Pillows
Melcro Products Ltd. Melcro House, Market Street, Tottington, Bury, Lancs. Tel. Tottington 4127. Pillows, washable, anti-suffocation, different sizes available.

Bibs, Cover-all Aprons
Boots
Mothercare
Philip & Tacey Ltd.

Bootees, Remploy Hillington, A043
Can be adapted for caliper wearers. Sizes 2-7, 5-11
Remploy Ltd.

Bootees, Thermo-Insulated
Husky of Tostock Ltd.
Large Department Stores.

Bootees – (see also SHOES)

Bowls, Suction
Homecraft Supplies Ltd.
Tiger Plastics Ltd.

Car Seats, Belts, Harnesses
Britax (London Ltd.)
T. Bowers and Son
Clippa-safe
Ellis, Son & Paramore
Halford Shops
K.L. Automotive Products Ltd.
I.N. Rankin Sales
The Spastics Society.

Catsuits for the Older Child
British Home Stores
John Lewis Partnership

Chairs
Reclining Platform Chairs
Powell Seat Co., 70 Lodge Lane, Derby DE1 3HB. Tel. 0332 47757.
Enables a person to be raised from near lying position to an upright position by a turning a handle. Can be operated by the sitter. Upholstered. Made to order.

Chair, Inflatable
Strong waterproof canvas, can be used in the bath. The Spastics Society.

CLOTHING
Clothkits, Lewes, East Sussex.
Fashionable, colourful designs, ready to cut out. Catalogue on request.

Miss Candy Cut Out Garments
6 Abbey Gardens, London NW8.

Maubri Fashions
Unit 2, Springfield Industrial Estate, Farsley, Leeds, Yorks. Tel. 0532 553274.
Clothes made to customers requirements. Specialists in clothing for handicapped people.

Clothing (See PUBLICATIONS for Clothing Advisory Services, catalogue)

Colostomy (The Schact Appliance)
Chas. F. Thackeray Ltd.

Cranes, Hoists
Houghton, Greenless & Associates.
Martonair Ltd.

Crawling Aids
J. & A. Carter Ltd.

Cups, Suction
Homecraft Supplies
Ships Chandlers
Tiger Plastics Ltd.

Cushions, Relief
Spenco Medical UK Ltd. Steyning, W. Sussex.

Cutlery
Antiference Ltd.
Boots
Ecko Plastics Ltd.
Mothercare

Draw Sheets, Underpads, Rolls, Wipes
Cellulose Products
Henleys of Hornsey
Luxan Hospital Supplies
Robinsons of Chesterfield
Vernon – Carus Ltd.

Dressmaking (See CLOTHING)

Exerciser, Cindico
Larger Model C. Enlarged and strengthened bouncer.
Weight range 30 lbs – 60 lbs. Larger models are intended for the treatment of handicapped children, and medical approval should be obtained.
Cindico Ltd.

Eggcup, Suction
Tiger Plastics Ltd.
Homecraft Supplies
Cup anchors to plate, egg gripped by plastic cup.

Feeding Bottles, Bottle and Beaker Combined, Bottle and Spoon Combined
E. Hill & Sons (Reading Ltd)
Playtex Ltd.
Thistle Products

Helmets, Protective
J. & A. Carter Ltd.
Pryor and Howard Ltd.
Remploy

Hobcart
Directorate of Industries and Supply

Medical Sheepskins
Antartex Sheepskin
Macarthy's Ltd.
E. & R. Garrould Ltd.
The Spalding Sheepskin Co. Ltd.
Walfix Fleeces

Medic-Alert (Medical identification jewellery)
9 Hanover Street, London W1R 9HF. Tel. 01-499 2261.
Jewellery carrying details of allergies, hidden disabilities, essential medication, etc. See also S.O.S. TALISMAN.

Mini-Bug (Hand propelled wheeled cart)
Byrdair Ltd.

Nappies
Courtaulds Ltd.
Lewis Wolf Griptight Ltd.
Molnycke Ltd.
Robinsons of Chesterfield
The Spastics Society
Vernon-Carus Ltd.

Nappies, Extra Large, Adult Disposable
Available from firms listed above.

Neck Supports
Bernt Bostrom
W.S. Rothband & Co. Ltd.

Odour Control
Liquid to deodorise nappies, bed linen, clothing, etc., and for ostomy appliances.
Dawn Bros.
Mayer & Phelps Ltd.
Nilodor Ltd.

Ostomy (HOLLISTER OSTOMY PRODUCTS)
Abbott Laboratories Ltd.

Pants (open crotch knickers for easier toileting)
J.H. Bounds Ltd. (mail order)

Pants, Plastic
Normal, large and extra large sizes, plus sizes for adults.
Bowman Marketing Group
Contenta Surgical Co.
Henleys of Hornsey
Home Nursing Supplies
IPS Hospital Services
R. & G. Associates
Robinsons of Chesterfield
Vernon-Carus Ltd.
Large and extra large infants size may be obtained from:
Brumas - chemists
Golden Babe – chemists
Twinletts, Boots chemists

Pillows, Waterproof
Melcro Products Ltd. Melcro House, Market Street, Tottington, Bury, Lancs. Tel. Tottington 4127.

Pillow, Safesleeper
Air channels in the self-ventilating, non-rubber foam pillow allows for free breathing.
Mothercare
Nursery Shops

Placemats, Non-slip
Dycem Plastics Ltd.
The Spastics Society

Plates, Stay Warm
Antiference
Boots
E. Hill (Reading) Ltd.
Mothercare

Potties
Jackel & Co. Ltd.
Mothercare

Potty Chairs
The Chaucer Co. Ltd.
John Lewis Partnership
Peckham Works Centre
Selfridges Ltd.
The Spastics Society

Plastazote (protective moulding material)
Foamed sheet, auto-adhesive. Can be moulded. Applications – pressure point protection, collars, foot supports, lining for plaster beds, carrying cradles, jackets, limb supports, head rests, boots, slippers. Smith & **Nephew.**

Putty, Plastic (Tufset CCL, Moulding Material)
A resin which is mixed, applied by hand and used for adaptation of cutlery, etc. Does not shrink. Can be sawn or filed to shape. Resistant to detergents. Manufacturer: CCL Systems Ltd. (Electric Division), Cabco House, Ewell Street, Surbiton, Surrey.

Rain Capes (For Wheelchair or Pushchair)
John Lewis Partnership
Mothercare
Selfridges Ltd.
Simplantex Ltd.

Riding Hats
The Wirral Saddlery Centre

Seats, CARRYING (See Baby Slings)

Sheets, GLOVE
Fitted sheets which stay in place better than ordinary sheets, cotton interlock. Waterproof sheet also available.
Heal & Son Ltd.
John Lewis Partnership and other department stores.

Shoe Guard, Protection Kit
Kit for strengthening soles and uppers of shoes which get excessively worn because of deformity or walking difficulty.
North Hill Plastics Ltd., 49 Grayling Road, London.

Shoes, Odd Sizes
Clarks Ltd., (School and Medical Liaison Officer), Somerset.
Fisher (Shoes) Ltd., The Market Place, Hampstead Garden Suburb, London NW11.
Freeman Hardy Willis Ltd. (to order only)
Masters & Son Ltd., 174/184 Grange Road, London SE1 3AH.
Start Rite Ltd., Crane Road, Norwich, Norfolk.
Sousters Bros. Ltd., 8 Clements Road, Ilford, Essex.
Truform Ltd. (to order only).
Shoes altered from left to right, right to left, where only one standard shoe is required, eliminating the expense of buying a superfluous shoe in a pair.
Messrs. J.E. Brown, 39 Kings Road, New Oscott, Sutton Coldfield, Warks. B73 5AB. Tel. 021-354 1449.

Shoe Problems or Queries

British Footwear Manufacturers Federation
72 Dean Street, London W1.
Will advise on all matters concerned with the shoe trade.

Childrens Foot Health League
3 Hyde Park Place, London W2 2LD.
Will provide details of retailers stocking unsual fittings and widths.

Society of Shoe Fitters
9 St. Thomas Street, London SE1.

Shoes to Measure Ltd.
Ken Hall Ltd., 39 Regent Street, Kettering, Northants.
Orders by post. Foot measured by their special measuring device (supplied on request).

Bury Boot and Shoe Company
Bury, Lancs.
A number of styles available, catalogue on request.

Baby Relax Ltd.
Wennington Road, Rainham, Essex.
Manufacture a special bootee for small children with abnormal feet.

Remploy
415 Edgeware Road, Cricklewood, London W2.
Manufacture felt boots, one for children, and a range of made to measure shoes, trainers, etc.

Disabled Living Foundation
Book, 'Footwear for Problem Feet' (See PUBLICATIONS)

Shoo Shoos
Shoes giving extra support, sizes 2-7.

Showers and/or Baths

Showers
Barking Brassware Ltd.
Dent & Hellyer Ltd.
Dolphin Showers Ltd.
Walker Crossweller Ltd.

Sunflower Special Bath
A 'false' shallow bath for bathing handicapped children and adults. Made to fit 5 ft, 5ft 5in. or 6ft British Standard Baths, it raises the bather to a level which requires less bending on the part of the assistant. Increase safety and reduces strain of entry and exit. If necessary, children and small adults can be undressed and dressed in the bath – if this is done, mixer taps must be used for the water.
From N.O.M.E.Q., 17 Ludlow Hill Road, Belton Road, West Bridgford, Nottingham, Notts.

Socks, (Tubular Stretch, No Heel)
Burt Bros. Hosiery Ltd.

Socks, Cotton
D. H. Evans Ltd., 318 Oxford Street, London W1A 1DE.
Absorba (will provide lists of local stockists)

Socks, Tabi (Divider between 1st and 2nd Toes)
Japanese Import Shop.

Straws, Flexible
Boots
Homecraft Supplies
Home Nursing Supplies
Portex Ltd.
Sweetheart Bristol.

Sweater and Tights Combined
Absorba.

S.O.S. Talisman
Details from – Mencap, 117 Golden Lane, London EC1Y 0RT.
Jewellery, pendants and bracelets, which carry an information strip giving vital information about hidden disabilities, allergies, blood group, essential medication, etc. *See also Medic-Alert*

Tables, Adjustable
British Red Cross Society
J. & A. Hanger & Co. Ltd.
The Spastics Society

Thermawear: Underwear, Footwear, Nightwear
Damart Thermawear (Bradford) Ltd.

Thermometer, Digital
"Ezotemp", digital thermometer. Re-usable, self-adhesive disc.
From most chemists, price £1.50. Or from Ezotemp Inc., P.O. Box 27505, St. Louis, Missouri 63141, U.S.A.

Tights
Messrs. Sunarama, 72/74 Eversholt Street, London, NW1.
Tights in sizes up to 54 inches, to fit heights up to 6ft. Available in 4 shades.

Tights, Indestructable
Hall and Son, (also "Indestructable Socks")

Tights, Divided Gusset
"Easytights" I. & R. Morley Ltd., Heanor, Derbyshire
Yellowtop Hosiery Co., Boston, Lincs.
Available in many department stores.

Tights Extra Strong
Hall and Son
John Lewis Partnership

Toilet Trainer Seats
Ecko Plastics Ltd.
Mothercare

Toothbrush, Automatic
Ronson Products Ltd.
The Spastics Society

Toothbrush, Tinkling
Tommee Tippee, available from chemists.

Treatment Mats
Lilleywhite International Ltd.

Urinary Appliances
Available on NHS Prescription
Dawn Bros. Mayer and Phelps Ltd.
Eschmann Bros. and Walsh Ltd.
Portex Ltd.

Walking Aids, Parallel Bars, Crutches, Tripods
Available through NHS.
J. & A. Carter Ltd.
Ellis, Son and Paramore Ltd.
Modern Tubular Productions
Pryer and Howard Ltd.
Remploy Ltd.
Seaco Products Ltd.

Wheelchairs
Available through NHS.
A.C. Cars Ltd.
Amesbury Surgical Appliances
Andrew McClaren Ltd.
T. & F. Barrett Ltd.
Biddle Engineering
Braune Ltd.
Gold Cross Ltd.
Modern Tubular Productions
The Spastics Society
Vessa Ltd.
Zimmer Orthopaedic Ltd.
Local Red Cross or St. Johns Ambulance, on temporary loan.

ADDRESSES OF MANUFACTURERS AND SUPPLIERS OF AIDS AND EQUIPMENT

Abbott, F. E. & Co. LTd., 104, Homerton High St., London E9 6JG.
Abbott Laboratories Ltd., Queensborough, Kent.
Absorba Ltd, 40, Great Portland St., London W1.
Amesbury Surgical Appliances Ltd., South Mill Rd, Amesbury, Wilts.
Andrews Maclaren Ltd., Barby, Nr. Rugby, Warks.
Antartex Sheepskin, Alexandria, Dumbarton, Scotland.
Antiference Ltd., Bicester Rd., Aylesbury, Bucks.
Ashtons Ltd., Unit G31, 14-16 Falcon Rd., London SW11.
Barking Brassware Co. Ltd., River Rd., Barking, Essex.
Barrett Co. Ltd., 22, Emery Rd., Bristol BS4 5PH.
Bernt Bostrom, S.V.C.R., Forsaljnings, AB, PO Box 4, 122-21, Bergen, Sweden.
Bickipegs Ltd., 43-37, Jopps Lane, Aberdeen, Scotland.
Biddle Engineering, Stourbridge Rd, Halesowen, W. Midlands.
Bounds, J. H. Ltd., Stethos House, 68, Sackville St., Manchester M1 3WJ.
Bowers, T. & Son., 266, Stamford St., Ashton-under-Lyne, Lancs.
Bowman Marketing Group, 154, Marylebone Rd., London N1.
Braune Ltd., Griffin Mill, Thruee, Stroud, Glos.
Britax Ltd., Byfleet, Surrey.
British Red Cross Society, 9, Grosvenor Crescent, London SW1X 7EJ.
Burt Bros. Hosiery Ltd., The Poplars, Wollaton Rd., Beeston, Notts.
Byrdair Ltd., 9, Widelands Rd., Hunsdon, Herts.
Courtaulds Ltd., Carrfield Mills, PO Box 19, Hyde, Cheshire.
A.C. Cars Ltd., High St., Thames Ditton, Surrey.
Carter, J. & A. Ltd., Alfred St., Westbury, Wilts.
Cellulose Products, 16 Dolphin St., Ardwick Green, Manchester M12 6HG.
Chaucer Co. Ltd., 71/73 Tooley St., London Bridge, London SE1.
Cindico Ltd., Skerne Rd., Driffield, Yorks. S623 7KH.
Clippa-Safe, Lenthwaite Rd., Clifton, Notts.
Contenta Surgical Co., PO Box 8, Long Ing Mill, Colne, Lancs, BB8 6BT.
Damart Thermawear Ltd., Bowling Green Mills, PO Box 23, Bingley, Yorks.
Dawn Bros., Mayer & Phelps Ltd., 22/24 New Cavendish St., London W1M 8BU
Dent & Hellyer Ltd., Walworth Industrial Estate, Andover, Hants.
Dolphin Showers Ltd., Weir Lane, Worcester, Worcs.
Dycem Plastics Ltd., Parkway Trading Estate, 15 Minto Rd., Bristol, Avon.
Ecko Plastics Ltd., Prittlebrook Industrial Estate, Southend, Essex.
Ellis Son and Paramore, Spring St., Sheffield, Yorks S3 8PB
Eschmann Bros. & Walsh Ltd., Church St., Shoreham-by-Sea, Sussex.
Garrould, B. & R. Ltd., 9 Hardwicks Way, London SW18.
Gewa Produkter Pantskogs, Vagen 5, 740, 22, Uplands, Balinge, Sweden.
Gold Cross (Hospital Equipment) Ltd., Coneyore Rd., Tipton, Staffs.
Hall & Son, Stoke Golding, Nr. Nuneaton, Warks.

Hanger, J. & E., Queen Mary's Hospital, Roehampton Lane, London SW15.
Heal and Son Ltd., 196 Tottenham Court Rd., London W1A 1BJ.
Henleys of Hornsey, Alexandra Works, Clarendon Rd., Hornsey, London.
Hill, E. & Sons Ltd., 38, Broad St., Reading, Berks.
Homecraft Supplies Ltd., 27, Trinity Rd., London SW17 2SF.
Home Nursing Supplies Ltd., PO Box 4, Westbury, Wilts.
Houghton, Greenless & Associates, Beach Ave., Clevedon, Somerset.
Husky of Tostock Ltd., Bury St., Stowmarket, Suffolk.
Industries & Supply, Directorate of, Tolworth, Surbiton, Surrey.
I.P.S. Hospital Services, Victoria Hill, Lower Vickers St., Manchester.
Jackel & Co. Ltd., Kitty Brewster Estate, Blyth, Northumberland.
Japanese Import Shop, 73A Lower Sloane St., London SW1.
K.L. Automotive Products Ltd., Homerton High St., London E9 6AT.
Learning Development Aids, Park Works, Wisbech, Cambs.
Lewis, John, Partnership, Oxford St., London W1A 1AB.
Lewis Wolf Griptight Ltd., 144, Oakfield Rd., Birmingham, Warks.
Lilleywhite International, 64-66 Battersea High St., London SW11 3H7.
Luxan Hospital Supplies, PO Box 8, Long Ing Mill, Colne, Lancs.
Macarthy's Ltd., North St., Romford, Essex.
Martin Russell Ltd., St. Albans, Herts.
Martonair Ltd., St. Margarets Rd., Twickenham, Middlesex.
Modern Tubular Products, 188 High St., Egham, Surrey.
Molnycke Ltd., 32-36 Great Portland St., London W1.
Morley, I. & R. Ltd., Heanor, Derbyshire.
Mothercare by Post, Cherry Tree Rd., Watford, Herts.
Myer, Horatio & Co. Ltd., 83/97 Vauxhall Walk, London SW11 5EN.
Nilodor Supplies Ltd., PO Box 8, Long Ing Mill, Colne, Lancs.
Peckham Works Centre, Southward Corporation, London SE1.
Philip & Tacey Ltd., Northway, Andover, Hants.
Playtex Ltd., 8, Baker St., London W1M 2DX.
Portex Ltd., Hythe, Kent.
Price Bros & Co. Ltd., Wellington, Somerset.
Pryer & Howard Ltd., Willow Lane, Mitcham, Surrey.
R. & G. Assocaites, 155, High Rd., Willesden Green, London NW16 2GS.
Rankin, I.N. Ltd., Bloomfield House, Clifton Villas, London W9.
Remploy Ltd., 415, Edgeware Rd., Cricklewood, London NW2.
Robinson & Sons, Ltd., Wheat Bridge, Chesterfield, Derbyshire.
Ronson Products Ltd., Leatherhead, Surrey.
Rothband, W. S. Co. Ltd., 21, Elizabeth St., Manchester M8 8WT.
Satra (Shoe Traders Research Ass.), Satra House, Rockingham, Kettering, Northants.
Seaco Products Ltd., 144, Old Lambeth Rd., London SW8.
Selfridges Ltd., Oxford St., London W1A 1AB.
S.E.S., Corscombe, Dorchester, Dorset.
Sherrards Centre, Digswell Hill, Old Welwyn, Herts.
Simplantex Ltd., Willowfield Rd., Eastbourne, Sussex.
Smith & Nephew Ltd., Bessemer Rd., Welwyn Garden City, Herts.
Spalding Sheepskin Co. Ltd., Clay Lake, Spalding, Lincs.

Spastics Society, The, 12 Park Crescent, London W1.
SVCR, Forsaljnings, AB, PO Box 4, 122 21, Bergen, Sweden.
Sweetheart Bristol Ltd., Badminton Trading Estate, Yate, Bristol BS17 5JT.
Talley Surgical Instruments, 47, Theobald St., Borehamwood, Herts.
Taskmaster Learning Materials, Morris Rd., Clarendon Park, Leicester, Leics.
Temple Engineering Co., PO Box 1, High St., Cowes, Isle of Wight.
Thackray, Chas. F. Ltd., Park St., Leeds, Yorks.
Thistle Products, 24, Beswick St., Ancoats, Manchester, M4 7HS.
Tiger Plastics Ltd., Carshalton Rd., Blackpool, Lancs.
Tri-Aid Co. Ltd., 17-19 James Watt Place, East Kilbride, Lanarks, Scotland.
Vernon-Carus Ltd., Penwortham Mills, Preston, Lacns.
Walfix Fleeces, Nursery & Sons, 12 Upper Ollard St., Bungay, Suffolk.
Walker Crossweller, Whaddon Works, Clyde Cresc., Cheltenham, Glos.
Wirral Saddlery Centre, Haddon Lane, Ness, Wirral, Cheshire.
Yellow Top Hosiery Co., 93 High St., Boston, Lincs.
Zimmer Orthopaedic Ltd., Bridgend, Glamorgan, S. Wales.

TOYS AND PLAY

The Toy Libraries Association
Seabrook House, Wyllyotts Manor, Darkes Lane, Potters Bar, Herts. EN6 2H. Tel. 0707 44571.
This is the best source of further information. They have a complete list of toy manufacturers and suppliers, including those specialising in toys for handicapped children. They produce an ABC of toys, which is arranged into categories, and a complete list of local Toy Libraries.

National Association for the Welfare of Children in Hospital
Exton House, 7, Exton St., London SE1 8UE.

Organisations concerned with play and play equipment
(Addresses in Hobbies, Leisure Sports and Clubs section).

Adventure Playground Association

Environment for the Handicapped, Centre for

Playground Association, National

Play Space.

EDUCATION

Organisations concerned with investigating or improving educational facilities. NB – Organisations concerned with specific disabilities will be fully informed about the educational provision for those affected by that disability, and will advise about the choice of special schools (i.e. schools for autistic children).

Advancement of State Education, Confederate for
1, Windermere Rd., Wembley, London HA9 8SH. Tel. 01-904 1722.
Pressure group of teachers and parents in local areas, concerned with improvements in educational facilities, including special schools.

Advisory Centre for Education (ACE)
18, Victoria Park Square, London E2 9PB. Tel. 01-980 4596.
Produces a regular journal, often containing articles on special education, many other publications.

Centre for Educating Young Children at Home
Dr. G. Waldon, 636, Wilmslow Rd., Didsbury, Manchester 20.
Individually planned programmes for parents and young mentally handicapped children. Privately run (non profit making). Fees charged, but financial help may be available in cases of difficulty.

Child Guidance Training Centre
120, Belsize Lane, London NW3. Tel. 01-435 7111.
Centre for children who have difficulty adjusting to schooling.

Home and School Council
Barbara Bullivant, 81 Rustings Rd., Sheffield S11 7AB.

Early Childhood Education, British Association for
Montgomery Hall, The Oval, London SE11 5SE. Tel. 01-582 8744.

Educational Development Trust, National
c/o National Childrens' Centre, Longroyd Bridge, Huddersfield, Yorks. Tel. 0484 41733.

Learning Disabilities, Centre for
Westhill College, Selly Oak, Birmingham B29. Tel. 021-472 7245.

Nursery School Association
89, Stanford St., London SE1.

Parent-Teacher Association, Confederate of
43, Stonebridge Rd., Northfleet, Gravesend, Kent. Tel. 0474 60618.
Will help with the organisation of a PTA where none exists.

Pre-School Playgroups Association, National
Alford House, Aveline St., London SE11 5DJ. Tel. 01-582 8871.

Remedial Education, Association for
77, Chignal Rd., Chelmsford, Essex.

Special Education, National Council for
Beaconwood, Borden Hall, Stratford-on-Avon, Warks. CV37 9RX. Tel. 021-1744 4162.

Young Children, Joint Council for the Education of
4, Old Croft Rd., Walton on the Hill, Stafford, Staffs.

Mentally Handicapped Children and Adults, Royal Society for
117, Golden Lane, London EC1Y 0RT. Tel. 01-253 9433.
For details of lists of educational provision, see publications.

FURTHER EDUCATION
(including training, assessment, rehabilitation, employment)

Camphill Village Trust (see also Rudolf Steiner Schools)
College and Rehabilitation Centre, Delrow House, Hilfield Lane, Alderham, Hants WD2 8DJ. Tel. Radlett 09276 6006.

Carrs Rehabilitation and Employment Advisory Service
48, William IVth St., London WC2N 4LS. Tel. 01-836 5506/7.
Advises and assists in improving employment prospects for people with any type of handicap.

Derwen Training College for the Disabled
Oswestry, Salop SY11 3JA. Tel. Gobowen (0691) 82 234/235/688.

Guardianship Society
Grace Eyre Woodhead Memorial, Old Shoreham Rd., Hove, Sussex BN3 6EW. Tel. Brighton 739887 and Brighton 738823.
Mentally retarded people admitted to the care of the society are placed in foster homes of various sizes and are then found part time or full time employment in accordance with their abilities. If unsuitable for employment training is given in one of the society's two Training Centres. Referral must be by local authority.

Home Farm Trust
57, Queen Square, Bristol BS1 4LF. Tel. Bristol 29060.

Horticultural and Rural Therapy Training, Society for
Goulds Ground, Vallis Way, Frome, Somerset, BA11 3DW. Tel. 0373 64782.

Lingfield Hospital School
Lingfield, St. Piers Lane, Surrey. Tel. Lingfield 832243.
Further Education unit for children with epilepsy or neurological impairments.

Royal Society for Mentally Handicapped Children and Adults
117, Golden Lane, London EC1Y 0RT. Tel. 01-253 9433.
Training establishments for mentally handicapped people
a) Dilston Hall Advanced Social Training Unit
2 year course, training and preparation for work experience.
b) Lufton Manor Rural Training Unit
Practical course in farming, market gardening etc. for those with the ability to work in open employment.
c) Pengwern Hall Transition Training Unit
Experimental unit using new ideas and methods in helping mentally handicapped people make the transition from school to work.
d) The Blendworth Centre, Cadlington
Agricultural and Horticultural work training.

Royal Society for Mentally Handicapped Children – Pathway Scheme
Aims – to place mentally handicapped people in jobs in industry, commercial enterprises, local government etc. An employer is reimbursed with the employees wages during the initial training and settling in period. A fellow worker, carefully chosen, is designated to keep an eye on the new worker. Scheme operating in a number of areas.

Radar
25, Mortimer St., London W1N 8AP. Tel. 01-637 5400.
Advisory service on all aspects of rehabilitation, training bureau, agent to local authorities, further education facilities for the disabled.

Remploy
415 Edgeware Rd., London NW2 6LR. Tel. 01-452 8020.
Sheltered workshops, advice for people with any kind of handicap.

Rudolf Steiner Schools
Rudolph Steiner House, 35, Park Rd., London NW1.
Guide to all schools, colleges, villages etc. available on request.

S.E.P.A.C.S. (Sheltered Employment Procurement and Advisory Service)
20, Albert Embankment, London SE1 7ST. Tel. 01-735 9431.

St. Christopher Trust
Redcourt, Glossop, Derbyshire, SK13 8JH. Tel. 4452687.
Residential accommodation for the mentally handicapped. School, industrial unit, special facilities for the study of Downs syndrome.

Wentwood Education
The Grange, Canon Square, Melksham, Wilts. SN12 6LX. Tel. 0225 706102
Education, training, social activities for mentally handicapped school leavers. Usually a 2 year course.

Wolfson Centre
Mecklenburgh Square, London WC1. Tel. 01-837 7618.
Assessment and advice at school leaving age.

RESIDENTIAL HOMES, SCHOOLS, COMMUNITIES, LONG AND SHORT STAY

Alison House
30, Abercorn Place, St. Johns Wood, London NW8 9XP. Tel. 01-286 9977.
All handicaps catered for. Periods up to 3 months, ages 2-30 years.

Barnardo's
Tanners Lane, Barkingside, Ilford, Essex. Tel. 01-550 8822.
Holiday homes, short stay -long and short stay. Fostering and adoption schemes.

Break
100, First Avenue, Bush Hill Park, Enfield, Middlesex, EN1 1BP.
Long term accommodation and short stay. 0-16 years. Bed reservation scheme. Sometimes older age groups considered.

Brookvale
167, Simister Lane, Prestwich, Lancs. Tel. 061-642 4624/2777
Mentally handicapped children, boys up to 14 years, girls up to 16 years.

Camphill Village Trust
(See Rudolph Steiner Schools, education section).

Care – Cottage and Rural Enterprises
Blacketton House, East Anstey, Nr. Tiverton, Devon.
Small rural community homes for mentally handicapped adults.

Ceres House
289 Dyke Rd., Hove, East Sussex. Tel. Brighton 551023
Children accepted with any handicap. Age 0-12 years.

Cheshire Foundation
Leonard Cheshire House, 26-29, Maunsel St., London SW1P 2QN. Tel. 01-828 1822.
Homes for handicapped children and adults, long and short term.

Collingham
57, Chignall Rd., Chelmsford, Essex CN1 2JA. Tel. Chelmsford 51788.
Short term care for up to 12 years, babies needing special care.

Dedisham School for Autistic Children
Slinford, Horsham, Sussex RH13 7RA. Tel. Slinford 257.

Elizabeth Fitzroy Homes for the Handicapped Trust
The Welfare Dept., The Coach House, Liss, Hants.
Homes for mentally handicapped children and adults, long and short term, including those with additional handicaps, incontinent, chairbound.

Grange Nursing Home, The
Hindhead, Surrey. Tel. Hindhead 4278.
All handicaps catered for, 2-9 years.

Hales House
Spastics Society Family Health Unit, Shakers Lane, Bury St. Edmunds, Suffolk.

Helen Allison School
29, Overcliffe, Gravesend, Kent. Tel. Gravesend 3781.
Autistic children and adults 2-25 years.

Helen House
Mother Superior General, 11 Saints Convent, 36, Leopold St., Oxford, OX4 1RU. Tel. 0865 40903.
Home for incurably sick or chronically ill children. Aims to help parents to care for their children at home by offering short stay care and support. In some cases, parents are able to stay with their children (scheduled for opening 1982).

Home Farm Trust
57, Queen Square, Bristol.
Permanent care in farming communities for mentally handicapped people.

Kingston Trust
The Drove, Kempshott, Basingstoke, Hants. Tel. 0256 21288.
Permanent and convalescent homes.

L'Arche communities
Rev. T. Hollis, 14, London Rd., Beccles, Suffolk.
Groups of retarded people living together with outside support.

Macintyre Schools
Westoning, Flitwick, Beds. Tel. 05 257 2343.
Village community, permanent care, school for mentally handicapped children and adults.

Royal Society for Mentally Handicapped Children and Adults
117, Golden Lane, London EC1Y 0RT. Tel. 01-253 9433.
a) Cadlington
Home for severely mentally handicapped children and young people 3-19 years.
b) Hales House and Pirates Spring
Homes for severely mentally handicapped people under 16 years.

HOBBIES, LEISURE, SPORTS, CLUBS

Adventure Playground Association, Handicapped
Fulham Palace, Bishops Ave., London SW6 6EA. Tel. 01-736 4443.
Illustrated booklet, information on play, play equipment and areas, advice for anyone wishing to start their own playground.

Art Therapy, British Association of
130, Northwood Rd., London N6. Tel. 01-384 6143.

Bird Watching
The Yorkshire Naturalists Trust, 20 Castle Gate, York YD1 1RP. Tel. 0904 59570.

Birds, Royal Society for the Protection of
The Lodge, Sandy, Beds. SG19 2DL. Tel. Sandy 80551.
Guide to reserves and facilities available on request.

Books (See Talking Books)

Cheyne Holiday Club for Handicapped Children
61, Cheyne Walk, London SW3. Tel. 01-352 4834.
Arranges all kinds of childrens' activities on a daily basis, during school holidays.

Cooking by Pictures, Step by Step
Hampshire Social Services, Trafalgar House, The Castle, Winchester, Hants SO2 38U.
34 wipe clean cookery cards for slow learners or people with little cooking experience.

Disabled Sports Foundation, The
10, Little Turnstile, Holborn, London WC1V 7DX.
Aims to set up sports associations all over the country, providing coaching and adapting existing facilities. All handicaps, all ages, all sports catered for.

Drama (see Sesame)

Music Therapy, British Association for
48, Lancaster Rd., London N6 4TA. Tel. 01-883 1331.

Music Association, The Schools
6, Newman Rd., Bromley, Kent.

National Trust, The
Guide-Facilities for the Disabled and Visually Impaired (see publications).

Paintings in Hospitals
Nuffield Foundation, Nuffield Lodge, Regent's Park, London NW1.

Playing Fields Association
57b, Catherine Place, London SW1.

Playground Association, National
12, Cherry Tree Drive, Sheffield, Yorks,.

Play Space
22, Frognal, London NW3. Tel. 01-794 6650.

Pony Riding for the Disabled Trust
Grange Farm Sports Centre, High Rd., Chigwell, Essex.

Riding for the Disabled
National Equestrian Centre, Kenilworth, Warks. CV8 2LR. Tel. 0203 27192.

Sesame
Christchurch Industrial Centre, 27, Blackfriars Rd., London SE1. Tel. 01-633 9690/9705.
Drama for and with the handicapped.

Sports Association for the Disabled, British
Stoke Mandeville Stadium, Harvey Rd., Aylesbury, Bucks. Tel. 0296 84848.

Sports Association for the Disabled, Scottish
1, St. Colme St., Edinburgh, EH3 1AA. Tel. 031225 8411.

Sports Association for the Disabled, Welsh
Llys Ifor, Crescent Rd., Caerphilly, Glamorgan, S. Wales CF8 1XI. Tel. 0222 869224/5/6.

Swimming Therapy, Association of
40, Gawsworth Ave, Crewe, Cheshire. Tel. 0720 662785.

Swimming Clubs for the Handicapped, National Association of
219, Preston Drive, Brighton, Sussex.

Talking Books for the Blind
RNIB, 224, Great Portland St., London W1N 6AA.

Tape Recordings for Hospital Patients, British Library of
12, Lant St., London SE1 1QR. Tel. 01-407 9417/8.

Wingfield Trust
24, Station Rd., Epping, Essex. Tel. 0378 73229.
Activities and music for handicapped young people.

HOLIDAYS AND TRAVEL
Across Trust
c/o Trade and Technical Press Ltd., Crown House, Morden, Surrey. Tel. 01-540 3897.
Takes parties of severely handicapped people on pilgrimage to Lourdes or across Europe.

Baden-Powell Holiday Home Trust
Baden Powell House, Queensgate, London SW7 5JS. Tel. 01-584 7030.
Caravans and chalets for families with a handicapped member.

Break Childrens' Holiday Schemes
20, Hooks Hill, Sheringham, Norfolk NR26 BHL. Tel. 0263 823170.

Buckets and Spades
Mr. L. Silverman, 20, Mersham Drive, London NW9 9PM.
Holidays and short term care at St. Leonards on Sea, Sussex. All types of handicap catered for, including multiple handicaps, 0-18 years.

Camps for Mentally Handicapped Children
Maggie Smith, 14D St. Charles Square, London W10.

Colwall Court
Pages Avenue, Bexhill on Sea, Sussex. Tel. 0424 211491.
Run by the Spastics Society but will accept children with other handicaps.

Elizabeth Fitzroy Homes for the Handicapped Trust
The Welfare Dept., The Coach House, Whitegates, Liss, Hants. Tel. 073082 3577.

Geoffrey Hazel Fund
135A, High St., Brentwood, Essex.
Fund to help children with chronic illness or crippling disease, to have a holiday.

Handicapped Childrens' Pilgrimage Trust
95, Carshalton Rd., Sutton, Surrey. Tel. 01-643 4431.

Handicapped Friends Service Council
Friends House, Euston Rd., London NW1 2BT.

Kids
16, Strutton Ground, London SWP 2HP. Tel. 01-222 1517.
Holiday Centre in Northamptonshire. Open all the year round. Pre-school to 15 years. Handicapped child may be accompanied by brothers and sisters.

Little Oyster Holiday Centre
Isle of Sheppey, Kent.
Run by Marlborough Enterprises Ltd, Enterprise House, 51, St. Mary's House, Tonbridge, Kent, TN9 2LE.
Chalets for mentally and physically handicapped people.

Mentally Handicapped Children and Adults, Royal Society for
117, Golden Lane, London EC1Y 0RT.
Several holiday homes and schemes (see publications).

Longfields
6, Bethany Lane, West Cross, Swansea, S. Wales.
Short term residential unit run by the Spastics Society. Will accept children with other handicaps from Wales.

Sussex Beach Holiday Village
Earnley, Chichester, W. Sussex. Tel. 07016 66151.
Chalet Centre for families or groups. Special weeks reserved for the handicapped at reduced rates.

Trans-Care International
Group House, Woodlands Avenue, London W3. Tel. 01-992 5077.
Escorts and transports sick, injured or disabled people.

Travel Well
Carlisle House, 8, Southampton Row, London WC1B 4AE. Tel. 01-405 9481.
A specialist holiday and travel service for the handicapped to enable them to travel with maximum enjoyment and minimum discomfort.

Appendix 3
PUBLICATIONS AND BIBLIOGRAPHY

(Publishers will send catalogues of their books, on request.)

Guides, Directories, General information
The major organisations catering for specific disabilities, or activities will have a range of literature and further reading lists, relevant to their field.

Local Facilities
Most local authorities produce a Directory or Handbook of services for handicapped people. Enquire at the Education Department, Health Department, Social Services Department, Citizens Advice Bureau or local reference library. Directories covering all aspects of disability.

Parents Information Bulletin A-Z
Information on all aspects of mental handicap. Supplements issued at regular intervals, keeping the information up to date.

Communications
A pack containing articles, leaflets on benefits, reports, new publications etc, relating to mentally handicap. Packs sent three times a year on payment of an annual subscription. Both the above from – RSMHC Books, 117, Golden Lane, London EC1Y 0RT. Tel. 01-253 9433.

Handbook for Parents with a Handicapped Child
Judith Stone and Felicity Taylor, 1977. Home and School Council. From bookshops or to order. Also, by post from RADAR, 25, Mortimer St., London W1N 8AP. Tel. 01-637 5400.

Help Starts Here
Phillipa Russell. 1976.
Voluntary Council for Handicapped Children, 8, Wakley St., London EC1V 7QE.

Source Book for the Disabled
Gloria Hale.
from bookshops or to order. Also by post from RADAR, (address above).

Directory for the Disabled
Ann Darnborough and Derek Kinrade, 1980.
Woodhead-Faulkner.
Also by post from RADAR, (address above).

A.A. Guide for the Disabled
Automobile Association, Fanum House, Basingstoke, Hants RG21 2EA. New guide produced each year. Free to A.A. members. Includes a gazeteer of hotel, restaurant and motorway service station facilities, toilets, car parks etc throughout Britain.

Compass
Disablement Income Group, Attlee House, 28, Commercial St., London E1 6LR. Tel. 01-247 2128.
A guide including organisations, social security provisions, holidays, leisure etc..

AIDS, EQUIPMENT, CLOTHING

Easy to Make Aids for Your Handicapped Child.
Don Caston, 1981.
Souvenir Press, 43, Great Russell St., London WCB 3PA.

Clothing and Dressing for
Disabled Child
Both from Equipment for the Disabled, 2 Foredown Rd., Portslade, Sussex BN4 2BB.

Clothing for the Handicapped Child
Disabled Living Foundation, 346 Kensington High St., London W14 8NS.

Footwear for Problem Feet
M. England, Disabled Living Foundation (address above).

Up to date lists of aids equipment and clothing produced by . . .
Scottish Information Service for the Disabled.
British Red Cross Society
Disabled Living Foundation
Equipment for the Disabled
(see information section, aids, equipment and clothing)

GENERAL BOOKS ON MENTAL AND/OR PHYSICAL HANDICAP

A Mentally Handicapped Child in the Family
Mary McCormack, 1978. Constable.

A Difference in the Family
Heather Featherstone 1981. Harper and Row Ltd.

More than Sympathy
Richard Lansdown. Tavistock/Methuen 1980.

The Handicapped Person in the Community
David Boswell and Janet Wingrave, 1974. Tavistock/Methuen.

Accident of Birth
Fred Heddell, 1980. B.B.C. Publications.

Help for the Epileptic Child
Jorge C. Lago, 1973. Macdonald and Janes.

The Handling of the Cerebral Palsied Child/Seating the Cerebral Palsied Child
Rosemary York-Moore 1981.
British Insitute of Mental Handicap, Wolverhampton Rd., Kidderminster Rd., Worcs. DY10 3PP.

Souvenir Press, 43, Great Russell St., London WC1B 3PA.
a) The Wheelchair Chair
Phillipa Russell, 1978.
b) The Hearing Impaired Child and the Family
Michael Nolan and Ivan Tucker, 1981.
c) Insights From the Blind
Selma Fraibert, 1977.

DOWNS SYNDROME
Downs Children's Association,
Quinborne Community Centre, Ridgacre Road, Birmingham B32 2TW
(a) **Early Training for the Infant with Down syndrome (mongolism)**
   Rex Brinkworth 1979.
(b) **Downs Syndrome – Let's be Positive**
   J. R. Ludlow 1980
   (an approach to help Downs syndrome children to reach their full potential).
(c) **I Can Talk** – guide for parents in promoting or improving speech for Downs syndrome children
   Lesley Streets LCST 1975.
(d) **Improving Babies with Downs syndrome and introducing them to school**
   Rex Brinkworth & Joseph Collins 1973.
   (revised edition).
(e) **Helping Your Downs Child to Talk**
   E. Mary Pryce LCST 1979.
(f) **Legal Aspects concerning the Mentally Handicapped**
   George P. Atkinson 1979.
(Many other publications concerning Downs syndrome are available from the DCA).

BOOKS FOR BROTHERS AND SISTERS OF THE MENTALLY HANDICAPPED
Sibs – a quarterly magazine written by and for brothers and sisters of the mentally handicapped. Contact Janet Bater, 13, Horwood Close, London Rd., Headington, Oxford.

My Brother Steven is Retarded
Harriet Lansam Sobol.
published by Victor Gollancz.

About Peter – leaflet for young children, RSHMC Books, 117 Golden Lane, London EC14 0RT.

GUIDES TO THE TEACHING OF SKILLS, AND BEHAVIOUR MODIFICATION
Souvenir Press, 43 Great Russell St., London WC1B 3PA.
a) Helping Your Handicapped Baby
Cliff Cunningham and Patricia Sloper, 1978.
b) Starting Off
Chris Keirnan, Rita Jordan and Chris Saunders, 1978.
c) Teaching the Handicapped Child
Dorothy M. Jeffree, Roy McConkey and Simon Hewson, 1977
d) Let Me Read
Dorothy M. Jeffree and Margaret Skeffington, 1980.

Methuen, 11 New Fetters Lane, London EC4P 4EE.
Teaching Plans for Handicapped Children
Franz Morgenstern, 1981. Tavistock/Methuen.

British Institute of Mental Handicap
Wolverhampton Rd., Kidderminster, Worcs. DY10 3PP.
a) Crossing The Road
Peter Taylor and Paul Robinson 1979.
b) Helping the Retarded – a guide to teaching new skills and coping with behaviour problems.

Royal Society for Mentally Handicapped Children and Adults
117, Golden Lane, London EC1Y 0RT.
a) Behaviour Modification in Mental Retardation
W. Gardner, 1971.
b) Behaviour Modification of the Mentally Retarded
T. Thompson and J. Grabowski, 1972.
c) Take Six Children
Hilary Cass, Karen Grant, Michael Lassman, 1978.

FEEDING
Souvenir Press, 43 Great Russell St., London WC1B 3PA.
a) Helping Your Handicapped Baby
Cliff Cunningham and Patricia Sloper, 1978.
b) Starting Off
Chris Keirnan, Rita Jordan and Chris Keirnan, 1978.
Feeding Can Be Fun
Mary Ryan, LCST.
The Spastics Society, 12 Park Crescent, London W1N 4EQ.

PLAY
All literature and toy guides from,
The Toy Libraries Association, Seabrook House, Wyllyotts Manor, Darkes Lane, Potters Bar, Herts. EN6 2HL.

Souvenir Press, 43, Great Russell St., London WC1B 3PA.
a) Lets Make Toys.
Dorothy Jeffree and Roy McConkey, 1981.
b) Let Me Play.
Dorothy Jeffree and Roy McConkey, 1981

Voluntary Council for Handicapped Children, 8, Wakley St., London EC1V 7QE.
Play and Toys for Handicapped Children - Fact Sheet No. 7

British Institute of Mental Handicap, Wolverhampton Rd., Kidderminster, Worcs DY10 3PP.
a) Teaching Self Help Skills to the Mentally Retarded/The Development of Play with Retarded Children.
J. Hattersley.

b) Play Activities for the Retarded Child
R. W. Carlson and D. R. Gingland, 1962. Cassell.

SPEECH AND LANGUAGE
Souvenir Press, 43, Great Russell St., London WC1B 3PA

a) Let Me Speak
Dorothy Jeffree and Roy McConkey, 1980.

b) Language Without Speech
Ruth M. Deich and Patricia M. Hodges, 1977.

c) Starting Off
Chris Keirnan, Rita Jordan and Chris Saunders, 1978.

d) Helping Your Handicapped Baby
Cliff Cunningham and Patricia Sloper, 1978.

Royal Society for Mentally Handicapped Children and Adults
a) Language Stimulus with Retarded Children
Mary le Frenais, 1971.

b) Communication and the Withdrawn Child, 1977

The First Words Language Programme
Bill Gillham 1981. George Allen & Unwin Ltd., P.O. Box 18, Park Lane, Hemel Hempstead, Herts.

The Spastics Society, 12, Park Crescent, London W1N 4EQ.
Feeding Can be Fun
Mary Ryan, LCST.
(good feeding practices as a preparation for speech development).

MOBILITY
Royal Society for Mentally Handicapped Children and Adults, 117 Golden Lane, London EC1Y 0RT.
Making Movement Fun
Fred Mortimore 1977.

British Institute for Mental Handicap, Wolverhampton Rd., Kidderminster, Worcs DY10 3PP.
a) Progress to improved movement for handicapped children and adults with poor posture.
Katy Hollis 1980.
b) Progress to standing for children with severe mental and physical handicap.
Katy Hollis 1980.

Souvenir Press, 43, Great Russell St., London WC1B 3PA.
a) Starting Off
Chris Keirnan, Rita Jordan and Chris Saunders., 1978.
b) Helping Your Handicapped Baby
Cliff Cunningham and Patricia Sloper, 1978.

TOILET TRAINING
Souvenir Press, 43, Great Russell St., London WC1B 3PA.
a) Starting Off
Chris Keirnan, Rita Jordan and Chris Saunders, 1978.
b) Helping Your Handicapped Baby
Cliff Cunningham and Patricia Sloper, 1978.

INCONTINENCE
Literature and personal advice is available from – Disabled Living Foundation, 346, Kensington High St., London W14 8NS. Tel. 01-602 2491.

HOBBIES, LEISURE
Souvenir Press, 43, Great Russell St., London WC1B 3PA.
a) Art Activities for the Handicapped
Sally M. Atack, 1980.
b) Puppetry for the Mentally Handicapped
Caroline Astell Burt, 1981.
c) Out of Doors with the Handicapped
Mike Cotton, 1981.
d) Horticultural Therapy
Audrey Cloet and Chris Underhill 1981/82.
e) Yoga for the Handicapped
Barbara Brosnan 1981/82.

Royal Society for Mentally Handicapped Children
117, Golden Lane, London EC1Y 0RT.
a) Drama Games for Handicapped People
Bernie Warren.
b) A Philosophy of Leisure in Relation to the Retarded
Kenneth Solly, 1975.
c) Recreation for the Retarded
Charles H. Jackson, 1975.

Just Me – a Songbook for Children
Jean Turnbull and Steve Storr.
24 songs for preschool or handicapped children. Also available in cassette form.
Pitman Medical, 57, High St., Tunbridge Wells, Kent.

ADOLESCENCE AND ADULTHOOD

Souvenir Press, 43, Great Russell St., London WC1B 3PA.
a) Learning to Cope
Edward Whelan and Barbara Speake, 1981.
b) Getting to Work
Edward Whelan and Barbara Speake, 1981.
c) Like Normal People
(the courtship and marriage of a mentally handicapped couple)
Robert Meyers, 1979.
d) A Home of Their Own.
Victoria Shennan 1981/82.
e) We Can Speak for Ourselves
Paul Williams and Bonnie Shoulz, 1981.

Royal Society for Mentally Handicapped Children and Adults, 117 Golden Lane, London EC1Y 0RT.
Housing for Mentally Handicapped People
Chris Heginbotham, 1978.

Voluntary Council for Handicapped Children, 8, Wakley St., London EC1V 7QE.
Guide for Handicapped Adolescents and Those Working with Them.

MENSTRUATION AND SEX EDUCATION

Royal Society for Mentally Handicapped Children and Adults, 117, Golden Lane, London EC1Y 0RT.
a) Sex Education and the Mentally Retarded
George W. Lee, 1977.
b) Sex and Social Training in an Adult Training Centre
Lindsay Lowes, 1977

c) **Help Your Child to Understand Sex**
Victoria Shennan, 1978.
d) **The Sexual Rights of the Retarded**
George W. Lee and Gregor Katz, 1974.

Growing Up Young
Guide on menstruation for parents of slow learning girls.
Mary Abbot.
Kimberley Clark Ltd, Larkfield, Kent.

Voluntary Council for Handicapped Children, 8, Wakley St., London EC1V 7QE.
The Sexual Needs of Handicapped Young People – Fact Sheet No. 6

Health Education Council, 78, New Oxford Street, London WC1 1AH
How We Grow Up.
Booklet, illustrated, dealing with physical development.

EDUCATION, FURTHER EDUCATION, ASSESSMENT, EMPLOYMENT

List 42 – list of all special schools (day and residential) in England and Wales.
Department of Education and Science,
From – HMSO offices, HMSO Mail Order, P.O. Box 569, London SE1.
List G – Provisions for handicapped pupils in Scotland
Scottish Education Department, 6/7 Coates Place, Edinburgh, Scotland.

Advisory Centre for Education
18, Victoria Park Square, London Bethnal Green, London E2 9PB.
A variety of publications on education including . . .
a) **WHERE – to find out more about education**
includes sources of information on handicapped children (leaflet available separately).
b) **WHERE – to look things up**
An A-Z of resources on major educational topics.
c) **Is Your Child Handicapped? – Parents Rights**

Voluntary Council for Handicapped Children,
8, Wakley St., London EC1V 9QE.
List of Voluntary Organisations Providing Further Education, Social and Vocational Training, Assessment or Sheltered Workshops. Fact Sheet No. 1.

Royal Society for Mentally Handicapped Children and Adults, 117, Golden Lane, London EC1Y 0RT.
a) **Directory of Educational Courses for Mentally Handicapped Adults**
Edited by Victoria Shennan

b) After Sixteen
Anne Henshawe, 1979.
A study of the courses available to the mentally handicapped at a college of Art and Design.

HOLIDAYS, LONG TERM AND SHORT TERM ACCOMMODATION
Royal Society for Mentally Handicapped Children and Adults, 117, Golden Lane, London EC1Y 0RT.

Residential Accommodation for the Mentally Handicapped in England and Wales, and Northern Ireland
List of statutory and private provision – schools, hostels, homes, communities for mentally handicapped children and adults.

Holiday Accommodation Lists
RSMHC Holiday Services Office, 119, Drake St., Rochdale, Lancs. OL19 1PZ.
RADAR, 25, Mortimer St., London W1N 8AP.
National Society for Autistic Children, 1A, Golders Green Rd., London N7.
Voluntary Council for Handicapped Children, 8, Wakley St., London EC1V 7QE.
(Fact Sheet No. 3)

FINANCE, RIGHTS, LEGAL ADVICE

Department of Health and Social Security
Information Division, Alexander Fleming House, Elephant and Castle, London SE1.
Publishes leaflets on all the benefits available. These can usually be obtained at local Social Security Offices, Social Services Departments or Citizens Advice Bureaux. If a leaflet is difficult to obtain, write to:
DHSS Leaflets Unit, P.O. Box 21, Stanmore Middlesex HA7 1A.

DHSS Booklets giving details of all current benefits available.
a) Help for Handicapped People – DHSS Leaflet No. FB2 HB1
b) Which Benefit? – DHSS Leaflet No. FB2
Allowances grants and benefits for handicapped people.
(See Chapter 00 for explanatory details).

Attendance Allowance	– DHSS Leaflet No. N1 205
Invalid Care Allowance	– DHSS Leaflet No. N1 212
Mobility Allowance	– DHSS Leaflet No. N1 211
Family Income Supplement	– DHSS Leaflet No. FIS 1
Free Milk	– DHSS Leaflet FW20

Rate Rebate – DHSS leaflet 'Rate Rebate for Disabled Persons'
Supplementary Benefit – DHSS leaflet 'Supplementary Benefits'.

Other benefits
Orange Badge Scheme. Anyone who has a child who is blind or has severe walking difficulties can apply for an Orange Badge to display in their car. This entitles the driver to special parking facilities as near as possible to the destination. Apply to Social Services Departments, Hospital Social Work Departments.

Organisations offering advice on financial welfare and legal matters.
Royal Society for Mentally Handicapped Children and Adults, 117, Golden Lane, London EC1Y 0RT. (Welfare and Rights Dept.)
Tel. 01-253 9433.
Disablement Income Group
Attlee House, 28, Commercial St., London E1 6LR.
The Disability Alliance
1, Cambridge Terrace, London NW1 4JL.
Citizens Rights Office
1, Macklin St., Drury Lane, London WC2.

Legal Advice and provision
Royal Society for Mentally Handicapped Children and Adults, 117, Golden Lane, London EC1Y 0RT.
Will advise on any legal problem relating to a mentally handicapped person.

The Trusteeship Scheme
A service for parents of the mentally handicapped, which provides for a specially appointed visitor to keep in close contact with each child or adult, and watch over his or her interests, after the death of the parents. Arrangements are made in which parents can either take out a simple form of insurance or leave a lump sum in a Will. Explanatory booklet available on request to RSMHC (address above).
There is also a scheme whereby parents can bequeath their houses to the RSMHC.

Making a Will (see Chapter 14)

Legal Advice Service for handicapped people and their families
Network, Bedford House, London WC1 3QL. Tel. 01-504 3001.

INDEX

(For ease of reference some clinical terms have been given a simplified form of spelling.)

Acceptance
  of the handicapped child, 23
  problems of, 55-57, 61-64
Accepting help, 64
Adolescence, 128-141, 187
Adoption, 38 (See also Information Section)
Adult Training Centres, 104, 131, 133
Advice
  Well meaning, 71-73
Aids Centres, 111, 159
Allowances and Benefits, 57-58, 115-117, 189
Another Child, 36
Attendance Allowance, 115, 189
Audiologists, 102
Autism, 6, 13, 17, 21, 32, 34, 36, 73, 83, 89, 123
Autistic Children, National Society for 109, 149

Barnardo's 110, 126, 127, 149, 175
Behaviour
  Modification, 81
  Problems, 43-44, 73, 81,87, 118, 123, 135, 139
Blind, Royal National Institute for, 126, 150
Blindness, 103, 126, 150
Blissymbolics System, 94
Books and Directories, 181-191
Brain Damaged Children, National Society for, 109, 150
British Institute for Mental Handicap, 108, 109, 155
Brothers and Sisters, 30-38, 63, 70, 71, 76, 183
Brownie Guides, 112

Campaign for the Mentally Handicapped, 110, 155
Camphill Village Trust, 126, 174
CARE (Cottage and Rural Enterprises), 126, 175

Careers Officer, 131
Castle Priory College, 111
Cerebral Palsy, 26, 28, 51, 76, 122, 140
Citizens Advice Bureaux, 111, 151
City and Guilds Syllabus, 79
Colleges
  of Further Education, 79, 131, 132
  Technical, 79, 131
Communication Systems, 94
Community Care, 121, 126 (See also Information Section)
Community Health Councils, 14, 111
Courses for Parents, 79
Court of Protection, 117
Crawling (See Mobility)
Crossroads Care Attendant Scheme, 114, 151
Cub Scouts, 112

Dancing, 113
Deafness, 19, 103, 183
Death of Parents, Provision after 117, 190
Diagnosis
  Disclosure of, 1-15
  Reaction of parents to, 1-15
  Pre-natal, 38
Diet, 44, 90
Doctors' Attitudes, 2
Downs Children's Association, 109, 152, 183
Downs Syndrome (Mongolism), 6-8, 9, 10, 11-12, 25, 31, 32, 33, 35, 36, 40-48, 54, 55, 59, 63, 64, 67, 75, 77, 89, 96, 120, 139, 144, 152, 183

Education
  Planning for, 62, 101-105
  Pre-school, 102
  Further, 104, 131
  Sex, 139-140
  1971 (Handicapped Children) Act, 101
  1981 Act, 105

Education and Science, Department of, 101, 102-103, 111, 126, 132, 188
Elfrida Rathbone Association, The, 110, 152
Employment, 133-134, 174, 188
Epilepsy, 6, 20,
and diet, 44, 103, 130, 133, 152
Equipment, 57-58, 98, 111, 112, 158, 182
ESN Schools, 22, 25, 76, 101-103, 132, 172, 188
Exercise (See Mobility)
Expectations, of Parents, 52
Exploitation and Vulnerability, 134

Family, The
 Fathers, 25-29
 Brothers and sisters, 30-38
 Grandparents, 18, 38-42
 Position of handicapped child in, 36-37
 Stress in, 43-51
Family Fund, The, 115, 153
Family Planning Clinic, 138
Fathers, Feelings of 25-29, 53-55
Feeding, 89-91
 Difficulties with, 91-93, 97, 184
Finance, 57-58, 115-117, 189
Fostercare, 113, 114 (See also Information Section)
Further Education, 131, 104, 174, 188

Gateway Clubs, 28, 113
General Practitioners, 1, 5, 8, 17, 19, 21, 54, 56
Genetic Counselling, 38
Grandparents, 18, 39-42
Guilt, Feelings of, 17, 26, 41, 55, 58, 119, 127

Health and Social Security, Department of, 6, 101, 111, 154, 189
Health Visitors, 6, 11, 13, 15, 20, 46, 58, 91, 98, 108, 111
Help, Accepting, 64-67
Help for Health, 108, 154
Hobbies, Sports, Leisure, Social Life, 112, 177, 186
Holidays, 114, 120, 178, 189
Home Farm Trust, 126, 176
Hospitals
 General, 113
 Mental Handicap, 113-114, 124
Hostels, 121
Hydrocephalus, 47, 50, 158
Hyperactive Children's Support Group, 44, 154
Hyperactivity, 43, 73, 83, 118
 Diet, 44

Hypercalcaemia, Infantile, 99
Hypercalcaemia Foundation, Infantile, 109, 154
Hypochondroplasia, 3, 34, 108

Independence, 123
Information
 Finding out More, 106-117
 Information Section 149-180
In Touch, 27, 49, 55, 59, 106, 145-148, 155

Joseph Rowntree Memorial Trust, 115, 153

Klinefelter's Syndrome, 11, 13, 107

Language, (See Speech)
L'Arche Communities, 126, 176
Leeds Fostercare Scheme, 114
Leisure, 112, 177, 186
Life Expectancy, Short, 48-51
Line 81; 108, 154
Long-stay Hospitals, 124

Makaton System, 94
Masturbation, 139
Meningitis, 47, 48
Menstruation, 137, 187
 inhibiting, 138
 pre-menstrual tension, 137
Mental approach, 61
Mental Handicap, British Institute of, 108, 109, 155 (See also Publications)
Mentally Handicapped, Campaign for the, 110, 155
Mentally Handicapped Children and Adults, Royal Society for (MENCAP), 6, 10, 27, 28, 65, 101, 108, 109, 112, 113, 117, 126, 131, 138, 145 (See also Information and Publications sections)
Mental Illness, 128
Metabolic Disorders, 49 51, 154
Microcephaly, 12, 59, 133
Mildly Retarded, 129, 133
MIND (National Association for Mental Health), 110, 155
Mobility, 94, 95, 186
 Allowance, 115, 117
Mobius Syndrome, 5, 97
Mongolism (See Downs Syndrome)
Moodiness
 in adults and adolescents, 135-137

National Development Group, 104, 132
Non-Acceptance, 24, 58
Nursery Education, 17, 22, 65, 102

Occupational Therapy, 88
Open University, 80
Orange Badge Scheme, 117, 190
Orthopaedic Consultant, 19
Over-Anxious, 16

Paediatricians, 1, 5, 8, 20, 21, 46, 50, 54, 55, 56
Paget-Gorman System, 94
Parents
  Acceptance of the handicap, 23-29, 52-57
  As Teachers, 74
  Expectations 52-57
  Financial circumstances of, 57
  Over-anxious, 16
  Pride, 143
  Reactions to diagnosis, 1-15
  Suggestions from, 59, 61-67, 69-71, 74, 82-84, 91, 99
  Training Courses for, 79-80, 94
Parents Voice, 101, 108
Pets, 85
Physical Handicaps, 44-51, 103, 142, 182
Physiotherapists, Chartered Society of, 96
Physiotherapy, 96
Play, 88-89, 172, 184
Playgroups, 88
Portage System, The 78
Prader-Willi Association, 109, 156
Pre-Menstrual Tension, 137
Pre-School Playgroups Association, 102, 156, 173
Progressive Disabilities, 48-51
Psychologists, 1, 14, 21, 79, 102

Questionnaires, 1, 3, 5, 31, 43, 45, 61, 106

R.A.D.A.R., 157

RNIB (Royal National Institute for the Blind), 126
RSMHC (Royal Society for Mentally Handicapped Children and Adults), 6, 10, 27, 28, 65, 101, 108, 109, 112, 113, 117, 126, 131, 138, 145
Religion, 58-60
Residential Care
  Community and rural homes, 126, 174, 175
  Decisions about, 71-72, 118
  Provision, 62, 113, 120, 121, 124, 175, 189
  Training courses, 126, 131, 174, 189
Rubenstein Taybi Syndrome, 13, 19, 21, 66, 157

San Fillipo Syndrome, 5
School Medical Officer, 1, 17, 103
Schools
  Ordinary, 103
  Residential, 103, 175, 188
  Special (See ESN Schools)
Secrecy, 107
Sex Education, 139-140, 187
Sign Language, 94, 185
Sisters, 30, 36, 71
Smith-Lemli Opitz Syndrome, 55
Social Education Centres, 104, 131-134
Social Life, 112, 177, 186
Social Services Departments, 6, 14, 15, 63, 88, 101, 104, 111, 114, 126
Social Workers, 6, 12, 14, 15, 58, 59, 63, 73, 108, 111, 114
Spasticity, 6, 26, 103, 130
Spastics Society, The, 111, 157 (See also Information section, aids and equipment)
Special Care Units, 102, 105
Specialists, 1, 3, 11, 13, 16, 19
Speech and Language, 93, 94, 185
Speech Therapy, 17, 93, 94, 157
Sports, 112, 177, 186
Sterilization, 138-139
Stress
  in the family, 29, 43-51
Supplementary Benefit, 115, 117, 189
Surveys
  CHC, 14, 15
  1971, 1, 106
  1977, 1, 31
Swimming, 96, 144

Tantrums, 18, 44, 81, 84
Telling Other People, 67-71
Therapists, 79
  Occupational, 88
  Physiotherapists, 96
  Speech, 93, 157
Toilet Training, 97-100, 186
  (See also Information section, aids and equipment)
Toy Libraries, 34, 79, 88-89, 112, 172, 184
Toy Libraries Association, 89, 112
Toys, 88-89, 172, 184
Training Centres, 102
  Adult, 104, 121, 131, 133, 136
  Residential, 126, 174, 188
Training Courses
  For parents, 79-80, 94
  For the mentally handicapped, 126, 131, 174, 189
Trusteeship Scheme, 117, 190
Tuberous Sclerosis, 2, 32, 46, 66, 158

Uncertainty, 3, 18

Vaccine Damage, 32, 258
Vulnerability and Exploitation, 134

Walking (See Mobility)
Warnock Report, The, 79, 105, 131
Will, Making a, 117
Work, 134

Youth Clubs (See Gateway Clubs)